'I have wholehearted admiration for this e
iatrist and psychoanalyst, Ahron Friedbe.
psychiatric patients and psychiatrists alike. It could also be subtitled "love in
the time of the COVID pandemic." The pandemic crisis transformed the close
face-to-face therapeutic situation into a remote screen-to-screen encounter.
As the pandemic is both danger and opportunity, the dark screen, paradoxic-
ally, shines a bright light on both therapeutic participants. Enlightened by his
own struggles with the pandemic, Friedberg compellingly renders the existential dramas and unique narratives of his patients and teaches them to cope
with the crisis, to maintain hope and resilience, to cultivate new contacts and
connections, to discover new meanings in their lives and loves.'

Henry Zvi Lothane, *M.D.*, *Clinical Professor of Psychiatry*
at Icahn School of Medicine at Mount Sinai

'*Through a Screen Darkly* is a remarkable achievement. In elegant, precise prose
it captures the personal suffering of individuals during the pandemic while
rendering the universality of their condition. Each essay is a version of how any
of us could experience these new complexities that will, one way or another,
determine all our futures. Dr. Friedberg's practice has been at the epicenter of
the pandemic for several months, and he saw it all – guilt, grief, fear, feistiness,
and self-reinvention. He helped people find their way towards some kind of
accommodation with post-COVID reality. His account of this straitened reality
is, therefore, tempered with possibility and hope. As we make our way through
these dark times, this inspiring book will become an essential read.'

David Forrest, *M.D.*, *Clinical Professor of Psychiatry, Columbia University*

'*Through a Screen Darkly* is a beautifully-written exploration of the human
psyche as it struggles with the uncertainty, anxiety, and fear prompted by the
pandemic. It is timely and fascinating. Dr. Friedberg's patients navigate from
the initial shock of lockdown, to venturing out into a "new normal," and ultimately to resilience. *A Screen* portrays the latest incarnation of an ancient human
challenge: to psychologically adapt to change and, even better, to learn how to
thrive within it.'

Heather Berlin, *Ph.D., M.P.H.*, *Neuroscientist and Assistant Clinical*
Professor of Psychiatry, Icahn School of Medicine Mount Sinai

'As a literature professor and poet, I am engaged with many issues in this book
from perspectives very different from the author's – for example, writing poems
about Covid-19. So, I'm indebted to this impressive collection for its valuable
new insights, notably its readings of literature. And *Through a Screen Darkly*
illuminates our personal experiences of the pandemic – we've seen the movie,
now read the book.'

Heather Dubrow, *Ph.D., John D. Boyd SJ Chair in Poetic*
Imagination, Fordham University

Through a Screen Darkly

This book offers real-time, intimate reflections on Dr. Friedberg's patients as they struggle with COVID-19 and its disruptive, dispiriting fallout.

Through a Screen Darkly identifies the psychological distress caused by the pandemic, examining how the particular elements of COVID-19 – its ability to be spread by those who seem not to have it, its intractability, the long-term uncertainty that it engenders – leave even relatively stable people shaken and unsure of the future. The book examines how, amidst radical uncertainty and the prospect of massive social change, such people learn to become resilient. The main theme of the book is that, of necessity, we learn to adapt. Though we still can only see "darkly," we can call on the resources that we have, as well as those we can reasonably acquire, so as to retain a sense of our dignity and purpose. *Through a Screen Darkly* examines what is possible now as the pandemic runs its course. It makes no predictions of how all this will ultimately play out, but offers a time capsule of how people have coped with a disease that landed suddenly and that we still do not fully understand.

Offering a series of intense encounters with worried, traumatized people, this book will be invaluable to in-training and practicing psychiatrists, as it points to the several possible directions for our national, psychological recovery from the pandemic.

Dr. Friedberg, M.D., is a Clinical Professor of Psychiatry at Icahn School of Medicine at Mount Sinai, and served twice as past president of the American Society of Psychoanalytic Physicians. He is editor of American Academy of Psychodynamic Psychiatry and Psychoanalysis *Academy Forum* and book editor of *Psychodynamic Psychiatry*, and a regular contributor to *Psychology Today*.

Sandra Sherman, J.D., Ph.D., was a Senior Attorney in the U.S. government and a professor of English at two major universities. She is the author of four books and over 60 peer-reviewed articles on 18th century literature and culture, and is co-author of several books on neuroscience. She currently works with scientists and physicians to support their research and writing.

Through a Screen Darkly

Psychoanalytic Reflections During
the Pandemic

Ahron Friedberg, M.D.
with Sandra Sherman

Routledge
Taylor & Francis Group

LONDON AND NEW YORK

First published 2021
by Routledge
2 Park Square, Milton Park, Abingdon, Oxon OX14 4RN

and by Routledge
605 Third Avenue, New York, NY 10158

Routledge is an imprint of the Taylor & Francis Group, an informa business

British Library Cataloguing-in-Publication Data
A catalogue record for this book is available from the British Library

Library of Congress Cataloging-in-Publication Data
Names: Friedberg, Ahron, 1963– author. | Sherman, Sandra, 1946– compiler.
Title: Through a screen darkly: psychoanalytic reflections during
the pandemic / Ahron Friedberg, M.D. with Sandra Sherman.
Description: Milton Park, Abingdon, Oxon; New York, NY: Routledge, 2021. |
Includes bibliographical references and index. |
Identifiers: LCCN 2020053318 (print) | LCCN 2020053319 (ebook) |
ISBN 9780367771515 (hardback) | ISBN 9780367764043 (paperback) |
ISBN 9781003169994 (ebook)
Subjects: LCSH: COVID-19 (Disease) |
COVID-19 (Disease)–Psychological aspects. | Resilience (Personality trait) |
Adjustment (Psychology)
Classification: LCC RA644.C67 F75 2021 (print) |
LCC RA644.C67 (ebook) | DDC 614.5/92414–dc23
LC record available at https://lccn.loc.gov/2020053318
LC ebook record available at https://lccn.loc.gov/2020053319

ISBN: 978-0-367-77151-5 (hbk)
ISBN: 978-0-367-76404-3 (pbk)
ISBN: 978-1-003-16999-4 (ebk)

Typeset in Bembo
by Newgen Publishing UK

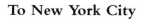

To New York City

Contents

List of figures   x
Foreword   xii
NATHAN SZAJNBERG
Acknowledgments   xiv

Introduction   1

Part I: Pandemic   8

Part II: Venturing out   48

Part III: The new normal   90

Part IV: Life, simplified (not really)   127

Reflections   168

References   173
Index   176

Figures

I.1   David sees the avenging angel punishing the people with the plague, National Library of the Netherlands.   11

I.2   Plague of Frogs from Medieval Haggadah, The British Library; 27210, f. 12v.   15

I.3   "I did not know I'd miss you as I do" (1903), Music Division, The New York Public Library. "I did not know I'd miss you as I do" The New York Public Library Digital Collections. 1901. http://digitalcollections.nypl.org/items/90c6a154-16ee-4f56-e040-e00a1806754d   25

I.4   String Fever (marionette), Library of Congress, Music Division, Federal Theatre Project Collection.   28

I.5   Still life with lemon and cut-glass wine goblet, Rijksmuseum.   38

II.1   Dixieland band, Music Division, The New York Public Library. "That funny jas band from Dixieland: song" The New York Public Library Digital Collections. 1916. http://digitalcollections.nypl.org/items/510d47da-4f0a-a3d9-e040-e00a18064a99   50

II.2   Kyoto Station, Hiroshige (1832), The Miriam and Ira D. Wallach Division of Art, Prints and Photographs: Print Collection, The New York Public Library. "Kyoto [Station 55]" The New York Public Library Digital Collections. 1832. http://digitalcollections.nypl.org/items/69f3e5ef-fcf0-0a54-e040-e00a180636a3   57

II.3   Teddy the Old Dutch Cleanser, Published by Keppler & Schwarzmann, Puck Building, June 5. Photograph. Retrieved from the Library of Congress.   60

II.4   Niwa no hanami, Women resting in a Park, Hosoda, Eishi, 1756–1829.   70

II.5   Death and the Miser, Hieronymus Bosch.   83

III.1   Miniature with man and mandrake plant, Plants from British Library, Sloane 4016, ff. 56v-57.   92

III.2	Coin purse, Brooklyn Museum Costume Collection at The Metropolitan Museum of Art, Gift of the Brooklyn Museum, 2009.	95
III.3	Brooklyn Bridge, 1916 New York: Success Postal Card Co. Durst Old York Library; Columbia University Libraries.	98
III.4	Lovers from the *Romance of the Rose*, The British Library, Harley 4425, f. 24.	103
III.5	Fire-stones, The British Library, Royal 12 C XIX, f. 26v.	117
IV.1	Dish with sailing ship, The Metropolitan Museum of Art, Harris Brisbane Dick Fund, 1966.	131
IV.2	Coronavirus.	134
IV.3	Statue with no face.	144
IV.4	Rabbis at Benei Braq, The British Library, 14761, f. 31v.	151
IV.5	Beast and Dragon, The British Library, Royal 19 B XV, f. 23.	154
IV.6	Chess board, The Metropolitan Museum of Art, Gift of Gustavus A. Pfeiffer, 1948.	161
IV.7	Vintage Map of New York City Subway System, Library of Congress, Geography and Map Division.	165

Foreword

Pandemic: a shadow across our lives. This book is a light across it.

We have all lived through the early phases of this pandemic, and have watched its effects spread across society like a vast black stain from a tipped-over bottle of indelible ink. Nothing seems like it will ever be the same. When we share our feelings, we stop ourselves: "Can I really acknowledge all of this? How much of someone else's troubles can I take on board?" The pandemic is testing our willingness to participate in the human condition. Sometimes, we feel numb.

Yet we're still here, you're reading this foreword, trying to make sense of a world where the simplest protocols – making friends, earning a living, shopping for groceries – have been massively altered until . . . who knows when? While we can't look for certainty, we have to find guideposts. We talk to people, join chat rooms. Perhaps our collective experience is itself a form of guidance: if others can sort out their options and find ways to cope, then maybe we can too. Maybe we can learn from these others, even be inspired as they navigate this challenging terrain.

Through a Screen Darkly: Psychoanalytic Reflections During the Pandemic offers a remarkable, multi-dimensional opportunity to encounter real-life human beings struggling through the first year of the pandemic. These people are patients of Dr. Ahron Friedberg, a New York City psychiatrist whom I have known for many years. Dr. Friedberg counsels these people as they lose jobs, watch loved-ones die, stress-out as ER doctors, try to keep their kids safe, try to maintain relationships, yet endure bouts of corrosive loneliness. He helps them work through self-doubt, guilt, and the temptation to just give up. None of these patients know any of the others, but – however vulnerable – they come together, as a creative community of determined survivors.

These people are a version of how we all may get through this. Working with Dr. Friedberg, they develop resilience and discover internal resources that they never knew they had. This pandemic forces us to rediscover our best selves. The people in *Through a Screen Darkly* find out that they have the ability to put one foot in front of another and keep going towards something better. In a couple of the essays in *A Screen*, the image of a bridge features prominently. We're on a journey out of this pandemic. Don't look down.

The title of *A Screen* derives from the Biblical phrase, "through a glass darkly," where Saint Paul suggests that our vision of reality is unclear. During the period covered in this book, Dr. Friedberg practiced remotely – the "screen" is literal, an iPad, a computer, maybe even an iPhone. This is one of the first books to examine how psychotherapy operates when patient and therapist are not face-to-face in the same room. I found Dr. Friedberg's conclusions (e.g. that remoteness may actually *promote* good therapy) to be fascinating, and a possible harbinger of how the profession may permanently change.

But most of all, I was fascinated by the nuanced depiction in these essays of the human dilemmas resulting from this pandemic. We find ourselves somewhere among all these individuals as they come up against problems that change shape spontaneously; seem never to go away; and consume all their energy, empathy, and faith in institutions. This book is focused on the personal – not on politics or the wider culture, although these externalities appear in the background. The action occurs in people's heads.

We also come away with a firm understanding of what it is like to treat a vast array of people during a time of stress and uncertainty. As in his previous book, *Psychotherapy and Personal Change: Two Minds in a Mirror*, Dr. Friedberg provides candid insights into how mental health professionals process their own stress, even while remaining attuned to their patients' fears, doubts, and consuming grief. When Dr. Friedberg turns to poetry, and shows us how he learns from it, we learn an immense amount about how the medical mind reaches beyond science towards other modes of knowledge.

A Screen begins as the pandemic first takes hold in New York, and follows it through people's slow progress towards venturing out; contending with a "new normal" that, in light of its uncertainty, is newer than it is normal; and finally, settling into a lifestyle that seems simpler on the surface (there are fewer choices) but for that very reason is perversely more challenging. None of these phases is starkly delineated; they are more like moods, shifting perspectives that go along with the opening of sidewalk cafes and reopening of businesses that have not permanently closed. When you finish reading *A Screen*, you think you've been immersed in a time capsule. This is what it felt like when life seemed to stop and then inched back towards being something else, alive, yet obviously different.

Dr. Friedberg has caught the psychological reality of this pandemic, its permutations and combinations, over a swath of time that will be studied for decades. I cannot imagine a better place to begin to understand it than *Through a Screen Darkly*.

Nathan Szajnberg, M.D.
Palo Alto, CA

Acknowledgments

First, I would like to thank Dr. Sandra Sherman, my co-author on *Through a Screen Darkly*. Initially, I published an article in *The Academy Forum* about my patients' experience with COVID-19, and did not think to follow up with a book. But Sandra proposed the project, and became its driving force. I could not have completed this effort without her intelligence, creativity, and awesome capacity for work.

Based on my original article, Hara Estroff Marano, former Editor of *Psychology Today* and now its Editor at Large, invited me to contribute to the magazine on the topic of resilience during the crisis. This provided a platform to describe the patients, along with others, whom I helped during this stressful period.

My clinical practice as a psychodynamic psychiatrist was informed by the work of Dr. Dennis Charney, M.D., Dean for the Icahn School of Medicine at Mount Sinai and President for Academic Affairs. His contributions to resilience as they relate to the treatment of Anxiety Disorders, PTSD, and Major Depression, as well as stress management and wellness, have been central to the treatment and care of my patients during this time.

Furthermore, since poetry sustained me during the pandemic, it appears throughout these essays. I would like to thank the following rights-holders for permission to quote:

"Love Song (I lie here thinking of you)" by William Carlos Williams, from THE COLLECTED POEMS: VOLUME I, 1909–1939, copyright ©1938 by New Directions Publishing Corp. Reprinted by permission of New Directions Publishing Corp.

Print rights for UK and Commonwealth for "Love Song," in William Carlos Williams, Ed: Walton Litz and Christopher MacGowan; Collected Poems Volume I, 1909–1939, acknowledgment is made to Carcanet.

"Dolor," copyright © 1943 by Modern Poetry Association, Inc. Copyright © 1966 and renewed 1994 by Beatrice Lushington; from COLLECTED POEMS by Theodore Roethke. Used by permission of Doubleday, an imprint of the Knopf Doubleday Publishing Group, a division of Penguin Random House LLC. All rights reserved.

For Non-exclusive English language permission throughout UK and British Commonwealth excluding Canada for Print rights to Theodore Roethke's "Dolor," acknowledgment is made to Faber and Faber Ltd.

"The Man with the Blue Guitar," copyright 1937 by Wallace Stevens; from THE COLLECTED POEMS OF WALLACE STEVENS by Wallace Stevens. Used by permission of Alfred A. Knopf, an imprint of the Knopf Doubleday Publishing Group, a division of Penguin Random House LLC. All rights reserved.

For print rights to "The Man with the Blue Guitar" in the UK and British Commonwealth, excluding Canada, acknowledgment is made to Faber and Faber Ltd.

From the song, "God Bless the Grass," words and music by Malvina Reynolds, Copyright 1964 Schroder Music Co. (ASCAP); Renewed 1992, Used by permission. All rights reserved.

Angelos Polychronopoulos provided technical assistance with the images, helping us to enlarge them to meet Routledge's requirements.

As *Through a Screen Darkly* has been a labor-intensive endeavor alongside my practice, I'd be remiss not to express my gratitude to my wife, Tania Friedberg, who tirelessly supported my efforts throughout this especially trying time.

Introduction

This book's title, *Through A Screen Darkly*, riffs on the passage from 1 Corinthians 13:12, "For now we see through a glass, darkly" – updating its technological premises without much altering the dilemma that it represents. As we come through and reflect on a 21st century pandemic, we still cannot see it in natural light. Our vision (what we see) is dark. In the Bible, St. Paul refers to a "glass" (perhaps a mirror) that provides only a darkened vision of reality; I replace that image with a screen which, since the pandemic began, has provided the digital means through which reality is backlit and only imperfectly interpretable.

Apart from the fact that my psychiatric practice has moved 100 percent onto screen-based platforms like FaceTime, Skype, and Zoom, I chose the "screen" image because, in our current environment, screens have a double, ambiguating function that affects almost every aspect of our progress through this pandemic (and, hence, how this book is designed). On the one hand, screens make possible whatever vision we have. Even though I am not in my office in Manhattan, I can see my patients and talk with them in real time while I watch their eyes and register whether they have bothered to get dressed. But on the other hand, the screen is a barrier, just like conventional screens in, say, hospitals, where they keep people apart. On digital platforms, I am with my patients but I'm not.

As I explain in Part I of *A Screen*, such remote connection took some adjustment on my part, since it diverged from how I had practiced for over 25 years: my patients and I had always sat opposite each other (or with them laying on a couch), picking up cues as people do when they talk naturally. I could watch their body language as, perhaps, we brought up a painful subject from the past. They could look at some art on the wall. But screens screen out most of how we naturally approach and avoid each other's gaze. No one has anywhere to look except at each other's torsos. The intensity can be unnerving, even overwhelming. What might have taken weeks to uncover, takes only a couple of sessions.

Psychiatrists' version of their reality is "dark," therefore, because this is not how we normally perceive that reality. Customary details drop out. In this sense, psychiatry becomes a darkened mirror of an equally dark, larger world that we cannot figure out (in the ways that we used to) but that we still have to live in. Psychiatrists, like everyone else, talk about normality as something remembered.

I was not sure how or whether this kind of psychiatry would work. But I was pleasantly surprised. In May, 2020, Adam Gopnik wrote an article in the *New Yorker* arguing that digital platforms had transformed psychiatric practice – and, in fact, made it better. I came around to believing, however tentatively, that he had a point. I wrote an essay, which appears in Part I, which said:

> Sometimes treatment can be more focused [on a screen] than is possible in an office visit; we get to the heart of an issue more quickly; we lock eyes (the windows and my artworks are out of bounds), and the patient can't as freely associate. This creates a more interpersonal, less intrapsychic experience. From a psychiatrist's perspective, what you see is more nearly equivalent to what you actually get.

There is an immediacy to remote psychiatry that sounds paradoxical but actually is not. The physical distance enforces a directness that intensifies our exchanges with patients. The essays in *A Screen* render that directness. They are a flash of light, so to speak, through the darkness of this time and of the medium that has come to define how we navigate through it. Thus, while they do not reflect the type of psychiatry normalized over analog decades, they are still the product of intense encounters with people upended by this pandemic. This book's subtitle, *Psychoanalytic Reflections During the Pandemic*, is meant to convey that they came out "during" this period, that is, in real time over the course of a long, still unfinished episode of our history.

These essays, which I began to draft in February, 2020, appeared in *Psychology Today* beginning that April. In *A Screen*, they are organized more or less chronologically along the time-line of the pandemic during that year. A year or two or ten from now, they will read like a time capsule of the period, present-tense moments in a past from which we may have diverged dramatically. The pandemic is changing us – changing everything – very quickly, and we may not even recognize who we were just a short time ago. In publishing these essays now, therefore, I am making that point in advance. I want to record some of the anxiety, fear – and ways of coping – as we lived these phenomena in real time, and as they characterized the onset of the pandemic through to its early consequences.

A Screen is presented in four parts: "Pandemic," "Venturing Out," "The New Normal," and "Life, Simplified (Not Really)." Together, the parts follow the arc of the pandemic from its sudden, overwhelming wallop; our tentative re-emergence from lockdown; the experience of a changed world; and development of new strategies for coping and rebuilding. But I want to emphasize that – notwithstanding when an essay first appeared – none of these parts represent discrete time periods, say, February through April or May through July. Rather, they represent a change in mood, a sort of shared sense that things had become somewhat different. Maybe it is okay to venture out, whereas before you risked your life. Maybe stores are open, but curbside pick-up is the rule. The differences are not stark, but it is possible to sense a change.

Yet because the differences are felt rather than marked off on the calendar, the moods that characterize these periods bleed into each other; they go back and forth; sometimes they are stronger than at other times. *A Screen* reflects these moods as a generality and as they waver over the pandemic's course. Thus, while none of the parts are arbitrary (we really did feel this way), neither are they clinically, scientifically, measurably precise. They resemble psychiatry, which deals with the human condition – which has ups and downs that are rarely exactly the same from day-to-day. Above all, they do not necessarily track the epidemiological facts on the ground. We may venture out, as a community, even as cases are rising. It's just that we're tired of staying at home.

For example, my subject throughout *A Screen*, however, and what ties all these essays together, is the psychological effect produced by the pandemic, followed by how my patients learned to cope. Anxiety Disorders are among the most commonly diagnosed psychiatrist conditions, and during the pandemic they surged. As described in the Diagnostic and Statistical Manual of Psychiatry (DSMV), these disorders are characterized by excessive anxiety or fear with related behavioral and mental disturbances. Anxiety focuses more on anticipation of a future threat, with an increase in vigilance, muscle tension, and avoidance; fear focuses on an immediate danger, and is associated with a fight-or-flight type response. Panic attacks can occur with either.

A patient with an anxiety disorder will typically overestimate the danger posed by situations causing them to be anxious or afraid. But in the case of COVID, it was hard for a clinician to know whether a person's anxiety and fear were excessive. It is entirely *reasonable* to show concern because even limited, indirect exposure can lead to infection. Moreover, infected individuals can be asymptomatic, leaving the whole world a potential source of exposure. When panic develops, the patient may be caught in a feedback loop where anxiety and fear feed on each other.

There is no rational way of stopping this intensifying feedback as the disease spreads, since the absence of any specific, tangible source of infection does not prove that such a source is not "out there," just waiting to materialize. Generalized Anxiety Disorder (GAD) develops when the anxiety becomes persistent and excessive. The person is not able to control it.

By definition GAD interferes with normal functioning, e.g. at work, at school, or in relationships and social settings. Some other features include difficulty concentrating, fatigue, irritability, and sleep disturbance. Some people that were chronically – but nonspecifically anxious – now meet formal diagnostic criteria for GAD and require treatment. In these cases, COVID-19 is the obvious determinant, whether or not someone has actually had the disease.

Like other psychiatrists and mental health professionals, I had to deal with the dramatic increase in anxiety disorders and related conditions during this time. People became ineffective at work; they had difficulty with friends and loved ones; it was hard to fall (or stay) asleep. I saw more panic attacks. Even people who, historically, had been resilient ultimately were impacted.

Over the course of these essays, I describe how my patients responded. In Part I ("Pandemic"), I emphasize how, amidst undeniable catastrophe, they nonetheless develop coping strategies and even learn to cultivate hope. They write songs and poems which become cathartic; they learn languages that connect them with tradition; they recover enough self-confidence to return to work. In effect, they equip themselves to keep going. They step onto the narrow, shaky bridge of this pandemic (towards no one quite knows where) but they don't look down.

They think they will get to the other side, but accept the idea of not knowing where they will emerge. Each Part of *A Screen* is concerned with uncertainty. Even as a new so-called "normal" takes hold, it is wise to hold your breath and cross your fingers. Part I examines the uncertainty of the moment and also as a component of plagues throughout history. It cites Daniel Defoe's *A Journal of the Plague Year* (1722) – a fictional account of the 1665 London plague – as the ur-text in English describing the uncertainty unleashed by a communicable disease for which there is no cure. Defoe's rendition of people's bafflement maps precisely onto today's epidemiological reports which, in turn, transfix us all. Uncertainty is the leitmotif of plague and, in *A Screen*, I do not pretend otherwise. Thus, while there is definitely "progress" from Part I to Part IV – we are eating in outdoor cafes, possibly getting our hair cut – the pandemic stays with us like a flashing yellow light.

However, while uncertainty is the theme of this book, its counterweight in Parts II, III, and IV is resilience – our capacity to bounce back from adversity. Thus, in Part II ("Venturing Out"), I talk about reconnecting, albeit gingerly, with others and with ourselves. I treat doctors who, for example, are stressed to the max; they figure out how to curtail a sense of failure. Other patients apply for jobs remotely, perfecting a screen persona. They let go of old assumptions about what they "should" be, and think in terms of what is possible. This is not a lowering of their sights; rather, it is a cultivation of peripheral vision. Such resilience requires hope, a version of the possible.

Possibility turns out to be a complicated term. If it replaces old certainties, it still allows us to consider the future from a new, unaccustomed angle of approach. There are no guarantees, but neither are doors to the future entirely shut. We simply have to adapt (there would be no *homo sapiens* if that wasn't in our species' ground game).

Part II also talks about my own ability to bounce back from stress by turning to poetry. Poetry provides me with metaphors to think about the pandemic. It helps me understand how it lingers, and how its defining attribute is loss. Reading poetry now does not make me happy in a conventional sense, but I feel stronger – more resilient – when I do.

Part II addresses the common dilemmas of venturing out, e.g. the safety of commuting and parents' concerns for children who insist on seeing friends. Even such mundane activities give rise to guilt and fear – I treat patients worried that their choices could spread the disease, even affecting people that they love. Ultimately, the Part concerns where and how to set limits, and how to enforce them. Many of my patients have never faced such questions so directly or with such psychologically potent consequences.

Parts III and IV ("The New Normal," "Life, Simplified (Not Really)"), extend into new patterns of life that emerge as the pandemic lumbers on. It will remain with us at least until there is a vaccine, and probably for much longer. Thus, Part III is about getting used to change – new ways of dating (what sort of physical contact? when?); going to school; traveling. Though many such activities may not be stressful in themselves, getting used to them – that is, making the transition – can call into question our judgment, even pitch us into bouts of guilt. We may worry, for example, that our resistance to change (or simple ineptitude) makes it harder for others to get on with their lives. On the other hand, we may resent those who accommodate more easily. We may *really* resent those who have done better financially. I counsel people who have trouble with changed circumstances, and help them to develop skills for dealing with change that (deep down) they do not want to accept.

Part IV concerns the apparent simplification of having fewer choices – a situation that, in fact, turns out to be just another complication. How do we navigate a world in which so much appears to be closed off or, worse yet, permanently closed down? How can we cope with a new kind of isolation – not indoors, precisely, but still cut off from the exploding capitalist phantasmagoria of pre-pandemic America? The only reasonable approach, which my patients come around to, is to adjust their estimate of what actually matters. They move further towards the connections that they have; they cultivate newer, more satisfying connections; they become more introspective to compensate for the loss of easy outlets to fun and distraction. In this sense, they become more like people used to be, say, at a time when access to fun and distraction was not so easy. Part IV is about the complications of living a simpler, more focused life, when we've become used to a plethora of choices (where, if something doesn't work out, we'll try something else). Commitment entails a heightened sense of consequentiality. This worries my patients; we discuss it.

Ultimately, Part IV is about managing a pandemic that has not gone away. The crux is that we are "managing" without a sense that we are in control. Such managing modulates into acceptance, and into an unwonted engagement with our community.

A Screen is not intended to predict where we go from here in the epic journey beyond this pandemic. Rather, it renders our very recent history, starting with the pandemic's onset and carrying through to our initial response. It's too early to be optimistic, pessimistic, or even anything in between. What I have tried to do, is to help put a human face on the period of the past several months. I have avoided the macro-issues of pandemic politics, as well as the large cultural issues of why this country was less able to remain in lockdown than some others. Professional historians will study those issues into the next generation.

A Screen is human scale, a series of intimate encounters between a psychiatrist and his patients.

I have so many stories to tell because I practice in New York City, the initial epicenter of the pandemic in this country. But still, my focus is on individuals, not on the mass of people affected. I focus on their mental state. Every day, stories recount the pandemic's psychological toll, which is even wider than its horrific physical impact. I see a tiny fraction of these people, but in many ways they are representative. As I write this, the unemployment rate rivals that of the Great Depression – my patients without jobs stand in for countless others. The physicians that I treat are as stressed as physicians anywhere.

Of course, the stories in *A Screen* are pointillistic dots (okay, pixels!) in a vast ongoing picture that will continue to emerge and, perhaps, become less dark. We can hope.

Finally, I should note that while *A Screen* may provide some guidance regarding how to get through the pandemic, it is not an instructional manual. It is not systematic. It describes the world as I have seen it. However, the examples that I include reflect general principles of resilience that I would like to emphasize. In "Building Your Resilience" (2012), the American Psychological Association suggests practices that, in some personal combination, can help us bounce back from trauma:

(1) Make connections with people and build strong relationships with family and friends.
(2) Avoid seeing crises as insurmountable problems.
(3) Accept that change is a part of living, and there are circumstances you cannot alter.
(4) Move toward your goals but make them realistic.
(5) Take decisive actions, and act on adverse situations as much as you can rather than being passive.
(6) Look for opportunities to discover more about yourself and gain an increased sense of self-worth.
(7) Nurture a confident, positive view of yourself.
(8) Keep events in perspective, and do not blow them out of proportion.
(9) Maintain a hopeful outlook, and visualize what you want.
(10) Take care of yourself by paying attention to your emotional and physical needs.

In examining the lives of my patients, I have touched on most of these. You can start with one or two, and then you can build out. The point is to remember that we are all in this, and that nobody will think you are acting out of turn by trying to survive with your sanity intact.

By now, we have all heard the cliché, "What does not kill me makes me stronger." It's from Friedrich Nietzsche's *Twilight of the Idols* (1888). Since that time, it has figured in the titles of several record albums (e.g. Bruce Willis' *If It Don't Kill You, It Just Makes You Stronger* [Motown, 1989]) and in the lyrics of popular songs (e.g. Kanye West's "Stronger" [*Late Registration*, Def Jam, 2005]). The point that I want to make is that we can learn from adversity, not merely adjust to it. Even though the pandemic has touched us in different ways – some almost to the point of dying, others not nearly so much – all of us are affected if only to be horrified at the effect on someone else. So, we can learn compassion. We can learn how to help. These are strengths, as much as any.

The stories in *Through a Screen Darkly* are based on those of real people, or composites of real people. However, everyone's name was changed and any identifying details were altered. If you think you recognize yourself, it's only because the stories recall people who are like you – but they're not you. We all have so many similar problems.

Part I: Pandemic

Part I of *Through a Screen Darkly* reflects on my patients as the pandemic disorders their lives. They struggle to understand it, as neither they – nor anyone else who's alive – has ever seen anything so encompassing. They're stunned. For a time, life is arrested, thrown against a wall, and made to keep its hands up.

Arrest and imprisonment feel like appropriate metaphors. How can normal people cope with outrageously abnormal limitation? How can they handle all the rest of life's problems, and then this too? But the fact is they can, and they do.

My role is to talk people through the initial shock towards some semblance of acceptance and, then, adaptation. First, however, I have to accommodate *myself* to the pandemic. It's not often that psychiatrists and patients share a common, massively disorganizing challenge. But this is one of those times. People who come through the screen barely have to explain themselves. We experience instant empathy (normally, this can take weeks).

As we talk, the present emerges as unnerving but also precious, given what might happen if we approach it incorrectly. In its perverse way, the pandemic is clarifying. It focuses our gaze. Where I and everyone once endured – even maybe embraced – our daily distractions, we now just address what matters: adapting, keeping safe.

It's like evolution unfolding in real time. We watch ourselves adapt and survive. It's existential drama.

However, since we're locked down and bored, we shuttle between drama and barrenness. The pandemic is in this sense an impresario of paradox. T-shirts say "Distant Together." My bank implores "Stand together by standing apart."

Part I is about how some of my patients learn to adapt. As soon as COVID-19 becomes rampant, its psychological fallout is as significant as its physical effects. The stress of having the disease, of knowing someone who has it, or of being on the frontlines of treating it is obvious. What makes this stress so challenging is its suddenness – no one sees it coming, no one is prepared. Do the old treatments work? Do we even have time to try them when people suffer so acutely?

Like everyone else, psychiatrists and their patients have to learn fast. COVID-19 is an immersion course in constraining stress and its progenitors in guilt, fear, loss of confidence, and loss of hope for the future. With our sense of time radically foreshortened to getting through the next day, it's hard even to think about the future except as more of the same.

I have to suggest approaches to this time that are not transparently anodyne, but that help people see hope as a necessary component of resilience, strength ... survival. No one can get anywhere if they have no idea where they're going. So, we talk about realistic bases for hope. In each case, there is some substrate that we can build on. Many of these stories are about reinforcing connections; developing old interests into skills; achieving small victories that remind us of our larger capacities. The point is to competently reimagine ourselves in a post-COVID world, different perhaps from our current selves but still here – and maybe better, more aware, increasingly sensitive to people with whom we still share this world.

In this process, each of my patients has his or her own narrative, reflecting the unique configuration of their lives. In choosing their stories (and some that relate to me personally), I want to demonstrate the multiple routes to beating back galloping stress and despair. The process is not easy, but it's possible with the necessary level of commitment. So, I try to develop in my patients the will to try – to keep going, to keep looking ahead instead of down. In looking ahead – literally -- Part II describes a rabbi and *his* story about a narrow, shaky bridge that defines how we can traverse perilous times.

Hope is the underlying thread tying these stories together. They examine how to ground hope in the resources that each patient can draw on. Psychiatry works through problems based on what a patient knows or has the capacity to learn. The pandemic is forcing us all to learn. My patient who learns Yiddish, as a way of drawing on the strength of cultural tradition, is a case in point. In this posture, hope is not some leap of faith. Rather, it is a *modus operandi*, a way of getting to another place that has to be better even if it is immensely different.

In the subsequent Parts of *Through a Screen Darkly*, hope emerges as the driver of resilience. My patients show signs of bouncing back because they had developed the confidence that they could. But in Part I, I illustrate how the pandemic's initial wallop forces people to hold onto hope despite the radical uncertainty of what's coming. Uncertainty is among the biggest challenges to any attempt at hope. It requires us to see around corners. But it also gives us grounds to see possibilities, and *realistic* possibilities are what I help my patients to formulate.

Of course, whenever psychiatrists talk about possibility they do so in the context of change. In my discussions with patients during the pandemic, I help them to be willing to accept change – in their work, their relationships, even in what they value. Throughout the early weeks of the pandemic, there is a yearning for some kind of "return to normality." That is, for everything to go back to just the way it was (people who disliked their lives, suddenly saw them as wonderful!). But quickly enough, we realize that what was normal in, say, February, will never be just the same. So, the question that I ask patients is whether, assuming that life is different as we go forward, they will allow life to change them or – ideally – they will be instrumental in changing themselves into the best-adapted people that they can be.

In virtually every case, these stories explain how people realize the need for change and move to embrace it. For all its horror, the pandemic is motivational, even inspirational. It brings out reserves of strength that we didn't know we had. So, while during this period no one congratulates themselves, they're able to survive the initial shock with a modicum of self-confidence and (yes!) hope. They develop momentum and assert control (at least where they can) when everything seems totally out of control.

If the pandemic is a centrifuge, they slow it down.

So, here are the stories, beginning with my own. They cover a period roughly from late January through late May, 2020, though, as the Introduction explains, the various feelings that we have all through the pandemic continually refract through each other. Thus, even in the early months, there is nothing simple (in the sense of being clear) about how we feel. Predominantly, we react to the initial onset of COVID-19. We are scared and worn down, as one would expect. Yet we still begin to venture out and glimpse the new normal, which will be more characteristic of later periods. Our focus continually readjusts to allow us to take it all in.

WAKING UP TO COVID-19

It's not like when JFK was shot or 9/11 happened. Everyone who was over the age of, maybe 7, knows where they were when those tragedies occurred, and exactly what they were doing. They remember being stopped cold, stunned. But this tragedy is different. As a psychiatrist, people come to me all the time with fears and anxieties. Heightened fear is nothing new. But slowly, over several weeks, the nature of this fear began to change. It was morphing into a terror of harming people, even oneself. It was guilt-ridden. In the space of perhaps a month, fear was laced with mistrust, anger, and dread. That's when it hit me that, in its slow insidious way, COVID-19 was right up there with JFK's assassination and 9/11 in its impact on people's psyches. Only it took time for us to see it that way.

Even though I am an M.D., and have over 25 years' experience, like many people I wasn't prepared for the bad news – probably because, like in the Phony War of 1939, nothing seemed to be happening. There were scattered reports. The first real sign of things for me was back in January when some Asians I commute with on the Long Island Railroad started wearing masks. But when I saw them, my frame of reference was wrong: political rather than epidemio-logical. Since I knew about an outbreak in Wuhan, I saw this face-covering as a show of solidarity – like wearing white for the suffragettes – rather than a proactive measure against what could happen.

It wasn't until it did happen, inescapably, that I realized that it had. Then suddenly I was scrambling. Whereas before I was practicing out of a Park Avenue office, talking to patients in an intimate but professional setting, I was now Skyping and FaceTiming in my attic study, trying to maintain some professional distance

Figure I.1 David sees the avenging angel punishing the people with the plague

when our screens were filled with each other's faces only inches apart. I struggled to mitigate the medium's intensity, afraid that my reactions might seem amplified – even extreme – when my patients expressed their own overwhelming fear.

Psychiatrists are not trained to refract their therapeutic approach through social media. I had tried it on my own a few times, but nothing major. But as I would discover as the pandemic progressed, there were no protocols for a situation so totally out of whack. Even in the aftermath of 9/11, which affected every person in the City, I was back in my office in a couple of days. My patients came there to feel normal, if only briefly. But nothing I can do now simulates normality. The stress is everywhere. It's intensifying. Some of my colleagues cannot practice under these conditions; they are disoriented by the makeshift adaptations that seem foreign to their concept of how we treat patients.

I am pushing on, but this is new territory. Among my patients, I have never seen such a sudden access of single-minded fear. All their usual, kaleidoscopic concerns – office politics, children, extramarital affairs – have snapped into abeyance behind one overriding worry: everything feels out of control. What comes out when we talk is a kind of hyped-up banality, a sense that quotidian tasks are potential inflection points along the road to their main concern: not getting sick. They ask about where to walk the dog, when to buy groceries, how to wash hands.

I try to offer realistic reassurance, but am afraid of lapsing back into that same blinkered frame of mind that I had in January. So, I say something about not panicking. But are people so panicked already that they're not listening to reassurance? I wonder if they can process advice, based on sound medical principle, that panic elevates stress levels even further. I wonder if some may resent when I offer what they hear to be platitudes, stock responses, when what they really want – perversely – is someone to share their doom and gloom.

I wish I could keep the chaos outside from enveloping the space that I share with my patients. But it's impossible. My simplest question is received as an existential challenge. I usually start a session with "How's it going?" or "How are things?" Now my patients ignore pleasantries. "I lost my job," "My dad is in the hospital," or "My wife has COVID" are common responses. If they've thought about their reply in advance, they seem to have concluded that whatever they say will not match the anxiety that they feel, so they just confess, "I'm not sure."

My regular patients know that I may press them to be more explicit, so they're surprised when I accept this response and appreciate their candor. I tell them we have to acknowledge the uncertainty surrounding this pandemic. The scientists who issue daily updates on infection rates, mortality, and when this will end are conspicuously uncertain. To them, COVID-19 is a moving target. Their imprecision is a form of honesty, the unalloyed outcome of number-crunching disciplines that prohibit certainty when data fails to support it. Moreover, since we *are* the data, we should adopt the same epistemology to describe our own lives. If our lives do not compute right now, we should say so. That extends to our employment status, our wavering confidence in the government – to whatever seems uncertain, and not just whether we will escape this plague.

Of course, honesty about ourselves may be received as an intrusion on others' carefully constructed composure. But for the most part, it sets others at ease, letting them know that they're not alone in feeling unsettled. If it is a paradox that shared unease is reassuring, this only reflects our need to be understood. In the context of mutual understanding while under the threat of plague, the old cliché, "misery loves company," has been newly renovated: now it permits us to be honest with each other when we are walking examples of the Uncertainty Principle. "I'm not sure," as a response, is the quintessential form of honesty.

So, as I settle into this pandemic and try to be honest with myself about the prospects of my patients, my practice, and my own mental health, I look in the mirror and say "I'm not sure." I have always tried to be honest with myself, but I was motivated by the belief that honesty is the first step towards improvement. If you admit that you're not perfect, you can find ways to do better. But now, amidst COVID-19, how do I make things better? Indeed, can I? Can I get a patient another job, and so keep her from despair? Can I keep her as a patient, when she can't even pay her rent? If I project a studied calm, so as not to rattle my patients, will they be bothered by it, or even resent me? How can I project *any* calm when everyone knows that today's advice may be useless tomorrow?

So, I'll keep an open journal. I'll try to be honest with myself and others, keeping track of our shared concerns. I want to learn more about what helps us become better and stronger – more resilient – as individuals and a community. Maybe succeeding entries will temper the uncertainties. But to be honest, I'm not sure.

WALKING THROUGH A PLAGUE

When I talk with patients now, we battle a sense of being stuck in the present. It's hard to imagine the near future, which just seems like a desert of dreary sameness; it's hard to remember the recent past, which seems infinitely longer ago than it really is. Time seems to have stopped or, rather, to have dissolved into a tick-tock routine that we are powerless to change. This frustrates me, since I always counsel patients that positive change is within their grasp (my forth-coming book, in fact, is titled *Psychotherapy and Personal Change*, 2021). But here we are, cemented in this moment, as if even our speech did not take time – 343 meters-per-second – to reach each other.

So, it's important, I think, to establish some perspective and, if we can't pre-dict the future in our current position, to at least learn from the past. The past has become more useful than it has been for some time: normally, we inhabit a culture fixated on the next deal, next date, next anything that satisfies our need for possibility. But as we find ourselves in this endless protracted moment of anxiety tinctured with boredom, we suddenly have time for the past. I mean the real, deep past, not just yesterday's news or the photos that fall from a drawer now that we fill our days with house-cleaning.

There is a website with 60,000 old books, Project Gutenberg, where vir-tually all the classics are available for free. While it was not made to liberate us from our current, stay-at-home navel-gazing, it might as well have been. Same with Eighteenth-Century Collections Online (ECCO) – thousands of titles, most of which I never heard of. With a New York City library card, ECCO is also free. Same with Early English Books Online (EEBO), for books before 1700. In other words, the past is extraordinarily accessible – even if the grocery store is not. After Skyping with patients all day, I wandered through these sites, looking for discussions of how to cope with extremity.

I found some of them. In the 17th and 18th centuries, repeated bouts of Plague felled millions, and people reflected in print on the devastation. In these books and pamphlets, I entered a world of antique English (ironically revived through modern technology), where everyone was as scared as we are. There were titles like *The mirror or glasse of health necessary and needful for euery person to looke in, that will keep their bodye from the sicknesse and pestilence* (1580), and *London's plague-sore discovered. Or, some serious notes and suitable considerations upon the present visitation at London wherein is something by way of lamentation, informa-tion, expostulation, exhortation, and caution* (1665). They make one shudder.

Of course, no one really had a cure. Medicine consisted in medical lore, circulating much like urban myth does today. Except for the utterly credulous, people developed psychological defenses – they compensated, like the blind who cultivate hearing. This is what interested me.

What I found in literary history was a useful epistemology, i.e. a way of conceiving plague. A lot of comparison has been made to the London Plague of 1665, and I suggest that for sheer psychological acuity – and the first real claim that uncertainty is the only honest response to pandemic – no one beats Daniel Defoe's fictionalized account in *A Journal of the Plague Year* (1722). Defoe's narrator, H.F., introduces his account by acknowledging that while the incidents he describes are "very near Truth," it is a fact that "no Man could at such a Time, learn all the Particulars." To be in the midst of the Plague was to see it incompletely. Later on, when looking into a pit of the piled-up dead, H.F. acknowledges the ineffability of plague phenomena and the inability of language to render them: "[I]t is impossible to say any Thing that is able to give a true Idea of it to those who did not see it, other than this, that it was indeed *very, very, very* dreadful, and such as no Tongue can express."

In an eerie anticipation of our own plague, H.F. asserts that the Bills of Mortality "never gave a full Account, by many thousands; the Confusion being such, and the Carts working in the Dark, when they carried the Dead, that in some Places no account at all was kept, but they work'd on." In example after example, H.F. demonstrates that the only honest response when trying to describe plague is to say you don't know because you can't know. In a time of plague, you accommodate to uncertainty. You must.

When I read through this old book, the irresolution it depicts was clarifying. It felt like a diagnosis. We are experiencing the same inability to grasp the situation. We don't know who is still going to get this disease; how long it will persist; how it will permanently alter our lives. Right now, while we must live in uncertainty and accept it, our chronic inability to fathom it produces enormous stress.

As I talk with patients, and they worry about getting the disease, they worry as much about the effect of all this worry. Like H.F., they see an infinite regress into a morass of unanswerable questions. I can't tell them not to worry. I can't simply say to focus on the important things, when they can hardly focus at all. There has been a discussion recently about how, during this pandemic, people's ability to focus has declined. One of my patients said, "I try to work, but I keep interrupting myself, and then I interrupt the interruption with something else." I think that lack of sensory stimulation, the effect of sitting at home day after day, turns the mind into a closed box where whatever's there just keeps ramifying. I have told some of my patients about H.F. and how he makes it through the Plague by means of luck and resilience. It's possible. I can help my patients to elicit luck by developing skills that contribute to resilience.

As we talk, I say "Look, we have vastly more resources than they did. And their first resource was themselves." That's encouraging. But the point is to approach our current dilemma by accepting it – in its complexity and uncertainty – and then trying to live our best lives in this constricted present. We should maintain our connections and feel part of the world, so that we can be there when the world returns. It's up to the world to return. We can't make it. But we can be ready for it.

I take walks, exercise, practice yoga. I focus on my family, seek support where I can find it. Writing helps. Creativity, now smaller scale, is no less real. We try whatever's possible.

PHYSICAN STRESS

Physicians on the frontlines of a crisis tend to open up to psychiatrists. We're physicians too. The assumption is that we can empathize at once, no lengthy explanations required. It's like when you meet someone and think "I've known this person for years." When physicians come to see me, they crave this instant response – they're pressed for time, stressed-out, and looking for support from someone who gets it.

Figure I.2 Plague of Frogs from Medieval Haggadah

Of course, working with physicians stresses me too. Their expectations are high and I don't want to disappoint. I also know, deep down, that my life is easier than theirs. I have to transpose my sheltered existence to the chaos of a hospital ward, where patients are wheeled in for emergency intubation and monitored minute-by-minute. I don't pretend to have been there, but I stretch myself to understand. So, while I admire their courage, and am sometimes in awe, it's helpful to us both if I don't show it.

Rick, a physician in his mid-thirties, drew on all my capacity for empathy. He presented over a year ago with anxiety and depression, stressed over his work in an ER and uncertain about his girlfriend. Then COVID hit. He'd been called over a weekend to work a double shift. Hospital beds were filled to capacity and medical supplies were dwindling. He had to use the same N95 mask for the entire day, which worried him, since a colleague had contracted the virus and died. I acknowledged how vulnerable that must have made him feel, and he teared up over the loss. He recalled his brother who died of an overdose and wondered if he might have done more to help him. I said that his present loss had brought up feelings from the past, and that while we could talk more about that over time, for now we had to help him with his current situation. I suggested that even though he was asymptomatic, he should be tested for COVID.

A week later, he developed symptoms and tested positive. He self-quarantined for two weeks and is now doing better. But he has asked to talk about his feelings – in particular, the continuing stress – so that he can process it before diving back in.

Some of Rick's stress is acute, as when a colleague suddenly dies. In responding, the body produces greater amounts of hormones that lead to increased heart rate, rapid breathing, and higher blood pressure – the fight-or-flight response. The body can generally return to a normal state through relaxation techniques like deep breathing.

However, other stress is chronic and, in the case of physicians, can lead to burnout. Chronic stress can weaken the immune system and contribute to conditions such as heart disease, diabetes, obesity, gastrointestinal disorders, sexual dysfunction, and mental health problems. With chronic stress, the body's immune system can become suppressed. It becomes more susceptible to infection such as COVID, and recovery becomes harder.

Stress can also intensify pre-existing stress. In a piece in the *New York Times* regarding the effect of our current isolation ("When the Pandemic Leaves us Alone, Anxious, and Depressed," April 9, 2020), Andrew Solomon wrote that "many who were already suffering from major depressive disorder have had their condition exacerbated, developing what clinicians call 'double depression,' in which a persistent depressive disorder is overlaid with an episode of unbearable pain." Moreover, extreme stress can shake loose stressors that the individual had previously kept under control.

For Rick, resilience will entail dealing with acute and chronic stress, sometimes at once. We spoke about grabbing moments to relax, basically to allow himself to recover. The harder that relaxation seemed, I suggested, the more crucial it was. Of course, Skyping from my home office, with none of my patients critically ill, I felt self-conscious about ordering relaxation. But I hoped that if I was honest and shared my feelings, Rick would take my advice.

One of the biggest challenges posed to psychiatrists by COVID is that it exacerbates a concern with emotional detachment: How can we give advice when we are outside the situation, looking in from a position of relative comfort? My response is that both Rick and I need to take a step backwards, remove ourselves from our personal psychological environment, and objectively think about how he can adjust to this crisis.

The fact is that Rick is starting from an enviable position, however precarious he may feel. He has a terrific education and has worked his way up to shoulder huge responsibilities. Often, it helps to recall the mountains we've climbed to bolster our resolve for the next attempt. One of my patients (who takes this M.O. literally) told me that every time she wants to give up, she pulls out her photos from the Himalayas. She trekked across the Thurong La (18,000 feet) and made a 300-mile circuit around the tallest peaks in the world. It was exhausting and at times terrifying, and she lost ten pounds. But she made it. Recalling past accomplishments can be a source of strength. It helps us maintain our self-esteem when guilt, exhaustion, or failure allow us to forget why we should be self-confident.

Dedicated self-care is not vanity. In a time of plague, it may seem vain to focus on oneself any more than is necessary to stay alive. But evidence demonstrates that dressing well and staying groomed – even if no one is around to appreciate the effort – can reassure us that we are not giving in or giving up. In a recent, widely quoted piece, the *Times'* fashion editor, Vanessa Friedman, suggested that thinking about one's self-presentation at this awful moment can "be a sign of faith in the future, and the idea that one day we will again be in public, dressing for the occasion, not hiding away from each other" (Friedman, 2020). That's a powerful message. So much of getting through this will depend on the belief that we *will* make it through.

Part of belief depends on acting "as if" we believe. Putting our money where our mind is. Belief becomes a performance, even if we are the only audience.

I have been reading lately about how mathematical models of this pandemic are in constant flux, and that no modeler is confident enough to predict the virus' course more than two months out. In mid-April, one of them admitted: "We are reasonably certain until approximately June 15 . . . After that, God knows" (Bui et al., 2020). It takes an act of will to live under that paradigm, much like climbing the Himalayas to 18,000 feet. My physician patients, who go back on the wards every day, have been trained to practice that. As best we can, so must the rest of us.

MEASURING RISK

None of us wants to be a statistic. But during the current pandemic, each of us is. An epidemiologist – somewhere, steeped in data – is studying the shifting potential for our getting infected; showing symptoms; surviving until there is an effective treatment, or perhaps a vaccine. When I pull up their graphs on my computer, I locate some pixel (on the up- or downswing) and think "Oh, that's me ... no, that's me," displaying my talent for dark humor. In truth, however, all the pixels bear little relation to what the number-crunchers are able to know. As the *New York Times* recently observed, there are many models for the trajectory of COVID-19 and "they don't really agree" (Bui et al., 2020).

The *Times* noted, for example, "you'll see differences in how high the peak of deaths is likely to get, and in how far we are from such a peak." This is because however good the modelers' mathematics may be, they still aren't sure about the rate of transmission or the rate at which infected people die. They don't know how many people already have immunity, or how long that immunity will last. They are not even sure how many have already died from the disease, since their deaths (at home, or pre-testing) may have been attributed to other causes. As the author of the Columbia model sighed, "We have uncertainty on top of uncertainty on top of uncertainty."

Indeed, none of the models goes out more than two months, even though epidemiologists believe that the disease will be around for a lot longer. They're hedging their bets.

In fact, an all-bets-are-off mentality is characteristic of communicable disease, where no one is quite sure who is sick and who will be infected next. Though our modeling capacity is vastly more sophisticated than in previous eras, the fundamental problem is the same. A lack of individualized human data bedeviled city administrators over 300 years ago, as they wrestled with the London Plague of 1665. In Daniel Defoe's fictionalized account, *A Journal of the Plague Year* (1722), the narrator's explanation for prognostic uncertainty could describe our own:

> People have it when they know it not, and that they likewise give it to others when they know not that they have it themselves; and in this Case, shutting up the WELL or removing the SICK will not do it, unless they can go back and shut up all those that the Sick had convers'd with, even before they knew themselves to be sick, and none knows how far to carry that back, or when to stop; for none knows when, or where, or how they may have received the Infection, or from whom.
>
> (p. 161)

The fact is, in a pandemic – where people cannot be adequately represented by numbers – we are up against the limits of epidemiology, and we always have been. We need to accept this fact, which was easier to do in Defoe's day when numeric systems were a lot less effective. As the *Times* noted, our current projections of COVID-19's course have ended up outside even the ranges of uncertainty surrounding our models, "a sign that the modelers have underestimated how little they know."

Okay, so back in a world that is so off the charts, how do I counsel patients? How do I help them to live their lives – to make choices, to take risks – when none of us knows how long this pandemic will last, how it will ultimately affect the economy, and how vigilant we need to be so that we can turn on a dime if things turn out worse than expected?

I'm thinking of a particular patient, Sally, whom I started seeing several years ago for a major depression (Major Depressive Disorder, Depressive Episode). She was referred by a colleague who specializes in the treatment of cancer. Her current stresses included financial difficulty with her interior design business and being a cancer survivor. She was status post a double mastectomy. At the time of presentation, in addition to a depressed mood, she had neurovegetative symptoms with difficulty falling and staying asleep, and decreased appetite with weight loss.

After discussing various treatment options, we decided on a combination of psychopharmacology for initial symptom relief and insight-oriented psycho-therapy. Sally responded well. I also coached her on the business, and things plateaued for a while. I suggested perhaps even cutting back our sessions. But then came COVID, which hit her business like a sledge hammer. It had only limited reserves, and had to close. But Sally did not give up. She was still able to maintain the payments on her house, so I encouraged her to reconnect with some clients and old friends – maybe meet outdoors – whom she had neglected during her cancer scare. One client offered her a substantial project. An old boyfriend showed renewed interest (admittedly, at a distance). She began to feel less dejected.

In Sally's case, resilience required exposing herself to people who might have moved on with their lives, might not have cared, might have left her feeling even more vulnerable. Resilience requires taking chances on people. When we need people, we have to swallow our pride. I observed, "It's a good thing pride isn't fattening, since I've swallowed so much of it." I wanted Sally to see that I had survived the same risks that I was asking of her. We can take chances when we can plausibly imagine ourselves benefitting from them. I offered my experi-ence as an example.

But still. My experience was long ago. When I try to situate taking even an ordinary risk *now*, in context with the existential risk posed by COVID-19, I have to ask: Is any risk worthwhile when we're already stressed to the max? Yes, provided it helps move us out of a difficult place to a better one. Risk can be an element of adaptation – the first principle of evolution. Throughout this crisis, we can't suppose that "sheltering in place" means staying fixed in old assumptions, habits, ways of doing things that don't work anymore. Resilience requires readi-ness to end up in a new place. We have to be willing to become different, to end up not even recognizing ourselves, or at least some aspect of ourselves.

So, Sally set off on a journey. If we look at risk-taking based on long-term outcomes, rather than short-term all-or-nothing leaps of faith, we often come out in a much better place. We have to acknowledge uncertainty, including the shape of its ultimate resolution – then we have to keep moving. Like epidemiologists, we hedge our bets, adapt, improve, and work out the imperfections as best we can.

It's also true that we never really know the results of a course-change until we're down the road. We have to give things time to work out. What's required is some roughly calibrated combination of belief and patience.

In this regard, I admired a recent article by Gabrielle Hamilton who had to close her restaurant, Prune, and imagine its place in a changed cityscape: "So I'm going to let the restaurant sleep, like the beauty she is, shallow breathing, dormant. And see what she looks like when she wakes up – so well rested, young all over again, in a city that may no longer recognize her, want her or need her" (Hamilton, 2020). Hamilton is hedging her bets. She is taking a measured risk. It's all we can ever do. But as her fairytale language suggests, she is not giving up. At least not until she has no other choice. Her subtext, of course, is that "Sleeping Beauty" has a happy ending.

LOOKING AROUND

During this crisis, we naturally focus on our own survival. Can I pay the rent? Do I have enough food? The "survivalist" fringe, holed up in Idaho and the badlands of Montana, suddenly seems prescient. The *New York Times* recently ran a story on techno-survivalists who hold down high-paying jobs by day while, at night, they prepare for the apocalypse with sophisticated gear – and, of course, cans of beans. In our own way, each of us is circling the wagons. Gun sales are up. More benignly but no less stressed-out, we rush to buy toilet paper. People who never uttered the words "supply chain" are suddenly terrified that, if they risk going to a store, the shelves will be bare. From a psychiatrist's perspective, the effect of COVID-19 is to have made us even more self-absorbed.

But I want to suggest that this kind of hunkering down, an extreme form of sheltering in place that excludes a concern for others, is really counterproductive. It creates a kind of stasis that prevents any acknowledgment of a changing reality, other than rigid resistance to it. It prevents nimble adaptation and, in fact, the psychological satisfaction that comes from engaging with the world and making it better. Frequently, the best form of adapting to a crisis is to do what you can to help yourself and then extend yourself – go beyond your comfort zone – to help others. The one entails the other and, I have found, that merely stopping to help oneself often leaves us feeling incomplete. When we reflect on the typical survivalist mentality, perhaps when we are into it for more than a few weeks or months, it feels profoundly unsatisfying.

Human beings were not designed to remain hunkered down, though with all our 21st century technology, there is a sense that we can do it. Physically, perhaps we can. But we have brains and psyches that evolved over eons to be social, to reach out and form communities in which we are mutually sustaining. New neuroscience research suggests that over the long term, we cannot survive without the reassurance of real, human-scale contacts that give us a sense of purpose and make us feel that we are of value to others.

You see signs of this need everywhere in closed-up New York City. A bakery on the Upper East Side posted a notice on its website that reads, in part:

> Although pretty much everything else is uncertain at the moment, one thing is clear: we love our community and are together in this.
>
> We commit to spending this time connecting with our loved ones and finding ways of helping our community so we can all be stronger than ever when we get to the other side of this.

The owners realize that however they plan to adapt to this crisis – and they may not even know yet – their plans must be intertwined with an effort to reach out towards others. Of course, it's good business to say so but, I think, when "everything else is uncertain," adapting within a context of communal outreach actually makes these owners feel better. If they can't feel good about next week's receipts, let alone how their bakery will look when all this is past, they can at least (and I wouldn't minimize it) feel good about trying to remain a part of other people's lives.

My patients have faced these issues as we've worked through recent challenges. For example, Bobby needed to change his business model when COVID upended Wall Street. His team at a major hedge fund includes over 100 analysts, traders, and support staff. It's a collaborative, fast-paced operation, but when no one could work any longer at the office, he moved everyone onto Zoom. He wasn't sure how this would work since much of the multi-directional spontaneity of the office would be lost. But Bobby saw no choice and, after a period of adjustment, things clicked. Bobby even found ways to hedge the risk with funds that stayed profitable while markets were tumbling. He never considered giving up. He adapted.

Yet though Bobby was doing well, he was sufficiently self-aware to recognize a case of "survivor's guilt" – he was barreling ahead while others were not so lucky. In response, I suggested that he consider donating some of his resources to charity, and he generously embraced the idea. This helped him feel better. But this was not because he could simply buy back his guilt, but because he could experience himself as part of the community, acting on its behalf as it struggles through crisis. In *The Altruistic Brain: Why we are Naturally Good* (2015), Donald Pfaff explains the neuroscience of why humans are designed to be generous. Sheltering in place tends to isolate us from any inclinations that extend beyond our immediate circle but, when we follow them, we're acting the way that we would in normal times. Resilience in a time of plague requires clearing out enough mental space so that we can replace non-productive inclinations with affirmative ones. We feel more like ourselves when we do.

Indeed, there is now an opportunity for people who have recovered from a COVID infection to donate plasma, which has antibodies to the virus for people in need of greater immunity. The actor Tom Hanks has done just that, giving enormous publicity to the need.

Adam Grant's *Give and Take: A Revolutionary Approach to Success* (2013), demonstrates that generosity is one of the best anti-anxiety medications in that it lowers the levels of stress hormones. Recent work by Emily Greenfield at Rutgers demonstrates that when we take responsibility for others, we feel better about ourselves. We believe in ourselves and, in effect, become more resilient.

In *Resilience: The Science of Mastering Life's Greatest Challenges* (2012), Dennis Charney and Steven Southwick observe that to survive stress, cognitive and emotional flexibility are crucial because they enable you to tolerate a highly stressful situation and reassess it. As in your own body, flexibility enables you to move, and to change directions as you continue to evaluate your position. During stress, movement is more important than knowing where you will ultimately end up. They argue further that assigning meaning and purpose to life can strengthen one's resilience and may help prevent the symptoms of stress from worsening.

Concomitantly, we should stop thinking about resilience in merely personal terms. Our own resilience frequently depends on that of others. We have now experienced the disastrous shortages of N95 masks and other Personal Protective Equipment. Food banks are under stress as restaurants close. The unemployment system was woefully unprepared for the surge in applications. Thus, in designing our own program of resilience, we need to think socially. Once this pandemic is under control, it would be wise to measure our own strength-building efforts in terms of how they strengthen society's responsiveness. As we form connections to resist the disorienting effects of isolation, we need to project that effort outward. By helping others, we help ourselves.

GETTING TO KNOW OURSELVES

One of my patients, an economist, told me that the macroeconomy has a counterpart in her swollen left foot. "You see, they keep trying to open everything up and I keep trying to get the swelling down, and we are both moving too fast." Okay, I can see that. Or, I sort of can, since on Skype I can only imagine her foot (on ice?) beneath the screen. But still, I appreciate the analogy: the swelling won't go down like the viral curve won't flatten – and the economy won't revive – since rushing interferes with natural recovery.

What's really interesting, however, is how my patient perceives the massive challenge of reopening the economy in terms of her own body – in terms of her own foot! Our unit of measure has become ourselves. Not GDP, or the latest unemployment statistics.

You see this contraction everywhere. I was talking with a colleague, recently, who said he has begun thinking in new, teleologically pinched eras: B.C. is now Before Coronavirus, A.D. is After the Discovery of a vaccine. The time in the middle is the messy present where the hands of the clock barely move. It's a time of distraction, when we will do almost anything – even what we don't like – so that we don't have to think about the virus or the economy.

I am working in my attic office and, for the first time within memory, I find myself emptying drawers of old papers, tossing year-old magazines, and generally triaging my personal space. I guess I would rather clean than think about COVID-19. Cleaning is a stress-reliever, and a form of meditation. We slow down; consider what we don't need; reintegrate on a smaller scale.

As our lives boil down to essentials, we jettison what seems foreign to newly "normal" habits. What do I absolutely need to do, right now, so that I don't entirely lose my cool? What makes me feel good? No, what should make me feel good, relative to . . . what?

We find ourselves analyzing our decisions, trying to discern our motivations, in an infinite regress towards the fundamental. If we catch ourselves choosing to act unusually, we ask: What really makes me tick? When we finally get past this pandemic (assuming that we do), we will know ourselves better. We may have developed habits of internal inquiry that, not too long ago, seemed uninteresting or even pointless. But now, with so much uncertainty and so much on the line, and with so many unaccustomed reactions to our immediate claustrophobic surroundings, all such inquiries seem normal. That is, normal for this odd, transitional time between B.C. and A.D. when we are becoming objects of our own personal inquiry.

However, even as our frame of reference seems to be getting smaller (spatially, temporally), new possibilities open up. Another of my patients said that she has always liked old cookbooks – really old ones, from 200 and 300 years ago. She would find them on eBay and the websites of rare book dealers. But now her favorite authors are all available for download! Take, for example, Martha Bradley, the Martha Stewart of the 1750s. Ms. Bradley's six-volume treatise, *The British Housewife: Or, the Cook, Housekeeper's, and Gardiner's Companion*, is instantly ready to provide instruction on "A Rabbit Pie," "Lobster Patties," and "Sweetbreads a la Dauphine." *My* Martha said she is cooking her way through these tomes, trying to figure out how to adapt the archaic recipes.

She is so determined that she organized a Facebook group for other enthusiasts, who can trade their experience in translating "spit-roasting" to gas stoves and "take a good handful" to some standard measure. The point is that as we still hunker down, what first seemed like deprivation and contraction can turn into something special – useful in its own right, without the stigma of its being a mere distraction.

Though we are becoming accustomed to compensating for what we miss, and are watching a whole lot more Netflix than going to the movies, we can discover new possibilities. This same patient told me that she has stopped going to the grocery store, and now orders online. Mostly, it's okay, although the selection can be limited. Sometimes, the warehouse is out of what she ordered and provides a "substitute." Uh, oh! Instead of a quart of oat milk, which she likes with cereal, two cans of coconut milk arrived. What do you do with *that*? My patient is learning to make Thai green curry.

There is no denying that things are out of joint, and that sadness is all around us. Some of my patients have become ill, or they know people who have died.

But in learning to cope with isolation and fear – as the one exacerbates the other – we are learning to salvage what remains, and what we might have overlooked. One of my patients, who is very industrious, is relearning Yiddish, which she hasn't spoken since her grandmother died. It makes her feel connected to a once-vibrant culture.

We are also developing aspects of ourselves that have lain dormant. A 50-something patient told me that she misses being on the barricades, going to demonstrations, even going to board meetings of her local NPR station. "Oh, before I had kids . . .", and her voice trails off into a sigh. But now that her children are grown, she feels ready to start up again – if she could. In recent days, however, she has started a campaign of writing to companies about their human-proof packaging. She tears her fingers trying to open plastic clamshells and other marvels of post-apocalypse engineering. She has since written to a cottage cheese maker, and even got a response.

We are improving the time, pulling together capacities that seemed, at best, inchoate. But we are also preparing for when free will is once again permissible. We are making ourselves better. Or hopefully so. In a funny way, those of us still functioning have started to push back on this plague, even to take our revenge. We have started becoming skilled practitioners of lost arts (or, maybe, lost arts and crafts), so that one day we can emerge as better versions of ourselves.

It has been shown that when butterflies emerge from their cocoons, they retain certain memories from when they were caterpillars. Tiny pieces of brain matter survive, enough so that if they would not eat something when they had a hundred legs, they still resist it when they have just six. I think the same principle may apply as we transition from B.C. to A.D. over the next however-many months (or years). We will take with us aspects of ourselves that, during the interim, we have refurbished, repurposed, or rediscovered. If we are paring ourselves down to fundamentals, we are nonetheless still there . . . cocooned, as it were.

At the moment, it may feel like endless waiting. But the time is not empty. We are recalibrating. We may be more austere when all this is over, and we will certainly be older, but we will know ourselves – and probably like ourselves – a lot better.

ALONE

During the lockdown, loneliness and isolation are everywhere. Nowhere to go, very few outlets. According to a recent study, more than 60 percent of Americans – over three in five – reported feeling chronically lonely even before the outbreak, when they were free to go anywhere! Now add in the current restrictions, and we are struggling with two pandemics, side-by-side. Each exacerbates the other since, as the science shows, loneliness decreases the body's defenses against disease. *The Guardian* cited John Cacioppo, the famous student of loneliness, as saying, "Chronic loneliness increases the odds of an early death by twenty percent" (Adams, 2016).

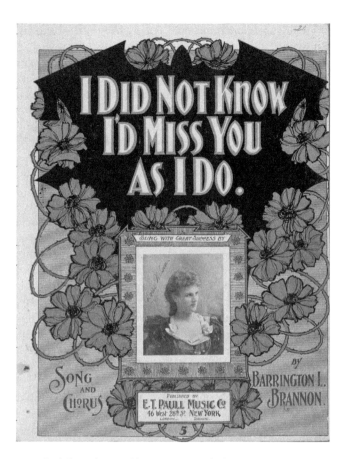

Figure I.3 "I did not know I'd miss you as I do" (1903)

Somewhere on the loneliness spectrum is my patient Teresa, an elderly French woman towards the end of her life. She never married and her only family is a brother, with whom she's been estranged for years. Teresa presented for treatment over 20 years ago for an episode of depression, and still sees me. Ostensibly, the cause was her retirement, which left her without a sense of purpose and colleagues with whom she could socialize.

Teresa had experienced a traumatic childhood. Her father was an alcoholic and would come home drunk, out of control. Her mother, who worked as a maid, kept late hours. Her older brother, the family's golden boy, had been violent towards Teresa growing up, at one point shooting her with a BB gun. Her one sexual relationship had been with a married minister, who promised his love and then left her.

Teresa finally settled in a community for the elderly, where she was treated well and made friends. But when COVID hit, her life narrowed to a couple of rooms. No more communal activities. The residents were not tech-savvy, so Zoom parties or even Skyping were impossible. Rarely, like on her birthday, her brother and a niece would call.

When we spoke (now by phone) she claimed not to mind being on her own and to enjoy the company of her cats, her books, and the occasional chat. She accepted the possibility of dying alone if she caught the virus. She wanted to be cremated, with her ashes spread at sea in the coastal village where she was born.

To be honest, I think I was more affected by her circumstances than she was. I had images of wartime France, no heat, people huddled in attics. A brutal brother in the next cot. I thought about how every day might have been their last, and no one would know, or care . . . or even possibly find them for weeks. Maybe not until La Libération!

Of course, I realized that my imagination was racing. But psychiatrists can't help running with their patients' stories. They get lost in a kind of reverie, and spin whole narratives around their patients in the mode of alternative history. Suddenly, they have to catch themselves before displaying sympathy for what never even occurred. When a couple of patients populate the same story, they know that it's time to refocus. Such drama, and the patient is blissfully unaware.

The point is that we care about our patients or, rather, we get to care about them, and the stories that we spin are curiously legitimated because they intensify our concern. They seem almost instrumental in that regard – I mean who couldn't care about a lonely old woman freezing in a wartime attic while the Nazis march through her town?

But in our sessions, I returned to reality. I asked Teresa if there was anything that might help her feel less alone. However, she was insistently stoic, even proud to be on her own. She was actually enjoying her solitude with hours of reading, knitting, and keeping a scrapbook. "You know," she said, "I'm an amateur historian, at least if you call scrapbooks history." ("Oh, if you only knew about my flights of historical fantasy," I thought. "They're a lot less accurate than yours!") She mentioned some old friends and work acquaintances to whom she was writing.

So, Teresa has set me thinking about being alone vs. loneliness. Loneliness is harmful. It's when you feel no one is there for you, and you ache to connect. John and Stephanie Cacioppo anatomized it into "intimate loneliness" (when you miss someone you love); loneliness for quality friendship; and collective loneliness, when a supportive group can no longer operate. I think Teresa probably fell into the second category, but not so much that it posed a problem. Like the French, she was philosophical.

Though Teresa was alone, she inhabited a kind of well-adjusted solitude. Such willing adjustment to circumstance is a personal achievement. It's making the most of what you have, rather than rebelling and falling into despondency. You recognize yourself as independent and self-sustaining. The psychoanalyst Donald Winnicott wrote of aloneness as a developmental milestone, when the child separates from its mother without feeling the anxiety of separation. This requires internalizing a sense of being loved by a parent and eventually oneself. As adults on our own, we have to recapitulate that feeling.

Over years of therapy, Teresa had come to enjoy her own company. But I asked if there was anyone with whom, after years of retirement, she might still consider establishing a connection. After a pause she said, quietly, "Well, maybe my brother." He had caused her real pain growing up, and their estrangement had only slightly abated with a few stiff phone calls. So, I wondered aloud if she might reach out. But the moment passed, and she talked about doing her laundry and paying some bills.

But today when we spoke again, she had news. She'd reached out to her brother with some anxiety, even trepidation, and he was delighted to hear from her. They spoke by phone for over an hour. He even put his daughter on, who was sheltering in place with him. He alluded to how he regretted his early harshness, and she told him how she had forgiven him long ago. They also shared memories about some good times like a birthday when he went to buy a bicycle with her. This helped her feel less alone, though she still disclaimed feeling lonely.

Certainly, physical touch can be important in feeling less lonely. The British psychologist and psychoanalyst John Bowlby, who pioneered attachment theory, discussed the importance of a secure base. When this was not present, such as with young children in orphanages, they failed to thrive. When loving care was present, they did better and were less prone to depression. Even when physical touch was not present, the emotional connection was meaningful. The same applies generally.

I felt proud of Teresa for reaching out to her brother after years of being estranged, and said so. Sometimes when we reach out to someone – even when it's not physical – we feel better. It becomes a source of energy, so that when we are alone – even if we not technically lonely – we feel as though we are in the world, resonating with others. The funny thing is that though we may be ostensibly self-sufficient, we never lose the desire for affirmation. That requires other people who appreciate us, and show it.

WHAT'S FUNNY ABOUT A PANDEMIC?

I have been catching up on old Woody Allen movies, and last night I saw *Hannah and Her Sisters* (1986). Okay, I know that Woody is controversial but, when he plays himself, he's acutely perceptive regarding human frailty. In *Hannah*, his escalating hypochondria is an essential case study for psychiatrists – though it's unsettling when, as a psychiatrist, you identify with the frailties he portrays.

Towards the beginning of this pandemic, and before we acknowledged that there was one, I thought I'd had a brush with COVID-19. Like Woody in the movie, I magnified *some* evidence into the looming likelihood of a potentially terminal illness.

It was late January, and I was still commuting to work on the Long Island Railroad. The train left at 6:27 a.m., and I usually caught the 7:14 home. Some

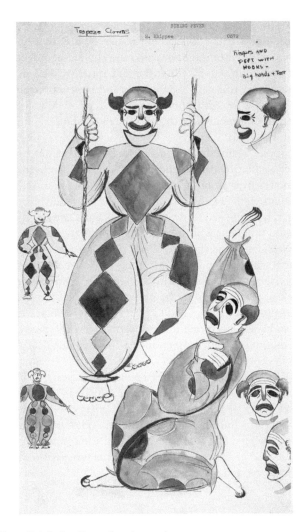

Figure I.4 String Fever (marionette)

Asians had begun wearing face masks, but I just assumed it was in solidarity with the victims in Wuhan.

One evening, I was on an especially crowded train for the 30-minute ride to Great Neck. A man near me was coughing uncontrollably. He looked sweaty and febrile. A woman started to yell at him, "Cough into your elbow!" and other riders chimed in. A short, bald guy applauded. But since this was before any talk of social distancing, I wondered what the big deal was and the moment passed. I got off at my stop.

But about a week later, I started running a low-grade fever; I had a dry cough, aches, and lost my appetite. Though there wasn't much talk of COVID-19 in the City, I thought perhaps I had caught the virus. I went to a City MD office, where a doctor said I had a low-grade fever, but not to worry. However, since it was towards the end of the week, I took a sick day so as not to expose my patients. By Friday evening, I was exhausted and short of breath. Saturday, I felt no better, and just slept.

When I woke up Saturday night, I was still short of breath, and was weak and achy. I wondered if I should go to the hospital. Bizarrely, I did some yoga. Then I read a while. As the evening progressed, I was still weak and tired, but I no longer had a fever. By Sunday, I felt much better, and on Monday I was well enough to go to work. But I still took another day off, thinking this would further reduce the risk to others. The rest of the week was full of patient care and the usual activities.

It wasn't until a week or so later, as the drumbeat of pandemic picked up, that I feared I had probably had a mild case of COVID and subsequently recovered. I thought I had exposed my family and patients. In fact, my wife felt under the weather for a few days, though she also seemed recovered; our kids, however, had felt fine. I was upset with myself. Had I been a "vector" (that disinterested epidemiological actor with very human consequences) who unwittingly had exposed his patients? Why hadn't I been more attentive, to the news and to everyone around me? Why hadn't I gone into quarantine the minute I felt sick?

Of course, I told my patients that I may have had COVID, and warned them to watch out for symptoms. One was pregnant and another elderly, so I was especially concerned for them – and I felt especially guilty on their behalf. As soon as the antibody test came out, I went to Quest Diagnostics to be tested, and told my patients about that as well. I assumed I was positive and said so.

I waited a week, counting the days. I had the thought that if I were positive, I at least had probably developed some immunity, though that would not have helped anyone whom I may have infected. I checked the Quest site daily for my test results and, when none arrived, I assumed that they were confirming a positive result. I dreaded telling everyone.

Then after nine days, an envelope came in the mail. I opened it hastily like a college rejection letter. It was thin, so I thought it must be a rejection, the equivalent of a negative result which, in this instance, translated to a "positive" finding. But to my astonishment, the result really was negative! I had not had COVID after all! It must have been some other bug. Of course, I was relieved. I hadn't been exposed or exposed anyone else. But I was also deflated, since the result was anticlimactic. Afterall, hadn't I righteously berated myself, expecting the worst?

I also felt ambivalent. If I had had COVID, I thought I would at least be immune now – or partially immune – so that I wouldn't have to worry about it, at least for a while. It was like I wanted those antibodies to be the Kryptonite to my Superman. But instead, I was just poor old Woody, scared when I imagined that I had the virus and just as scared now that I hadn't. The absurdity of the situation amused me, as I realized how this virus is forcing us into a hall of mirrors: every fear is magnified and distorted while all we can do is stare at ourselves.

But I couldn't really laugh. Not having had the disease, I was still in the same boat as most people, one that can easily tip over and dump us into very choppy seas. We live in times of loopy logic, when the hope is to contract an infection to avert contracting the infection! One of my patients, a Democrat, said he hoped to become immune so that he could sell his immunity – but not to a Republican. We are making feeble jokes, in an effort to salvage any available humor.

My patients recount the gallows humor circulating on the web. Maybe it makes them feel better, sort of distancing them from dread for a few seconds. "Did you hear the one about Vincent van Gogh? His mask was hanging off one ear." Van Gogh was famously crazy, and cut off his left ear in a fight with Paul Gauguin. Or how about "If you've ever eaten at Papaya King on the Upper East Side, you're immune to COVID-19." I have!

This propensity for humor has not escaped the medical establishment. A scholarly article in *Foot & Ankle International*, a journal for orthopedists, suggests that "an active pandemic presents ample opportunity for the use of [gallows] humor" (Chiodo, 2020). However, it cautions that jokes about death are best kept among physicians so as not to terrify "outsiders." It intones: "Imagine an outpatient overhearing health care providers employing gallows humor about ... a bleak prognosis." Perhaps they haven't got the message that "outsiders" are already making the jokes.

In my own case, I can imagine the joke on myself. I was not quick enough to react to the threat, and then too quick to over-react once I had recovered. I may have agitated my family and patients. But I think a lot of us are imagining the worst right now, since so much is uncertain and it's dragging on forever (like a bad joke).

DRESSING UP

As this pandemic drags on, I've become an epidemiologist – of sorts. I consider my patients' demographics, their changes and trends, even while I focus on them individually. I notice, for example, that their grooming is increasingly casual: more beards, hairdos that are don'ts. Over the past two months, my patients have emerged *au naturel*. I see lines on women's faces, muscles (or fat) bulging from men's t-shirts. Before the pandemic, when most patients came during work-days, they were made-up, dressed up, generally put together. They obviously cared about how they looked. But now there has been a regression, of sorts, towards work-at-home indifference. Because Skype and FaceTime reduce us all to talking upper torsos, it's impossible not to focus on the few – but significantly altered – details of my patients' heads and shoulders.

I wonder whether these people are self-conscious about dressing down or, whether, the devolution towards some unkempt, unadorned state seems normal in this liminal New Normal.

So far, I haven't asked anyone, but I wonder whether the lack of obvious self-care reflects some worrisome letting-go. Have they given up, stopped caring about themselves? Have they concluded that the world outside barely exists anymore, so why play the game (with the right moves, the Botox, and good clothes)? If every day is Sunday now, there's no reason to bother.

But still. Each of us needs to maintain his or her own dignity, even if the only person to acknowledge it is the one in the mirror.

I don't expect people to dress for work just because they are Skyping with me. However, because they are so ... um ... oddly turned out, I expect that their days are empty of significant contacts. I worry about encroaching isolation. Are people losing face with themselves; are they embarrassed by idleness? If so, then maintaining a sense of dignity may seem merely pompous, even pretentious. In a bid to be honest with themselves, to look themselves in the face and say YUCK, they put on the worst stuff they own.

This is a problem for the especially busy (or formerly especially busy). Some businesses are still paying employees even though they have shut down. So, people can eat and pay rent, but they are at loose ends. This concerns me. When left entirely to our own devices, we often don't know what to do with ourselves. We fill the time with worry, if only not to get bored. We focus on the immediate, the acutely awful, and allow it to seem irreversible – as if now were forever, since amidst a pointless emptiness that's how it seems. One patient said to me, "I see all the red ink in my 401(k), and it looks like blood." She conveys a sense that she's bleeding to death. From her perspective, dressing down is the objective correlative of her losing faith in her life. Irreversibly.

So, while I don't mention my patients' devolved new "look," I do try to address with them what I suspect it represents. I try to assess whether they feel as though things may not turn around soon enough for them to get back to feeling *able* to navigate the world, and make useful changes. I approach this enquiry gingerly, since I don't want to presume too much based on a newly hirsute face or absent lipstick. But sometimes, patients actually bring up their altered appearance, and this gives me permission. "Oh, please forgive my sweats but, you know, I've gotten lazy." Lazy is a freighted term, and tells me that they know that I know that they have fallen off their customary standard. They are inviting me to ask why.

In such instances, we talk about how the present constriction seems like it will last indefinitely, limiting their options to express themselves, pursue relationships, carry out quotidian chores like shopping and going for check-ups – and just having fun. Maybe, if there is no improvement, their generous employers will start furloughing people – then what? More limbo? Even more nowhere and nothing? We discuss the need for differentiation in their lives. After all, why change your outfit (or fix your hair or trim your beard) if every day is also yesterday, the equivalent of solitary confinement? We need to see glimmers of possibility, each day, to believe in the return of possibility.

Existentialism declares that we are our possibilities.

As my patients and I explore these concerns, we turn back to the issue of clothes and self-presentation. Grooming ourselves for each day is one way to affirm that something new – and, ideally, interesting – may happen. It allows us to feel as though we have not resigned ourselves to a world of infinite time and no space, where a thin trickle of events has nowhere to go in any direction . . . except maybe drop-by-drop onto our heads like slow Chinese torture. If we let ourselves go in one major area, like appearance, we are inclined to let go in others. We can't allow ourselves to risk not liking ourselves. If we do, then decline is easy, just when we need to be ready for things when they do turn around. And things will be different when they do, which makes being ready all the harder.

I have begun modeling self-care to my patients. While I am not wearing ties as much, I don't wear sweats either. I talk about exercise and eating well. I let my patients know that caring for oneself is work, worth as much as the work they do at the office. Nobody is suggesting that sheer vanity is a worthwhile motivation, but self-respect and dignity are. As we age, dignity becomes more a concern, since aging is not always pretty. Our hair gets thinner, we may stoop. The passage of time and the pull of gravity are inevitable. We may dwell in our minds, but we can't escape our bodies. So, we still need to show the world and ourselves that we have not abandoned appearances.

I read recently that fashion magazines like *Vogue* and *Harper's Bazaar* will never be the same, and that some of these publications may disappear. Clothes have come to seem more utilitarian; disposable fashion is dismissed as wasteful. I can appreciate that. But without being fashionistas, we can treat each day as an occasion, indeed as multiple potential occasions to which we have invited ourselves. It's good to be an active participant in one's life. If we skype with our friends, or even talk on the phone, we can spruce up. The phone is perhaps even better than Skype, since we can imagine our friends imagining us. When we prepare dinner (however so humble), we can wear something clean, take a shave, fix our hair (gender-specific gestures, for those of us identified with a gender, are an advance over unisex jeans and a t-shirt).

The point is that in these days of isolation, we each need to perform our identity and practice who we want to become. We need to make personal choices that reflect our taste, our sense of our own value, and what we might still be to other people. We need to perform our roles even if no one is presently clapping, or even in the audience. This is because we need to envision ourselves as potentially the object of other people's thoughts. At this point in the pandemic, reality is a consensual process, where each of us helps each other affirm our shared existence. This is now a more acute version of the usual case.

So, we need to give each other material, to be there for one another. As we perform, we give each other material. We rehearse each other. We help each other believe that it's not the last act.

THE VIRUS AS MUSE

Over the years, patients have offered me various gifts: homemade cookies, coffee mugs, theater tickets, Yankees tickets. I've received invitations to weddings, bar mitzvahs, a baptism. A dowager, who was a trustee at a local museum, offered me a work of art. A professional baseball player sent tickets to a playoff game.

It's natural to want to give back to someone who is helping you. Patients think about me personally – even apart from what I represent to them – and our relationship resonates beyond our once- or twice-weekly sessions. This comes with being part of people's lives. So, of course, I'm grateful. While patients understand the need to maintain a certain professional distance, they sometimes feel the need to test the limits, or even breach them slightly, if only to acknowledge our relationship with something more tangible than just showing up and talking. Yet despite all these tokens – really, gestures of goodwill – I was unprepared for the outpourings I've received during this pandemic.

Patients have begun giving me their poetry, songs, diary entries, and, in one case, a novella about surviving the Holocaust. These are often works-in-progress, which patients find a hedge against isolation and despair. One patient, who studied Renaissance poetry, is writing a crown of sonnets or sonnet "corona," an interlocking series of sonnets that elaborate on a single theme, in this case the eponymous virus. The form dates back to the 15th century. But where the sonnet conventions usually address love and its loss, this current corona extends into scenes of suffering, chaos, and death. "No one else has seen this corona," she says. "I write them for catharsis." It's okay.

This woman's gift to me is very personal, an attempt to share aspects of herself that she could not describe – or bear to describe – in a Skype session. She reads some sonnets out loud, then looks up, expecting that I will have construed the lines into meanings that transcend words. So, what can I say? At a literal level, I have heard an avowal of deep pain; fear that we are headed into crazy-making times; disgust at institutional incompetence. But there is more, and I reach for an adequate response. "I understand," I say. Old poetic forms can give shape to the present. They announce endurance, mixed with pain.

I'm not often called upon to be a critic of poetry, and that's not what she was looking for anyway. My patients are imposing new demands – even by their gifts. This woman needed me to hear her through another, unaccustomed medium, so that I might access feelings that she could not otherwise express. In effect, she was telling me that there are limits to psychotherapy, which is conducted in prose. She needed poetry to articulate her most acute, most disturbing responses, and to share these with me. I am beginning to realize that as we proceed through this pandemic, the conventions of my profession – not just of Renaissance poetry – will be upended. Patients will ask that we listen with different capabilities to different forms of self-disclosure. Their gifts may do double duty as primers on their sense of themselves.

I am bemused if not slightly concerned by this development (am I up to it?), but I also see it as a hedge against complacency. Patients can teach us how to expand ourselves as therapists, and respond with new abilities that suit altered circumstances. It's humbling, of course, since patients look to *us* for guidance. But I must remind myself that in the long run, at least part of my role is to help them find their voices, to speak candidly and live authentically. If that takes responding to poetry, or some other medium that's congenial to them, then I *should* be up to it.

My patients have various temperaments. Apart from the deeply thoughtful, some are whimsical, albeit with a Charles Addams twist to accommodate COVID-19.

A grim humor is creeping into sessions as patients use funky, alternative media to express themselves. One patient, a woman in her 70s, likes to give pop tunes new lyrics, turning disco, rock, and Afrobeat into conspicuously off-kilter dirges. She took an old Bee Gees' standard, "Stayin' Alive" (*Saturday Night Fever*, 1977), and weaponized it as a cri de coeur: its "Barely Alive" lament targets the government, the virus, and the misplaced optimism of anyone predicting a vaccine within a year. "Just drink Clorox then wash your hands. . ." goes one line, as the refrain keeps ironically upending the point of each claim. Actually, it's pretty good.

There is a tradition of assigning new words to old songs, where memory of the original jars with the revision. Tom Lehrer, a celebrated practitioner of this (minor) art form, raised it to such heights that he became a hero to the '60s anti-establishment set. But my patient just needs an outlet. She sings the lyrics while she cleans her apartment, since the maid is furloughed indefinitely. She wishes for a karaoke back-up, then laughs at the implausibility. Yet beneath the whimsy, there is worry, a growing awareness that her cushy life is fraying. During our last session, she told me that the maintenance staff in her toney Manhattan building are not allowed into apartments except in the direst emergencies. ("I'm glad we have two bathrooms," she confides.) She frets about her investments; about when she can resume physical therapy; about her declining bone density for which she receives (or, rather, had been receiving) injections. For the first time in a long time, she feels unsettled.

The songs, however, help her to express her fears so that they don't just fester. As she sings a few lines to me, I see her brighten rather than turn grimmer. The songs are coping mechanisms. She sends them to friends, and they sing together on Zoom, impromptu duets against despair. In this time of pandemic, shared creativity, shared complaints, shared anything become bulwarks against feeling isolated, static, stoppered up. Also, creativity is a riposte against sameness and boredom. If you can invent, however modestly, you change the reality around you. Don't feel embarrassed. "If it feels good, do it," by the Canadian rock band Sloan (*Pretty Together*, Murderecords, 2001), never had a better title . . . my patient may discover it next.

Another trend I've encountered in this period, one not so much creative as confessional, is the renewed interest in diary-keeping. Suddenly, my patients have time, and it seems that the less that's going on to fill that time the more they want to explain how they feel about the emptiness. Old yellow pads with neat blue lines, which lawyers use to take notes, are repurposed as repositories of daily reflection. Some patients have ordered blank notebooks on Amazon, and are filling them up – even, occasionally, with illustrated versions of their semi-pointless days. If they bake bread, there is a description of kneading it, maybe even a drawing. It's interesting that there are no photos. Only old-fashioned, retro art forms: careful handwriting, nice pen-and-ink images. People know it's quaint. But, for that reason, they find it oddly soothing.

In the 17th and 18th centuries, the Puritans kept diaries. If you wrote enough, God's purpose for your life would be revealed. In the 19th century, women kept diaries, especially if they were literate and not in the work-force. It was a way to fill the day, more acceptable than reading novels, and a private refuge from the chaos of large families. But what I find now is that old forms of creativity and self-revelation, or at least forms that do not require technology, are resurfacing. They provide, I think, direct contact between the individual and language in ways that allow language to be shaped more exactly to that individual's feelings. If *anything* positive emerges from our current siege, this recursion to basics may be one such development. I think that the importance of all this writing extends beyond any one writer's life. In whatever genre, we are writing history.

CYBORGS

Now, in the midst of a pandemic, I can see how video-therapy affects my work as a psychiatrist. I see it play out in real time.

Actually, I've practiced using video-therapy for years, but I never thought much about it. It was always at the margins – mostly where someone could not physically attend a session; or had moved out of town; or was from another area. I saw it as useful, occasionally, but nothing I'd practice full-time.

In a weird way, it evoked a sort of *Twilight Zone* of man-machine cyborgs that didn't belong in the staid, traditional world of psychiatry.

But all that's changed now. Fast.

Ever since the pandemic made cyborgs of us all – in everything we do – video-therapy has become my *modus operandi*. It has, indeed, for most New York psychiatrists. So, I was interested to see Adam Gopnik's opportune article ("The Empty Couch") in the *New Yorker* (2020), examining how the current crisis – with everyone sheltered in place – is reshaping psychiatric practice.

For starters, Gopnik observed that video-therapy facilitates easier access to care and psychological services. True. But that's also true of almost any non-invasive medical treatment. What interested me more about the article, was the claim that some psychiatric patients might actually be *better* treated remotely. That seemed radical. We leak our feelings though our pores. We get the scent of someone in the room with us. We "feel" the concomitants of their presence. How could that translate to a screen with two talking heads? We'd each miss the body language.

But I wanted to test Gopnik's claim. So, I wondered what was therapeutic in psychotherapy. That is, what elements in a complex process actually make it work? When you've practiced for over 25 years, as I have, you tend to see the process holistically, and never stop to analyze whether any specific element – including physical presence – is responsible for the empathy and understanding that lead to recovery.

My background is as a neo-Freudian. Intense, frequent psychoanalytic treatments were the "gold standard"; anything else would not expose a patient's unconscious conflicts and underlying issues. In fact, this is still the prevailing view at traditional psychoanalytic institutes. So how would diluting the intensity by eliminating the in-person connection increase the therapeutic effect? It sounded like a paradox.

Admittedly, I had treated patients in Beijing, Hong Kong, and Dubai without meeting them in person. We had even worked through significant psychological issues. But was the treatment better?

I thought some more about the type of connection that we achieve through a screen. Sometimes treatment can be more focused than is possible in an office visit; we get to the heart of an issue more quickly; we lock eyes (the windows and my artworks are out of bounds), and the patient can't as freely associate. This creates a more interpersonal, less intrapsychic experience. From a psychiatrist's perspective, what you see is more nearly equivalent to what you actually get. Less wandering down byways that, only years later, may turn out to be productive. So, after some reflection, I granted Gopnik the benefit of the doubt.

At least, as a thought experiment. What about with a real patient?

As a case in point, I offer my patient Sam. I spoke with Sam remotely today. He is (or was) a successful businessman in his 50s, but his company was clobbered by the pandemic. He'd lost millions. Then his business partner defrauded him. He felt devastated.

He felt the same way back in prep school, when the wealthy kids made him self-conscious. He was that self-conscious kid again, he said. "I feel like people are looking at me, laughing. Could I have done something different?" I wanted to reassure him, but was concerned (notwithstanding my provisional concession to Gopnik) that the distance between us was an emotional barrier. I imagined how we would have talked, *mano a mano*, had we been seated across from each other. But instead, I ticked off his accomplishments; I suggested that his self-worth should not reflect his net worth. It sounded rote; it was cliché. We both knew it.

But then the mood quickly shifted. It was like a phase change – ice into vapor. Sam's focus narrowed from generalized despair to specific recollection of his life as a young man. He recognized that the intrusion of memory into the present was aggravating his despair.

He talked about how his father had sacrificed so much for so long and, in the end, had so little to show for it. "He was left with a five and dime store, and now I'm just like him." He recalled how his father would travel weekends for a second job, and how he was still just a hapless loser. "Maybe I'll start working for Uber Eats. I hear it's a growth industry." You could hear the self-mockery. You could hear it through what Sam always wished he had said to his father.

In that moment, Sam stood in for his younger self, jabbing at a father who left him vulnerable to schoolboys. He was standing in for his prep school classmates, re-enacting their silent taunts.

I had worked with Sam for several years, and I had never seen him so piti- less towards himself. He'd always had a sense of irony, but usually this sense was tinged with the comedic – more pratfalls than tumbles into darkness. But this time he was dead serious. He drew out the connection between a grim past – at home, at school – and his current, grim sense of drawing the short straw.

But here is where I am going with this. "You know," he said, "it's because your attempt to reassure me fell flat that I've had to figure all this out for myself." He said he didn't think he could have made the connection between himself, his father, and his current state of mind if we'd been talking in my office. "I might have appreciated your attempt, and then the moment would have passed."

What happened, is that the video-therapy concentrated Sam's mind. When you stare at someone, and everything else falls away, you're actually almost all mind. Your mind moves easily, back and forth through your personal history and its demands on the present. You take control of your mind. That's key. Rather than allowing it to wander, you force it into channels that can run very deep. Like the businessman that he was, Sam took charge. For a short while, he dismissed me. It's like I wasn't there, even though he was looking me straight in the eye. He became his own facilitator.

Ultimately, he told me what I needed to know so that – together, finally – we could work out the circuitry of his current despair. This might have happened over weeks in my office, but here it happened virtually (pun intended) in a flash.

I think that when you stare into someone's eyes, it drives you inwards. That's what Gopnik understood, albeit implicitly.

So, while I would say that the jury is still out, I have to acknowledge that Gopnik is on to something that could signal a paradigm shift. Video-therapy does not mean that "therapy," now paired with "video," diminishes the value of personal contact. Rather, it means that the process of therapy may be altered as we apply the capabilities of its video component. If my experience with Sam is any indication, we may be surprised by how quickly and intensely patients respond.

WHEN YOU HAVE LEMONS . . .

The logic of coziness – when it's grim outside, we're safe at home – has pitched into reverse, and marooned us in stay-at-home sensory deprivation. Three months into this pandemic, not having to "be" anywhere is no longer a nov- elty. Some days, in fact, the verb "to be" seems as though its rich, multi-layered meaning has been scrapped. Existence is now pared back to the essentials.

Normally, we rarely think about how we exist in a sensory maelstrom. The life around us clatters, hums, sparkles, and shines. We shake hands. We dance. We

Figure I.5 Still life with lemon and cut-glass wine goblet

window shop. Usually, there is music in our ears, jostling with the traffic noise, sirens, car alarms, and garbage trucks of the average day. On the subway ... don't ask. It's part of being alive. Indeed, as neuroscience has shown, our brains inter-pret sounds and images even at a distance, and our face recognition capacities exceed that of any AI currently available. We have evolved to be highly sensate, able to defend ourselves and, by the same sensory token, able to connect.

But what about now? Several of my patients find the sensory deprivation extremely depressing. They play music, look at photos, watch TV, but these now seem forced, rarefied, unhinged from reality without the real-life noise and the sights in the street. Apparently, my patients are not unique: the New York Public Library has made available a recording, Missing Sounds of New York: An Auditory Love Letter to New Yorkers, a "new immersive experience . . . a collection of audio landscapes that evoke some of the sounds" of the city (New York Public Library, n.d.). The premise – that some vital sounds are "missing" – suggests that our jigsaw puzzle lives are losing vital pieces that, one-by-one, provide the complexity, color, and shape of our existence.

The condition of feeling detached from sensory reality is made worse, during this pandemic, because it's not only against our nature but because we see the direction that our situation is taking. At its extreme, sensory deprivation is a recognized form of torture. In the manhunt film about capturing bin Laden, *Zero Dark Thirty* (Bigelow, 2012), prisoners were locked up in boxes as a way of forcing them to talk. The idea was that they would crumple as they slowly went mad. Offscreen, the European Court of Human Rights found that sensory deprivation techniques used by the British to interrogate prisoners in Northern Ireland amounted to inhumane and degrading treatment. Of course, while no one (in the pandemic) is now subject to such treatment, people are starting to chafe at what feels like forced isolation from normal human activity.

Recent studies have measured the effect of sensory deprivation on the brain. When volunteers were placed in a blackened sound-proof room for 15 minutes, several reported psychosis-like experiences similar to those of recreational drug-users, e.g., hallucinations of faces and shapes, and in some cases the "presence of evil."

In 2008, six individuals agreed to be shut in a cell inside a nuclear bunker, alone and in complete darkness for two days and nights. Half experienced auditory and visual hallucinations. All lost their sense of time. They had trouble thinking of words beginning with the letter "F." One subject remarked that it was hard to stimulate your brain with no light, and that his brain just didn't want to do anything.

So, I see this pandemic as posing a conundrum. On the one hand, people are isolated and deprived of the basic stimuli of everyday life. It's driving them nuts. Several of my patients have invoked Edvard Munch's famous painting, "The Scream" (1893), and I recently saw a video of a music teacher screaming as she strums a ukulele. But the complication – the "other hand" of this problem – is that the very condition that leaves us stressed, exhausted, and wanting to scream also creates a need for the relaxation that some sensory deprivation techniques provide. The trick in all of this, therefore, is to turn our current isolation into opportunities for relaxation rather than for driving endless stress.

It is well-known that short-term sensory deprivation can be deeply relaxing and conducive to meditation. Technically, the various therapeutic techniques come under the heading of Restricted Environmental Stimulation Therapy (REST). They include chamber rest (where the subject lies on a bed in a dark, sound-reduced room for up to 24 hours), and flotation rest (where the subject literally floats in a pool, unable to feel much). Both of these have been used to lower stress, though there is a debate over which is more effective. Combined with other therapies, they have been used to treat smoking addiction and alcoholism.

The point is that when you have lemons – lots of boring simulacra that make you want to scream – then you need to make the kind of real lemonade that is relaxing, and that makes the world's withdrawal seem therapeutic, even enjoyable. In other words, sensory deprivation can be turned on its head, producing effects that actually mitigate the deprivation and produce feelings of well-being. It's a way of beating our enforced isolation at its own game.

Towards this end, it's okay to indulge, if not in the type of REST techniques employed by researchers, then in DIY knock-offs that have some of the same calming effects. It's okay to take a long, hot bath, or turn off the TV and just meditate. There are dozens of videos showing you how. One of my patients has taken up complicated baking: she makes puff pastry, Danish, and braided challah from scratch. She makes marmalade, a two-day process that involves skinning the oranges, pitting them, soaking, boiling – a very 19th century process that reflects a slower time.

Now is the time to give yourself time. Find an immersive project that takes you out of yourself into strings of serial micro-challenges that don't allow you to declare victory until the project is done. Buy a book of crossword puzzles . . . and do them all. Take up quilting . . . and make a quilt. Order 20 pounds of vegetables . . . and put them up before they spoil. Commit to making a quantity of face masks. Commit to anything that will keep you engaged. One of my patients is learning Czech, another is reading *War and Peace*. It is actually stress-reducing to work towards a goal and experience progress. Progress towards attainable goals is integral to happiness. It creates positive feedback that is continually reinforcing and makes us feel good about ourselves.

Enduring this pandemic is a balancing act. If we must live with sensory deprivation, we can at least turn it to our advantage. We can find activities that remove us from the stress of our environments and provide a sense of well-being. If we can induce plausible states of well-being, we are on the way to promoting resilience. Plausibility is the key. We need to believe that we really are doing well by ourselves. We need to train our brains away from feeling stressed and anxious, and towards acknowledging our efforts on our own behalf. The point is to start somewhere, while we can.

SMART PEOPLE, DUMB ACTIONS

Even smart people act stupidly during this crazy period. Sheltering in place, keeping a safe distance, and wearing a face mask have been shown to slow the virus' spread. But they can also affront one's sense of independence and, ironically, ramp up one's fear. The resulting stress is disorienting. It leads some to ignore socially acceptable behavior, and to wander around in smug indifference; others withdraw to the point of self-annihilation. Neither response is smart.

Compounding the problem, a smart person can exhibit both (contradictory) tendencies. I'm thinking of my friend David, whom I called today just to check in. David, a distinguished man in his late 50s, is always the smartest person in the room. After becoming an Ivy League law professor, he morphed in his 40s into a high-priced consultant. Now divorced, he lives with his teenage son in California.

During our conversation, David talked about how he was presently "cloistered," but planning a musical salon at his home in a few weeks. I asked who was performing, and he named a famous violinist in his 70s. He asked if I could come, but I said that it was unwise to expose a septuagenarian and other possibly vulnerable people to the risk of COVID-19. I asked, "How would you feel, even if the violinist were willing to play and other people to come, knowing the risks they faced?" This gave him pause, and he agreed to wait at least until autumn before holding the event.

Yet I was stunned that he would even contemplate such an occasion. Was it that he just wasn't thinking? Unlikely. So, I had to assume that holding the soirée – and featuring someone notably at risk – was an act of misguided self-care. It was a means of suspending his intelligence to make himself feel better. His use of the term "cloistered" tipped me off, suggesting that he knew the risks all too well; he just didn't want them to apply to him.

Intelligent people often act in contradictory ways. In "The Crack-Up," F. Scott Fitzgerald (1936) observed, "The test of a first-rate intelligence is the ability to hold two opposed ideas in the mind, at the same time, and still retain the ability to function." The trait (noticed perhaps as early as Shakespeare) is known as Negative Capability, as if the forces pulling in one direction cancelled out those in the other, leaving the mind perfectly stable. For such people, unpredictability (in which direction will they swing?) can be a point of pride.

But I was, predictably, mystified, and asked David how he remained "cloistered." "I haven't been out of the house in five weeks," he said. He acknowledged the importance of fresh air and sunlight, but didn't want to get the virus. "Well," I asked, "then how do you square that with potentially exposing others to it?" The moral dimension had never entered into his calculation, allowing him to subsist in Negative Capability.

The point, of course, is that while we can manipulate our intelligence, we do so at a cost. We become moral relativists – balancing the cost in human lives against other seemingly desirable objectives – or, at the extreme, we obliterate the moral factors altogether. David did the latter. I should have called him on it. However, I guess I indulged in some moral relativism of my own, choosing to preserve our friendship over starting a fight. I've heard a lot of stories from my patients lately about similar situations, where they're inclined to challenge someone's anti-social behavior but then fall back, sighing "discretion is the better part of valor."

Except when it isn't, i.e., when lives could be at stake. It could be a moral failing not to speak up for morality.

So, alas for me. Before our conversation ended, I told David – speaking as a doctor, rather than his friend – that he needed to take walks in the sunshine. I made the discussion into a little wellness lecture. I knew this was a compromise – given the lecture that I might have delivered – but I consoled myself that I was doing some good, even if it wasn't the existential good that I should have done.

Yet to be fair, I realized that David and I were both under stress. What may not be the best course of action in normal situations can be excused, and may even be appropriate when adding even a little to the stress-level can make things disproportionately worse. Even if the effect of enhanced stress is subclinical, it can still cause real symptoms and contribute to physical and mental illness.

So, David has opted to stay in lockdown. I am reminded of a sonnet by William Wordsworth, "Nuns fret not in their convent's narrow room" (2006). The sonnet, a precisely defined form in poetry, nicely echoes the image of a nun's feeling free in her room to think and pray. Perhaps, for a while, David feels liberated by confinement. Perhaps he will, in time, reflect on his own contradictions. Confinement does funny things – it can drive us nuts or, ultimately, it can be clarifying. Often, we just go back and forth, sometimes seeing our circumstances clearly, other times "fretting" in just the way that nuns seek not to do.

A classic example of the uncertain mental states that disturb intense confinement is Alexander Pope's "Eloisa to Abelard" (1717), based on the medieval imprisonment of Eloisa in a nunnery after her affair with Abelard, her teacher. Addressing the walls of her cell, she cries:

> Though cold like you, unmov'd, and silent grown
> I have not yet forgot myself to stone,
> All is not Heav'n's while Abelard has part,
> Still rebel nature holds out half my heart.

It is memory that plagues Eloisa. During our current plague, David and everyone else remembers how it *used* to be. Confinement is not the perfect solution, and it can drive us – as, apparently, it drove David – to take equal and opposite actions that serve no real purpose other than to complicate the situation and make survival that much harder. I can't really be angry at David, therefore, even though his reaction to confinement has radically discounted the moral dimension of *how* he comes out of confinement. As a therapist treating many people like David, I wrestle with similar dilemmas every day. No one means to do ill; it's just that this whole situation creates unaccustomed stresses that lead us away from our best selves.

Ultimately, we all have to live with ourselves and find our own way. When all this is finally past, everyone is likely to reflect on themselves and on conduct that they can hardly imagine was theirs. We will have to live with our remembered selves. It hurts to remember all the fun of just a few months ago, and it will hurt to remember the sad irrationality of our negatively capable now.

HONESTY

Normally, my patients have one or two issues – anxiety maybe, or an extra-marital affair. But since the pandemic struck, they offer litanies of reasons why things are bad. "Look," said Jeanette, "We're over 100,000 dead, Minneapolis is burning, Trump just picked a new fight with China, and I feel compelled to read *Frankenstein* again." Does she want me to laugh or to cry? Probably, the pandemic excites the performance artist in us. We turn our troubles into schtick.

As I listen to Jeanette, I hear someone who feels like she is losing control. Who can stop a virus, or tell the President to lay off? No one. So, we package our helplessness into a routine. We perform it. We put it on display, like a flag in a window, so maybe the performance – and not us – will become the topic of conversation. We really don't want other people to hear about how awful we feel, since we're afraid it might offend them. It might seem like we want to take up what mental space they have left once they've processed their own issues with this pandemic.

Jeanette, like so many of us, is formulating a new etiquette – a pandemic politesse. It's based on the assumption that people have had Enough Already, and don't want to consider all the dimensions of this all-encompassing siege. It assumes that empathy is now a luxury, which most people can't afford just now. It assumes that when people ask how we are, they want some anodyne response that elicits no action on their part, no further concern.

Jeanette said that even when she Skypes and Zooms with her friends, they all talk about what they'll do when it's okay to do anything. "I'm going to *Hamilton* – I deserve it." "I'm going to the zoo." Their conversations are exercises in imagination, sweet but polite excursions beyond their current reality. Nobody wants to admit that they feel depressed; that their finances are suffering; that their relationships are under strain. Nobody even wants to talk about the election which, as we all understood just a few months ago, would be the most pivotal expression of the popular will since Reagan.

According to Jeanette, "we've retreated to a Hallmark world" in the midst of so much sadness.

Implicitly, I hear this from other patients as well. One of them, who lives on the Upper East Side, told me that every day she sees fewer people wearing masks – even as pleas go out from the CDC and the governor that masks are *de rigueur*. It's as if, with COVID-19 all around them, the anti-maskers prefer to believe that it's not. I am reminded of a condition, rapture of the deep, which occurs when divers act erratically once they've descended below 30 meters. As the nitrogen dissolves into their nerve membranes, they become giddy, exhilarated, and pull off their diving gear . . . swimming unencumbered (barefaced!) until they drown.

Not wearing a mask when we should is a marker of denial.

Yet while the pandemic is still "pan-," meaning everywhere, a certain mutual consent is required for denialism to have a major impact. We have to *allow* other people not to be empathetic, and we have to allow them to act as if no one is harmed by their anti-social indifference to wearing protective gear. So, maybe we *should* tell our friends how worried we are (instead of hiding behind some Borscht Belt performance), and maybe we *should* remind people about how to behave in public (instead of diving into the deep along with them). By not being up-front, we are not just being reticent – we are being complicit in creating a community that in the long run is anti-communal.

No one wants to call attention to themselves just now: "Hey, I'm hurting. And, by the way, you're hurting me too." With all the trouble that we know is out there, it feels terribly self-important. But the trick is to learn to pick our occasions, i.e. when we should talk candidly with people and, indeed, when is it okay to confront them. Perhaps, as a counterweight to the new politesse, we must develop a new assertiveness. People who have never actually shared themselves – whether it be their private fears or their indignation – may need to learn to master the skill.

In a grim – but not altogether inappropriate – way, this liminal time is not unlike the '80s, when New York was waking up to the epidemic of HIV-AIDS. There were crusades among the gay community promoting safe sex. How could you not wear a condom? How could you have unprotected sex with multiple partners? After a while, the answers emerged that you couldn't and you wouldn't. There were demands for honesty, for concrete action, for concern. It finally sank in. We don't like to think about awful analogies when our present problems are bad enough, but in fact we have to. Honesty became the norm back then, and it will have to do so now.

So, I talk with Jeanette, and finally the schtick starts to crack. I remind her that friends may actually be relieved by her candor, since it can open the door for their own. I pose a leading question, "Do you think you're each performing for each other?" Perhaps the repression is mutually agreed upon, based on each person's fear of alienating the other. She thinks that is likely so.

Isolating at home has had the effect of isolating us in our minds. We are more than usually self-conscious and, as a result, we have a hard time extending ourselves to others whom, we assume, are equally self-conscious inside their mental cocoons. In a misbegotten effort to maintain our friendships through this crisis, we pull back from exercising the prerogatives of friendship. We refrain from talking about what's really on our minds and indulge instead in mutual entertainment.

It's probably easier just to stay in this mode, indulging our inner Mrs. Maisel when, in reality, we'd prefer to ditch the performer for real, one-on-one human connection. Sometimes, the hardest part of maintaining relationships is not providing empathy, but seeking it for ourselves. We don't want to have that emotional cup in our hands. So, it is useful to remember that our friends, in isolation, may feel just as we do – aching to let it all hang out and, as part of the bargain, aching to participate in shared rituals of support. That is, the people that we know may want to provide us with advice and virtual hugs, if for no other reason than they'll feel better about seeking the same from us.

As we sink into this new normal, we should not normalize emotional self-blackmail, and justify every possible reason for repressing justifiable feelings. It's okay to be out there, telling our own truths. Actually, it's necessary if we plan to survive this pandemic with our sense of ourselves intact.

READING A POEM

During his tenure as Poet Laureate (1997–2000), Robert Pinsky published a small anthology, *The Handbook of Heartbreak: 101 Poems of Lost Love and Sorrow* (1998). I pulled it off the shelf recently since I remembered how much I had enjoyed it. Maybe, I thought, rereading the dog-eared pages would encourage me during a day's worth of fretful, unhappy patients.

But then it occurred to me: why had a book full of star-crossed lovers ever made me feel good? As a psychiatrist – and not one particularly inclined towards schadenfreude – I was interested in the answer to that question.

In fact, Pinsky anticipated that most readers would be. The very first paragraph of the introduction (p. xiii) states: "This is one of the great human mysteries: why do works of art about bad things such as loss and deprivation make us feel good?" Well, I thought, if it's still such a mystery, then that could be a rhetorical question. Any answer is bound to be inadequate, most likely related to nuances of individual psychology rather than to the species *homo sapiens*.

But still, since I couldn't think of any nuances in my own psychology that led me to enjoy the *Handbook*, I was curious about Pinsky's approach to the question.

In fact, Pinsky concedes that there is no one answer. He suggests, instead, that the truth is distributed across an array of more or less truthful responses:

> The great answers to this mystery probably have, each of them, a measure of truth; by the artist's gift, we have our own unarticulated feeling expressed; by catharsis we get the woe and the fear of woe out of our system; by sublimation we convert neediness into a possession; by recognition we feel companionship; by contrast we relish recollected or imagined misery because it heightens the tranquility of our present state; and because we are not, at the moment, being attacked by chain saw or betrayed by our beloved, we can take voyeuristic, secure pleasure in the spectacle.
>
> (pp. xiii–ix)

At one time or another, I've probably experienced each of those emotions. Certainly, each of them is worth a separate essay. But because I needed a jolt of positive emotion just then, I decided to let some of the poems – one way or another – take me out of myself for a while. The daily onslaught of COVID-related "woe," "fear of woe," and "misery" was taking a toll.

One poem, William Carlos Williams' "Love Song" (1938) really affected me, as it had 20 years ago when I first read it:

> I lie here thinking of you:–
> the stain of love
> is upon the world!
> Yellow, yellow, yellow
> it eats into the leaves,
> smears with saffron
> the horned branches that lean
> heavily
> against a smooth purple sky!
> There is no light
> only a honey-thick stain
> that drips from leaf to leaf

and limb to limb
spoiling the colors
of the whole world –
you far off there under
the wine-red selvage of the west.

But now I read it differently.

What's striking about this poem – now – is that it expresses, in such a tight compressed compass, how I feel about a virus that is "spoiling the colors" of a world so usually full of color. I think about the image of thwarted love which, unable to express itself except in despair, is turning the vegetable color of decay. So many people feel a version of this deprivation, right now. I picture that tree whose discoloration inexorably spreads.

As I read the poem a second time, I realized that it had made me feel better – though not, necessarily, for any reason that Pinsky suggests. Instead, it gave me a metaphor (the virus = spreading yellow decay) to think about our current state, and to understand it in terms of a natural process that I can visualize. It gave me a lens through which to think about the virus as this concrete thing, moving through life, "spoiling" it, cutting off the possibility of human contact when that is really what we need.

In other words, the satisfaction that I derived from "Love Song" was primarily intellectual, rather than emotional. However, there is an emotional satisfaction in being able to understand a phenomenon more completely, possibly even through new eyes. In this sense, we engage in an act of sharing with the poet, who enables us to see the world through eyes that have seen a lot more, or seen more acutely than we have. I wanted to thank Williams for what seemed, in the end, an act of generosity.

Of course, I realized that my reading of "Love Song" was idiosyncratic, and very much determined by my seeing patients and needing some respite. But so-what? One thing that will come out of this pandemic is that we'll be free to use the tools that we have in novel ways – like using church-keys to open Amazon packages – so long as the tools work. We'll read poetry, for example, to help us think about a newly configured world in ways that the poet may never have imagined.

Why should the poet care? I doubt that poets are such disciplinarians that they would hold us to reading their poetry only for some "official," intentional meaning. If Williams' ultimate purpose was to make me feel good (or, at least, better than I did), then he shouldn't care how I used his poem to get there.

In a post-COVID world, we will need resilience to make the most of whatever may still be possible. My encounter with "Love Song" – my reinterpretation of it to suit the times and my own personal need – made me feel resilient. That is, capable. Art is no less artistic because, in a different light, we see it differently, use it differently, make it our own.

Now perhaps more than ever we need to be in conversation with art. Art that we didn't think had anything to teach may, in fact, teach us a lot. This is because we are now different people, able to pry meaning from art that we couldn't have even a short while ago. I hate to admit this, but the pandemic – with all its "woe" and "fear of woe" – has made me able to imagine death and its expansive consequences in ways that I never imagined I would ever have to.

"Love Song" is about a world that dies in the absence of love. Equally, it is about the spread of death. Because I think about death a lot now, and how big and encompassing it can be, I found the poem congenial. I read it literally and metaphorically, as one might do Scripture. The poem made me happy because, in part, I felt better equipped to appreciate it.

Lately, we have seen old works of creative imagination become newly relevant – Defoe's *A Journal of the Plague Year* (1722), Camus' *The Plague* (1947). We read them against our own plague. So now, it may not be so great a leap to read poetry about a sere dying world, even though the worlds in those poems are dying differently.

Part II: Venturing out

This Part follows my patients as they re-enter a world still largely in suspended animation. When we hear the term "re-entry," we think of satellites crashing through Earth's atmosphere, almost too fast to be seen clearly. In the last mile or so, astronauts drop with precision on some stretch of waveless ocean. The Navy turns out to swoop them up . . . okay, wrong analogy. Forget the Navy. Forget the speed and excitement. Re-entry post-COVID is often lonely, lumbering, in no way part of a fabulous adventure. The goals are modest, even perhaps uncertain, and the experience is utterly mundane. Someone plants a garden. Someone applies for a job. Rarely does anyone make a big splash.

But what is lacking in bravado is more than made up for by the vast array of people involved. Everyone, sooner or later, has to try to get out of the house. They have to deal with their fears. They encounter frustration. The point is to navigate, to keep going. Human beings – whether descending from outer space or just returning to work in the ER – somehow find resilience to pursue some reasonable goal. They find a way.

As I wrote these accounts, I realized that the common thread was personal creativity, the capacity of all these individuals to devise ways of problem-solving that worked for them. They appeared, instinctively, to have taken their own measure, and to understand what they could accomplish when the whole notion of possibility still seemed so constricted. They took the sort of risks, made the sort of accommodations, that suited their personalities and capabilities. In other words, they knew themselves pretty well, if only because the pandemic had thrown them back on their own resources, forcing them to think about themselves as perhaps they had never been forced to before.

If any good thing emerges from this siege, it will be that people had closer encounters with themselves than they had ever thought necessary (in effect, venturing out precipitated an inward turn). My role was to facilitate that encounter, to assure people that – however unaccustomed – their inward turn would be outwardly useful as the world opens up.

This is not to say, however, that Part II is a fount of optimism. The first two essays present somewhat conflicting views of how well we are likely to navigate the world that COVID has left behind (or rather, reluctantly, slowly, uncertainly, sort-of leaves behind). If I suggest that we are likely to be less hedonistic, I also suggest that we will have to deal with a straitened set of services, unresponsive at times and likely to be robotic. We will have to find work-arounds, even as we work on cultivating patience.

Will we get used to these new co-ordinates? I come back to that term, suspended animation – we'll have to make the most of what animation there is, and hope that the suspension dissolves into something more tolerable.

However, I have not arranged the essays in this Part to send a message *merely* by their arrangement – even though I hope that you'll read them all the way through. I wanted the essays to seem kaleidoscopic, to convey the extraordinary variety of approaches that my patients adopt. One chooses to write a biography of Hieronymus Bosch, convinced that his moment has come around again from the 15th century (Bosch practically invented surrealism in art). Another has to rein in a rebellious pre-teen. Still another, an expert on French literature, starts a Facebook group for aficionados of vintage French clothes. If it works for them, then hooray. One coping mechanism can open up into the next.

Of course, several of these patients are still looking for ways they should choose to cope. Their stories are the hardest to tell: the balance between suspension and animation decidedly tilts towards the former. But still there are avenues to explore. They understand, at least, that their worlds have not hit a wall. They may need to find a new direction. They may have to rely on the support of their extended communities – not just until they find a new direction, but rather as a type of direction filled with mutuality and trust.

Nobody said any of this would be easy. However, it is possible to say that the possibilities are as varied as the people who pursue them.

I was going to end this introduction with "the people who pursue them" until I realized that the phrase included me. During this period of venturing out, my caseload has increased; as people try to recoup some sense of reality/their lives/ fun, they need advice. Moreover, working with patients remotely is intense – the focus never lets up, even for a second (to look away might seem natural in a face-to-face meeting, but any such movement is magnified onscreen and both parties try to avoid it).

I've noticed too that the very fact that some people are venturing out is a cause of anxiety in others ("If they're out, then there's more chance for me to get infected"). So how do you deal with a paradox? The more things reopen, the more that becomes a portent of bad news. I have to deal with a No-Win mentality where, no matter what I say, there is an equal and opposite possibility. This is also tiring, in the sense that it's Sisyphean. There is a sense of likely futility.

Reading poetry, writing these essays, and exercise have been part of my routine for maintaining well-being. I'm also encouraged by the fact that life goes on, however haltingly. The essentials are coming into clearer focus, which may be the ultimate take-away of venturing out.

SHARING A POST-PANDEMIC WORLD

COVID-19 put TV-show writers in a bind. Recently, some told NPR that they weren't sure how people would watch TV once the pandemic was past – would they want shows that reflected their ordeal, or pure escapism that allowed them to forget that it ever happened? A lot is riding on the answer to that question in terms of which pilots actually get made into full seasons.

As a psychiatrist, I thought about that question because its commercial aspects stand in for how people will feel about themselves on the other side of intense, combined personal loss and social devastation. Will they want to look deeply into how – as individuals and as a society – they responded to this crisis, or will they just go on their way, trying to shield themselves from the pain, guilt, and hard work of evaluating their response?

It's natural, after a period of psychic overload, to look for some surcease. Everyone is entitled to kick back, relax, and even congratulate themselves for having survived. Even during the midst of this pandemic, mental health experts

Figure II. 1 Dixieland band

are assuring us that it's okay to use this time to slow down and take up a hobby. But at some point, we must emerge from hibernation and look around. If I were promoting a TV series, I would be willing to bet that most of us will want to understand the world from a post-COVID perspective, and be anxious to think about our place in it. We'll want to look at our habits of consumption and consider whether they still make sense. (Okay, so that's why I'm writing these essays!).

One of my patients, an inveterate traveler, theater-goer, and restaurant aficionado, told me that her life up until this period has been one long effort to amuse herself. "I want to be happy," she said, "and I feel no need to apologize." My thought was "Then why are we even talking? Something's not right." But I just said "That's interesting." Many of us were already in an escapist mode before the pandemic, trying to get past what was gnawing at us by pursuing still more escape. It was a vicious circle that suddenly collapsed when all the opportunities collapsed. Now, with a protracted period of constricted outlets for pleasure-seeking, we are forced back onto ourselves. We will need to start building inner resources for honesty, generosity, resilience, perhaps from the ground up.

That is, choosing to amuse ourselves as if nothing has changed is now a false choice. Even the most inveterately self-absorbed will need to think about their place in a radically changed world, where disruption, displacement, disappearance, and decline offer a constant reminder of how we all need to adjust our consumption in the interest of society and our own self-respect. I think it's no longer possible to accept indifference.

Where before we may have spent $200 on a Broadway show, we may now understand that perhaps half that should go to a food bank. We may want to spend time thinking about how to tutor children who have fallen behind in school; we could serve on our condo board, so that the building stays child-friendly; we could join a church or synagogue group that reads to the elderly. One of my patients has begun supporting a dance company devoted to bridging the divide between Western and Middle Eastern art forms (albeit they're largely in lockdown). Another, a former theater professor, has agreed to volunteer at a bookstore once it reopens to save it from closing. The need for rebuilding will be immense – but, more importantly, unavoidable for anyone concerned with maintaining their mental health.

Those of us who have been less devoted to pleasure may feel that we deserve to indulge to the extent that it's possible. In fact, everyone deserves a break, especially from the crushing routine of hanging around the house. But how do we want to think of ourselves over the long run? I expect that organizations like Volunteers of America will experience a surge in applicants. There will likely be thousands more responses to the Volunteer, non-profit section on sites like Idealist.com, offering positions to people intent on making a difference.

Psychiatrists help people to think about themselves in ways that are conducive to their personal well-being. We want to produce positive change. But in many cases, this is not just a matter of helping people to confront their submerged demons and, by confronting them, understand and dispel them. In many instances, we ask that people evaluate their responses as life changes around them. The collective effects of COVID-19 are shaping up to be the biggest cultural tectonic shift in our lifetime. This transformation will have a drastic impact on how we see our place in the world. It will influence the value that we place on ourselves.

Recently, the *New York Times* had an article concerning the "value" that economists and government agencies place on a human life. Figures ranged from the hundreds of thousands of dollars into the many millions. But when psychiatrists talk about such value, we mean how each individual considers their place in society – are we merely consumers, or do we contribute at least as much as we consume in terms of increasing the ability of those around us to cope with life and even thrive? In these terms, we need to calculate, on a daily basis, whether we are so involved with living for ourselves that we are insufficiently integrated into the world at large.

In 1985, Neil Postman wrote the seminal book, *Amusing Ourselves to Death: Public Discourse in the Age of Show Business*, in which he argued that television has reduced our capacity for rational thought by substituting entertainment for information. We have come to see ourselves (he argues) as extensions of this medium, and live our lives as if defined by it. Thus, for example, politics is no longer concerned with rational debate, but with one-liners, zingers, and gotchas. News is fragmented into sound-bites. Everything is about image rather than truth – it's advertising writ large, 24 hours a day. Little wonder, therefore, that until an earth-shaking crisis like COVID-19 we were content to live as if constant amusement was not just acceptable but normal.

The fact that TV writers now question that assumption or, at least, raise the possibility of an alternative reality, suggests how profoundly we have been shaken by COVID-19. If the very source of our amusement society is now unsure of its premises, then you have to believe that those premises are not as sound – not as responsive to our humanity – as our good fortune has allowed us to pretend that they are. Once we are past this pandemic, and even starting right now in the midst of it, we will need to begin rethinking how we connect to other human beings. That is, we will need to reconsider how we practice our basic humanity.

COVID-19 has called into question the basic premises of our lives. It has captured everything from how we buy food (in the grocery store? online? in bulk?) to what we eat, where we eat, when we socialize, when and where we work, and the place of technology in routine communication. It has forced us to think about ourselves as fragile, and to appreciate the fragility of everything that we took for granted. In this new environment, and in the climate yet to emerge, our only option is to define ourselves so that we can respect ourselves in a more demanding, less comfortable world that we inexorably share with everyone else.

We can still have a good time, but thoughtfully.

SILENCE

I've started a small nonprofit dedicated to jump-starting medical research. A lawyer is helping me file the forms: we reserve the name, incorporate, and declare a "mission." Ultimately, we will seek tax-exemption. But during this pandemic, even the ordinary is hardly *pro forma*. When I send in the forms, there is no response. So, I wonder and wait. I can't call anyone because everyone is furloughed. Before COVID-19, you could pick up the phone – "Did you receive my submission? How long will it take to process?" Now it's anyone's guess. What used to seem like government is now a mail-drop.

There were guidelines for when to expect a response. Once upon a time, there was even Albany and Washington; there were people at the end of a phone-tree who assured you that government still "cared" . . . but now there is just silence. This disjunction between the requirements of bureaucracy – all the forms, all the payments – and the minimal human follow-through, strikes me as unsettling. It suggests that while I am still expected to perform my duties as a citizen, I cannot expect an equal and opposite response. Not forever, perhaps, but for a very extended meantime.

As the effects of this pandemic play out, the lack of response to our pleas, queries, filings, and even offers to help will become increasingly unnerving, and act as reminders that some basic instruments of connection have defaulted. Several of my patients report that feeling alone is bad enough, but that feeling bewildered makes the condition a lot worse. Whom can you ask? Whom can they ask whom to ask? With no one designated to respond – except first responders, whom we hope we'll never see – there is a sense that expecting a response is somehow, for now, unduly self-important.

We are questioning what we deserve as survivors, as if still being able to ask for assistance is reason enough not to get any. If we expect a response in the ordinary course of things, do we demonstrate a misplaced reliance on others? Do we arrogate to ourselves more than we are entitled to, like kids with bad manners? Some of my patients, who are already frail, now feel as though their limited capacities are beside the point, and that they must fend for themselves along with everyone else not yet totally incapacitated.

I counsel these patients that the echo chambers they seem to inhabit are temporary, and that sooner or later everything will come back. But they tell me of trying to call Amazon, which shut down its help-line, and even trying to call the local police precinct, which shunts them to 311 or 911, depending on whether they are merely upset or afraid they could die.

My elderly patient, Teresa, who is French, told me that she dreamt about Versailles or, rather, the Hall of Mirrors in Louis XIV's great palace. Normally, it reflects your image reflected as your image in an infinite regress toward *de minimis*. It was probably Louis' idea of a joke, with all his subjects dwindling inexorably as they set foot inside. Accordingly, I expected Teresa to say that Versailles now defined the world for her, with her "self" receding into a non-entity. But instead, she surprised me: "You know, it's like all the mirrors were tilted so there is no image at all. You keep walking, but there is no way to know if you're even there."

I found that idea to be chilling. Living amidst COVID-19, there is so little feedback – even from the most likely sources – that we don't even know whether we exist. For many people, especially those living alone, existence depends on affirmation, often from impersonal sources that, in any case, can still look up your name and respond to your queries – maybe about Medicare, or taxes, or incorporating small nonprofits. Teresa recently called the IRS about the three-month extension for paying taxes, and received a recorded message that the branch responsible for answering queries had temporarily shut down.

It's not as if institutions are not trying to serve. But they are encouraging us to deal with them by rote, without the nuance of human intervention. There are rows of FAQs and, when you get to the bottom and are none the wiser, a sheepish little question of their own asks "Was that helpful?" Who is going to read your response? When? You feel like screaming "I am not a zombie. This is not a zombie movie." Really?

Recently, my bank suggested that I make deposits and pay my bills online, not because it's convenient but because it's safer. Okay, but this reduces the concept of a bank to a vehicle for circulating cash when, in fact, I sometimes want to talk to someone – like, for example, what kind of bank account is best for a nonprofit? Does a nonprofit pay taxes on the interest that it earns? Someone can answer questions from 3:00 to 5:00, three days a week. Too bad, I'm working.

So, I wonder about the long-term effect of this silence, this chronic lack of response to our gesturing for help. When the economy "comes back" (if it does), will we be conditioned by then to expect much less from it? If we are, will this have a negative effect on ordinary people who already feel as if they have been written out of the new normal?

There are so many ways to feel unrecognized, and I fear that we are multiplying them. I think about how corporations will respond when responsiveness is offered as a luxury that only some of us can afford. Maybe there will be tiers in the new service economy, where you pay extra for access to a human when you have a query or need advice.

I don't believe in conspiracy theories. But I do think that ideas spread; they get taken up; they become institutionalized. Remoteness, I think, will be one of those ideas, and with it a reduction in access to human beings. During this protracted shutdown, the roboticists have been busy. They have been designing ways to eliminate the need for people in places like call centers and behind bank windows. With government coffers deeply depleted, they will design websites purporting to answer Frequently Asked Questions. Too bad if your question is anomalous.

As a psychiatrist, I am concerned that the world will appear more impersonal, and suggest to people that the loneliness they experience is irremediable. I am concerned that when the noise returns from jack-hammers, cars, and crowds in the street, there will still be silence. I have told my patients to prepare, to find out all they can about everything in their lives so that they don't have to ask as many questions. It's the cognitive equivalent of saving money.

I have told them to join groups of people that share their interests. As the opportunity for connection diminishes, the importance of connection increases. Now we will have to be curators of connection. As we watch how most other connections recede.

WRITING THE PANDEMIC

My patients' professional lives reflect how they see the world and, not surprisingly, how they cope with COVID-19. I have a range of patients – economists, actuaries, professors of Creative Writing. Over the years, I've learned what spikes their stress levels – quarterly reports, tax season, the Writer's Digest annual awards. So, I've learned how to talk them down from the accompanying anxiety ("Hey, next year you'll submit another story!"). That is, until now. The pandemic brings out qualities of mind in my patients that are submerged during typical bursts of stress, so I'm no longer dealing with their reactions to discrete stressors. Because the stress is now unrelenting, patients approach it as if it were encompassing, a boiled-down version of the whole world.

How you think about the world – your intellectual prism – defines how you think about crises, and (in the present crisis) whether you're sanguine or immensely depressed. My patients who are number crunchers are mostly depressed. They plot the tallies of the dead and infected, watch the economy collapse, and register the rising number of the unemployed. "Numbers don't lie," they insist, and do not respond to magical thinking. Since current numbers tell a depressing story, they argue there is no way *not* to be depressed. "I'm just being rational!" which is spoken like a Pythagorean proof. Even if they acknowledge some progress, maybe a 2 percent increase in the Dow, they demur: "Well, that's 2 percent of a much-reduced average. We're nowhere near where we were."

How can you argue with rationality? That is, how can you suggest to someone that apocalypse is not at hand when, every time they Skype you, they cite an unimpeachable method for concluding that it is? All you can say is that if numbers do not lie, neither do they tell the whole truth. Extreme rationality – uninflected by warmth, or kindness, or anything human – can pitch into reverse, and produce an irrational result. I suggest to these patients Book IV of *Gulliver's Travels* (1726), where Swift skewers Enlightenment excesses in a herd of ingenious horses lacking any trace of human empathy. During this pandemic, humans are caring for people; becoming everyday heroes; juxtaposing empathy to sheer numbers and, thereby, helping to reverse a calamity that in the logic of exponential increase should be all but inevitable.

The question is: Do I get through to the number crunchers? I wonder. Psychiatrists can help to change someone's mind regarding how to solve a particular problem ("Stop seeing your mother in your boss"). But it's much harder to change someone's entire habit of mind, i.e. the way that they approach every problem. As I argue with economists, actuaries, accountants, and securities analysts that the world is not yet lost, I am trying to get them to think beyond their habitual way of thinking. I am trying to get them to see around the corners in their brains to other, more edifying possibilities. It's too early to tell yet whether I'm succeeding.

On the other hand, my patients who are creative – the poets, copywriters, even an English professor – are coping rather well. Lured by protracted days and unaccustomed quiet, they are writing about how they feel, transforming feelings into art. At day's end they sit back, assume the role of their own most favorable critic, and assure themselves that they're still in the game. Maybe Giovanni Boccaccio did pretty much the same when, fleeing to the hills above Florence, he wrote *The Decameron* (1358) while the Plague was wiping out everyone below.

These patients are writing constantly now, turning out stories and poems about their new constriction; they are surprised by themselves, discovering irony in routines whose very inability to change is in itself new. A sense of discovery has firmly taken hold. They are still worried, of course, but even in their constricted environments they do not seem intellectually pinched. In fact, they seem quite the opposite, open to the possibilities that their own curious natures generate. One patient told me, "Okay, my world has shrunk to a pinhead, but a thousand angels are dancing on top of it."

Among Medieval scholastics, there was debate about how many angels could dance on the head of a pin. Now, since the question has no theological resonance, it suggests only contriving and responding to questions of no intellectual consequence. But wait a minute! That's the point! My creative patients whose world is a pinhead are permitting their minds to play. They are approaching the pandemic as an opportunity to see things differently precisely because there is no consequence – no editors, no clients with products to sell, no deadlines. The pandemic has become a jumping-off point into the undiscovered where, if you create something, you have the right to love and admire it.

During the pandemic, some of these writers are happier than they have been in a long time. They realize that while they are "coping," and that all is not as it should be, they are also living in a little sealed bubble of their own minds. They are their own companions, along with a thousand dancing angels – nice work if you can get it. They realize, of course, how lucky they are to have talent. But most of them knew that anyway. What's new and different is that they have learned how to use it to ride out a plague.

I think that when new, immense challenges emerge, they will look back on this period as one that was not just about survival through intellectual escape, but about developing an all-purpose survival mechanism, good for whatever transpires. The formula would not require isolation but, rather, the ability to focus on – and describe – one's own recalibrated feelings. The point is that however terrible the situation, we are ultimately our own best resource.

As someone who is always trying to write, and has accepted being perpetually rewritten, I see an opening. Could I adapt my patients' writing the pandemic to suit my own critical devices? Well, when the next catastrophe occurs...

Just as I may learn from my patients, I think about introducing them to each other. What would happen, for example, if a few of the number-crunchers met some of the writers? Perhaps they would pivot, and learn the utility of inwardness. In a way, numbers – which have their own pristine beauty – are entirely "out there," dissociated from an inwardness that entails thinking hard about oneself, mapping some part of one's own terrain until the details are clear. It's hard work. Since the creative types do it as a matter of course, and even relish it, my question is whether such a turn of mind can be taught. If it can be, can it be practiced at a level where it is fun, perhaps even edifying?

Because we are spending so much time alone during this pandemic, the situation exposes how different habits of mind produce different capacities to cope with the circumstances. I suppose that we have always known this but, right now, the differences could not be starker. There will be so much to reflect on after this pandemic (assuming, as the creatives will tell you, we actually get there).

THE RABBI AND THE PANDEMIC

An epigram attributed to the Hasidic rabbi, Nachman of Breslov (1772–1810), seems appropriate just now, "The whole world is a narrow bridge, and the

Figure II.2 Kyoto Station, Hiroshige (1832)

essential thing is not to fear at all." This notion of the world – shaky, spindly, not easy to navigate – has passed into song, and is the title of a recent novel, Aaron Thier's *The World is a Narrow Bridge* (2018). Nineteenth century Jews had a talent for describing impending disaster.

Yet while this epigram seems poignantly appropriate to the world of COVID-19, and we should take it to heart, it is not what Nachman actually said.

Research by a modern scholar, Rabbi Daniel Pressman (2009), demonstrates that what Nachman said is actually more nuanced, indeed more modern in that it throws responsibility for making one's way specifically onto the wayfarer: "When a person must cross an exceedingly narrow bridge, the general principle and the essential thing is not to frighten yourself at all." The more famous, but inaccurate version of this saying is an example of Jewish "telephone," where meaning curves and warps and is ratified by repetition in popular culture.

Apart from the vagaries of Hebrew translation, however, the actual version of Nachman's saying calls on us not to originate fear – not to be its first-instance cause. This imposes a heavier burden than imploring us not to give in to fear that is already present in a world that, like a narrow bridge, creates an environment of fear through its mere existence. The real epigram demands self-control, perhaps even belief that on either side of the narrow bridge there is hope. It's the difference between the world's *being* a narrow bridge – which is a pretty encompassing idea, likely to frighten anyone – and there being a narrow bridge *in* the world, which we can navigate if we take control. So apparently, according to Nachman, fear comes from ourselves. We can repress it by not originating it in the first place.

I think about Nachman as we emerge on Memorial Day like soldiers emerging from bunkers. We stick our heads up an inch or two, and worry that the enemy may mow us right down. I can see the irony, since I'm not supposed to feel like someone in a war movie on Memorial Day – I am supposed to remember real soldiers. But it's how I feel. It's how we all feel in the upended world of COVID-19.

So, what would Nachman have to tell me today? He would talk about courage. He would not say not to be afraid, but he would cite the examples of other people on the bridge who are still moving along. That is, don't look down. Look ahead. Keep going. One of my patients once told me that when she trekked the Himalayas, there were all these narrow bridges over rivers and gorges. At first, she was terrified, but she watched how the Sherpas crossed and tried to imitate them. They never looked down. I think they would have been amused at the notion of some Hasidic rabbi . . . but they applied his principle. So, she did too.

During the course of this pandemic, I've introduced Nachman to several physicians on the frontlines who are stressed, traumatized, burning out. My regular practice is full of people in need. I tell them all to keep looking ahead, to keep going, to acknowledge what is scary but not to nurture fear. That is, not to project horrific outcomes based on our own worst imaginings. I think that is what Nachman is getting at – while we cannot just put fear aside, we must not ruminate on it and allow it to take us over. We must not be the source of our own terrors.

In Nachman's sense, fear is like the virus. It cannot replicate outside human beings but, once inside, humans become its agent. Nachman is the great epidemiologist of fear: his warning is that we not allow ourselves to be complicit in allowing fear to grow.

Many people have had to overcome fear. For example, my patient John is an art dealer in his mid-30s. He had broken up with his live-in boyfriend before COVID-19, and was still trying to cope with life on his own. Moreover, because he is black as well as gay, he is self-conscious in an art world that is largely white. When he heard the recent news of a black man who was shot in Atlanta while jogging, he was concerned. But then he went out for a run.

John had been on the track team in college, and running made him feel strong. It was a source of self-esteem. He could have let it become a reason to fear, but he turned it to his advantage.

But perhaps even braver is my patient Sherry. She's an accomplished writer in her 70s; never married; more on her own just now than she would prefer. During the pandemic, she remained in her apartment, except to pace the hall and pick up the mail. "What am I supposed to do if I get sick?" It's a fair question. But life is a series of trade-offs.

Over the Memorial Day weekend, she wanted to mail some letters, in particular her application for an absentee ballot. The deadline was early June. She debated whether to venture out, and decided that having to show up in person for the June 23 primary was a greater health risk than crossing the street to the mailbox. After all, she is well-equipped. She has N95 masks and latex gloves. She understands social distancing. I urged on her the benefits of fresh air, and explained that the viral load is lower outside than on a crowded bus or in an emergency room. So, she took the plunge.

When we spoke, she told me that the sun felt warm. Before she knew it, she had walked to the mailbox and then a few blocks more. In effect, she had crossed the bridge. Just as John had. Both of these frightened people kept looking ahead, rather than down. John knew he was a runner, and wasn't about to forsake it. Sherri knew she wanted to cast a mail-in ballot, and (literally!) took steps to make that possible. Neither of these people allowed themselves to proliferate fears that, like the virus, will multiply exponentially if we give it a favorable environment.

I like this idea of a bridge in the world. We are not crossing to a better world, but learning to traverse the troubles in this one. We are making up our minds to traverse them. My patients put one foot in front of another – and they are still here.

LOOKING FOR A JOB

One of my patients is looking for a job – right now, during a pandemic. Millions of others are in her shoes. She needs practical advice and moral support. I don't know that anything I can do will make a difference, but we are making a plan.

Margery is an Associate Professor at a small, sectarian college outside New York City. Colleges like these are cutting their budgets, closing departments, furloughing staff as they wait to see whether students return in the fall. Actually, they have been financially strapped for years, as enrollments sink due to fewer students and rising tuitions. In a bid to attract what students there are, they have added amenities and taken on debt that they now fear they cannot repay.

Morale has deteriorated, and Margery wants out before she is given the ax. But amidst a pandemic, when virtually every institution of higher learning is

Figure II.3 Teddy the Old Dutch Cleanser

postponing capital projects; not hiring anyone; and essentially holding its breath, what is an academic to do? "Kill, if it's possible," Margery quips.

I like Margery. She is funny, brash, an unreconstructed feminist. She wrote her dissertation on the origins of vegetarianism in the 18th century. She is an eco-feminist, and campaigns around the world to call out men whom, she contends, destroy the planet in testosterone-crazed meat-eating bravado. She wears a ring in her nose, an emblem of her days in an Indian ashram.

Academics like Margery deploy their positions as spring-boards to radical change. They thrive in these little colleges, which are perversely proud of the excitement they generate. The colleges, which don't pay very well, also leave professors to their own devices – it's possible to experiment, teach new courses, change the world one student at a time.

So, up until recently, Margery was content. But, as she's since told me, "you know what's hitting the fan." Her course-load was increased, even while colleagues were eased out. She became scared, depressed, then desperate. On top of it all, she is a single mother.

We decided to draw up a list of potential alternatives. How about working for a nonprofit? Margery has a lot of friends in Birkenstocks. Publishing? Prep schools? Tutoring? Margery consulted her dissertation adviser ("Hang on for a while. The market's tanked"). She wrote to everyone she could think of. Nothing. Dead silence.

I tried to light a fire under Margery – which shouldn't be hard, given her irrepressible nature. But it *was* hard. Margery had fallen into desuetude from a toxic brew of fear, bewilderment, and daily reports that the economy will get worse. "In a few months, 20 million people will be looking for jobs," she said. "Who am I?"

But then I saw an opening. Margery's rhetorical question – who *was* Margery? – was actually the answer. I insisted that we approach the job search from the other direction, that is, not in terms of jobs that were available but, rather, according to what Margery could do for anyone so lucky as to get her.

We made a list of Margery's experience that demonstrated her essential qualities – she is a fiercely articulate firebrand with a head for organizing. She can write stuff that draws on history as much as on current politics. She is committed. A fount of ideas. Exciting. In another era, and based on her Irish background, she would have been Maud Gonne, the great revolutionary who captured the heart of William Butler Yeats. I wanted Margery to envision herself being herself, just in another place.

So, Margery began drafting letters to colleges that had Women's Studies programs. She suggested that no matter how badly they were short of funds, they needed someone like her to take those programs public, open them up to the community, and excite women to think of themselves as activist, political beings. She suggested that she could turn ivory-tower theory into streetwise praxis. She said that if those places meant what they said within their own confines, then the inevitable consequence was to let everyone know.

In other words, Margery pulled out all the stops. It was clear that COVID-19 was a formidable obstacle to anyone's hiring anyone, least of all in an academic institution, but for that reason we felt that nothing should remain unsaid. Let it all hang out. Go for broke. There is a concept in tort law called Last Clear Chance where, if you know about a danger and fail to avert it, then you can still be liable even though the other person was also negligent. In other words, if Margery didn't give it all she had – right now, full stop – then she couldn't complain when those 20 million other people came looking for the same jobs.

COVID-19 has made "plans" of any sort seem tentative, but within that massive sphere of limitation one still has to try. One's own best resource is oneself. I helped Margery write letters that sounded optimistic about what she could do for an institution without sounding ridiculously optimistic that things were back to normal – or that it would be by the time the new semester began. We spoke about how raising consciousness is slow, laborious work even in the best of times, so that if Margery began work in the fall, she could help build programs that would begin rolling out as things opened up. We made optimism sound plausible.

We held our breath. There were a few responses. Now our sessions are largely practice interviews conducted over Zoom. Margery is worried about how she looks on Zoom, more or less like a reflection in a fun-house mirror. She has not done her hair in months. Her apartment looks like a mess in the background. But these are the worries, I assure her, of everyone else. What matters is the answer to that fundamental question – "Who am I?"

We spent ten minutes discussing the nose-ring – by now, as much a part of Margery as her nose. But she agreed that it had to go.

We had to work on maintaining authenticity when an interview is conducted remotely, mediated by a screen. "I feel like I am acting, like I'm a performer." I tell her not to look at her image on the top right-hand corner of the screen. I tell her that everyone else will be in the same boat, that Zoom-faces have become emblematic of the distortions in every phase of our lives. "Don't apologize for looking like a rubber doll."

We don't know yet how Margery's venture into the job market will develop. It could come to nothing and be a crashing disappointment after a whole lot of work. But Margery's situation will not get any better as colleges continue to consolidate, close, or, at the very least, shudder in response to continuing pressures. Mostly, I want Margery to think of herself as a survivor. Survival is not just a matter of luck, though luck is an undeniable factor more times than most survivors will admit. To continue and indeed prevail, you have to play all the angles and give yourself utterly to meeting the challenges. You have to think outside the box if you want to get outside the box.

That is what Margery has started to do.

THE PROBLEM OF CHOICE

As the pandemic winds through and disrupts our lives and livelihoods, it leaves behind impacts of geographical proportions. It's like the glaciers of 10,000 years ago, which first threw up mountains and then left moraines on the land as they receded. Glacial movement is instructive to think about during this crisis, since it is at once slow and, ultimately, totally transformative. Once we are finally past COVID-19, the flat planes of ordinary life – which we thought would more or less go on forever – will be strewn with outcroppings of radical change. The terrain of our lives will be harder to navigate as we learn what's safe; what's permissible; what's even possible. All of this will take time. Adjustment will become a lifestyle, littered (like a post-glacial landscape) with fissures that we can fall into.

I think it will become easier to make mistakes because, with fewer opportunities to enjoy life and advance professionally, every action will seem more consequential. We may overthink what we undertake, afraid that we'll blow it . . . and then we *will* blow it because our fear will show. We'll give the wrong impression. In exaggerated fits of self-protection, we may seem like wimps or, worse, like flawed specimens concerned about revealing too much of ourselves.

I can already see this *terror mundi* among my patients. It's a form of PTSD (Post-Traumatic Stress Disorder) where, in this instance, we act in ways that may prevent us from suffering when confronted with uncertainty. Essentially, we go into hiding, afraid to commit; afraid to expose ourselves; afraid of anything whose outcome we cannot entirely control. We exhibit an extreme anxiety in the absence of ordinariness.

Exhibit A is my patient Jack. Jack had been seeing me for three years, mainly concerned about recovering from a divorce that left him feeling "discarded in the couples world of suburbia." He hated dating again, and he hated being alone. It was like nothing was right anymore. When he lost his job in a paint company due to the pandemic, he became suddenly desperate. He felt that however badly he'd felt already was now made much worse – "How am I supposed to recover when I'm emotionally wrecked and I've lost my job when there are no jobs?" I was afraid he would act out his desperation and, as a result, prove the point of his rhetorical question.

We tried to explore strategies for coping with his compounding crises so that he would not act rashly. But you never know when any such action is likely to occur. We didn't *think* it would occur if things started turning in his favor. So, of course, that's exactly when it did.

Jack had actually managed to get a job interview with a wall and floor coverings manufacturer in another part of the country. He knew he had great experience, and actually liked the idea of leaving the suburbs for a small, mid-western city. He was hyped. There was going to be a Zoom interview which he thought he would ace. But there was still that desperation – so few jobs, if not this job then what? Another glacial wait? He was an unsteady mix of confidence and anxiety.

Predictably, the interview went well and Jack felt confident . . . up until the last question. They wanted to know whether they could call any of his past employers, including those he had worked for several years ago. Jack was startled. He'd given them names of all the managers at the company that had just let him go, so why did they need to dredge up his history, maybe from ten years ago? "What are they, the FBI?", he asked. The request struck him as an affront, a surprise attack from out of nowhere. He lost his cool.

COVID has sensitized us to threats from every quarter. It has pricked up our ears, intensifying flight-or-fight responses inherited from hominid ancestors. Thus, without even considering the risks that the request actually posed, or the consequences of responding without thinking, Jack said he'd have to think about granting permission and would get back to them.

What an unforced error! As soon as Jack signed off Zoom, he called me, distraught. "How could I have been so dumb? I *had* to give them permission, so I should have done so gracefully, immediately, though I still think they were wrong." That evening, after my scheduled appointments, we discussed what to do.

Jack was inclined, at first, to explain that he had been startled by the request because there had been no hint of it previously and, in fact, it was unorthodox. He thought that once he'd provided some context, he'd grant permission. But I went negative on this approach. "You're implicitly criticizing them, suggesting that it was bad judgment to take you by surprise." I also said that he'd seem as though he couldn't handle the unexpected. Fundamentally, he'd seem as though he was hiding something, and only reluctantly acceding to the inevitable.

I thought my reaction would persuade him, but it provoked him even more. He insisted on being honest, and thought that his candor might actually impress them. "Maybe I could even give them some guidance as to who in my past they could call."

I told him that he was digging himself even deeper. He'd made a mistake out of overabundant caution – excusable by the times that we live in, but most likely irrelevant to a potential employer. "Just email them tonight, and let them contact whomever they wish." The best part of valor, I said, was to act as if he had not missed a beat.

Jack thanked me but, by the end of our session, I was not sure what he might actually do. Perhaps, consistent with his low-grade PTSD, he would keep thinking, tying himself into knots.

The funny thing is that I have not stopped thinking about Jack's dilemma either. It may be that as we exit this pandemic, all that we have to hold onto is ourselves. Maybe being "honest," as Jack calls his likely admission against interest, will be more satisfying in the long run than an expedient that prevents our being the person we feel that we are. Maybe in fleeing to certainty, we are fleeing to core values that no pandemic can dislodge.

In these next several months, choices that once may not have fazed us may suddenly seem momentous. This happens when there are far fewer choices available. We may feel that we are choosing whom we are supposed to be because do-overs will not come along to make things right.

I am reminded of that much-anthologized story, Frank Stockton's brilliant "The Lady or the Tiger" (1882), where life and death hangs on a choice presented as an incalculable conundrum. It will be hard to advise my patients in this difficult environment. Like them, I am making hard choices, anxious about what is right, acknowledging that we are both picking our way among the detritus left by this new landscape.

STEPPING OUT

As we emerge from this pandemic, however gingerly, we try to keep things together. We avoid crowded places. Make sure we have enough masks. Oh, and remember to get a flu shot. The rush of little mandates is like a clutter of post-it notes, insisting on what must be done. Now. Next. Soon. There is still not enough time, let alone distance from COVID-19 to take the long view. How can we develop perspective on the ways this experience is altering our lives?

There are several predictions, of course, like how fashion is likely to change – less fussy, since we're used to working at home; no, fussier than ever, since we won't want to be reminded of sweat pants. In light of our delayed response to the pandemic, some expect a health care revolution. Perhaps a realignment in politics. But it's still anyone's guess.

The data that you choose will determine how you see the world that we're just stepping into.

I am once again turning to poetry, which allows me to reflect on the larger issues embedded in tragedy and loss, no matter the cause. Thus, while no poem can speak to whether we'll become a more efficient society, or more capable of allocating resources humanely, it can still shed light on how to approach the profound experience of loss that we have all just recently shared. Because it is so condensed, poetry abstracts from experience; it allows us to see through to what persists – what inexorably remains – beyond what is merely incidental.

As an abstract of experience, poetry provides structure. I think we're aching for that now – not just because of all the chaos we've endured, but because we sense that we'll desperately need it in the coming months. Where are all the old bodegas, barbers, restaurants? So much ordinariness seems to have disappeared. What we thought we could take for granted has collapsed like origami construction. This morning, I felt as though I needed a poem, like I couldn't start my day properly without one.

I found "Dolor" (1943) by Theodore Roethke (1908–1963). I think it puts a frame around our new reality, telling us the signs to look for in a landscape conspicuously lacking in any prominent signs.

"Dolor" deploys the drab surroundings of a 20th century office to convey the idea that, beneath its commonplace artifacts, there is a looming threat. At first, the threat seems only to come from the lack of sensory stimulation; but it's really from something "almost invisible" and far, far worse. I'm actually stunned at how closely this poem seems to model a post-COVID world, weary of COVID but still perhaps unaware of its lingering potential:

> I have known the inexorable sadness of pencils,
> Neat in their boxes, dolor of pad and paper-weight,
> All the misery of manilla folders and mucilage,

> Desolation in immaculate public places,
> Lonely reception room, lavatory, switchboard,
> The unalterable pathos of basin and pitcher,
> Ritual of multigraph, paper-clip, comma,
> Endless duplication of lives and objects.
> And I have seen dust from the walls of institutions,
> Finer than flour, alive, more dangerous than silica,
> Sift, almost invisible, through long afternoons of tedium,
> Dropping a fine film on nails and delicate eyebrows,
> Glazing the pale hair, the duplicate gray standard faces.

In this office environment, with its "endless duplication of lives and objects," there is an image of a world drained of individuality. But how do I know that it's us, maybe a few months from now? Because just beneath the surface – or, rather, falling from the walls – there is a substance that seems almost deadly. The picture that emerges is one of stasis ("the unalterable pathos of basin and pitcher"), of desolation and loneliness made worse by a deepening film that is "alive" and "dangerous." Sounds like it could be 2021.

In the world of the poem, the film falls on "duplicate gray standard faces." Just yesterday, my patient Rosemary told me that she feels like she's lost her personality after being alone in her house for two months. "I used to have an imagination, but you need stimulus to imagine things." She claims that without the wherewithal to be creative, she is just like everyone else, reduced to common humanity, hell-bent on mere survival. In the poem, even survival is at stake.

I want to be cautiously optimistic about our emergence into post-COVID reality, but "Dolor" feels convincing, backed up by patients like Rosemary. The poem suggests that in the near future, our surroundings will lack the personality they used to have. We may lack the personalities we used to have – the virus was a sort of pre-Xerox "multigraph," producing an "endless duplication of lives and objects."

My feeling is that if this turns out to be the case, then any remedy must entail an effort to get our personalities back. This could be hard, given the continuing threat "through long afternoons of tedium" (which, I think, will continue while there are still very few places to go and few things to do). We have to resist – somehow – the vicious circle of not straying beyond our comfort zone and, therefore, not extending our comfort zone beyond where we are willing to venture.

Maybe the first real step is to start venturing mentally. I have gone back to reclaiming a literary predisposition that I've more or less put on hold for the past several years. I am writing poetry again, not just reading it. But in order to write it, I have to read poetry intently. It imparts a way of thinking that does not come easily in the lock-step logic of prose. Poetry skips a lot of beats, and requires you to make mental leaps. It requires you to make leaps of faith into meanings that, at first, may be beyond immediate apprehension. This takes practice. So, I am practicing, building up faith in my ability to do it.

My patient Gregory, who also lives alone, told me that his relationships became frayed during the lockdown. He was isolated. His friends were isolated. Nobody shared much. They used to get together for poker sometimes, and shoot the breeze afterwards – but with all that impossible, no one stayed in touch. Now he feels that his relationships were merely convenient – not based on anything consequential – and that no one will bother to repair them. "I think I learned I could get along without those guys, and they learned they could get along without me." In any case, poker games may still be out of the question.

We discussed why Gregory tended to think of himself as socially undesirable. While socializing may still be dicey, we can make an effort to make ourselves interesting. "Go out and learn something new, like the history of aviation, and then find a group where you'll be valued." Online relationships can still be reinforcing, and can develop into intensive sharing.

The point is that amidst the "Dolor" left behind by COVID, we can't allow ourselves to remain any more dolorous than we have to in order to stay safe. While the world remains dusty, drab, and only slowly on the road to Normal, we can work on ourselves. We have to hope that, eventually, the world will be ready for us.

PARENTS, RISK, AND THE PANDEMIC

My patients talk to me about issues with their children. As life now turns towards some inkling of normality, they want to know, "How do I teach my kids about risk, even while I encourage them to make their own judgments?" Indeed. How do parents honor a child's right to grow up, while still ensuring that a parent's experience and wisdom will keep them safe?

The short answer is that kids should make their own mistakes, but not when it might kill them. They have to be taught to respect risk, especially when our new normal is a very long way from risk-free.

Take, for example, my patient Rachel, who fretted over her daughter's desire to socialize again with her friends. Dawn is 12 going on 21, fiercely proud of how nothing can stop her. She makes stunning videos on TikTok. She aspires to be a YouTube influencer. Her motto is: "I know what I'm doing!" Predictably, she chafed at her parents' reluctance to allow anything beyond Skype, FaceTime, and Zoom. A remote birthday party she attended was "odd." Today, she wanted to meet a friend at her house, though Rachel said, "Maybe soon. Let's see."

But Dawn did not want to see. She thought her mother was being irrational and, in fact, unfair. (In Dawn's hierarchy of values, fairness outranked thinking straight, since brains were a matter of luck but morality is a choice.) In fact, during the past few months her family had sheltered in place. They'd had virtually no contact with anyone. Her friend's family had done the same. "So, we have a *de facto* bubble," Dawn asserted, "I read about bubbles. They keep you safe."

Oh, dear. How do you answer a kid when, logically, they make sense?

Rachel had encouraged Dawn to keep in touch with friends, and thought she was in sync with other mothers in prohibiting physical contact. But now Dawn's friends were starting to meet up, and Dawn wanted to also. Desperately. She told Rachel about her fear of being "left out," even of becoming the object of helicopter-parent jokes.

I wondered whether Dawn wanted to make Rachel feel guilty. Maybe Rachel already felt guilty, and was trying even harder to explain her thinking to herself.

Dawn had called her mother "risk averse," "overcautious," and "fearful," citing several distance biking and swimming examples that had gone off without a hitch. Dawn may make a good lawyer someday.

Still, Rachel was uncomfortable with the idea. I suggested that in approaching it, therefore, there should be two levels to her decision – the practical and educational. That is, after making her decision, she should share her thinking and how she came to it with Dawn. Rachel reminded me that she had already talked with Dawn. However, since Dawn did not accept that decision, the point was to explain it in terms that Dawn could appreciate, following up on desiderata that Dawn herself had raised. Why was it *not* irrational? (Her friend was planning to have other friends at her house, and who knows where they have been?) Why was it *not* unfair? (Because rational decisions can be justified on their own terms, without making comparisons to the results of possibly other, irrational decisions.)

I suggested that Rachel talk with Dawn as if she were an intelligent person, not just a pre-teen concerned about her reception by other kids. "Look," I said, "it's not too early to teach Dawn about the pernicious effects of peer pressure." While it's rage-inducing to pull rank with your kids ("I'm your parent, so do it"), it's important to impress on them the value of your experience.

But it wasn't easy. Dawn suggested that if she and her friends got together outside, wore masks, and maybe just played volleyball, everything would be fine. It sounded okay, but still . . . Rachel was sure that no one would stick to the rules. Was there going to be a parent present? When she had asked Dawn, Dawn groaned "I can't ask them that" (as if she feared being thought of as her mother's wooden dummy).

So, you just have to set boundaries, allowing some leeway but not so much that you find the risk intolerable. When my daughter wanted to go skateboarding, we allowed it, but not without a helmet. When she balked at the helmet, we cited a talented skateboarder who'd refused a helmet and ended up in the hospital. She wore her helmet. Boundaries that make sense to kids – that stand up against a demonstrable risk – will usually be accepted.

Usually, but not always. Rachel said she told Dawn that whenever she goes to her friends' – tomorrow or in the next couple weeks – she'll need to wear a mask. Dawn said that her friends did not wear masks, and to just forget the whole thing.

But Dawn did not forget.

After a pause, Rachel shared what she called Dawn's "ultimate try": tears, with Dawn exclaiming, "You don't trust me." Rachel was taken by surprise – what to say, what to do – because Dawn is treated as the most responsible, careful child in the family. So, Rachel responded "No, dear, that's not true, you have our full trust and confidence." But, she added, "It's not only about trust. It's about knowledge and experience."

Ultimately, reasonable people can disagree, and parents are entitled to say "I trust you to understand that."

Each of us makes a calculation as we venture back into the world. We ask in meeting with others – friends, family, and loved ones – how much risk we are we imposing on them and ourselves. Each person we expose or are exposed to can potentially be infected; without knowing they're infected, some people are "super carriers," able to infect many more. For most of us, no symptoms will mean no infection. But at this point in the pandemic, without universal and frequent testing, you can't be sure of anyone.

Parents need to explain that to kids.

So, parents' concern is not just paranoia. As the government allows us to remove our masks and resume hanging out in public, there will inevitably be some uptick in cases. We have to balance that risk with staying cloistered forever.

For parents, the question is how to accommodate oneself and one's child to each level of risk as it presents. Each situation will be different, though there will be some common questions: (1) Who is the person venturing out; whom are they meeting with, and how at risk is that person? (2) What is the situation (e.g. Will there be social distancing, masks, indoors or outdoors)? (3) Why are people getting together, and can the function be carried out remotely?

As Rachel and I talked, and as I reflected on my own daughter, I realized that setting community standards may become increasingly useful – no child will feel "different" or left out. But the main consideration must be to talk to children, not as adults but in terms that make sense from their perspective. Children need to feel that parents respect their ability to assess and assume risk. Parents need to start from the assumption that children can, in fact, evaluate risk provided that it is carefully, respectfully explained.

KEEPING IT TOGETHER

Here are some events that were cancelled in New York City on account of the pandemic:

New York City Peace Film Festival
Annual Dinner of the Lesbian, Gay, Bisexual, and Transgender Community Center
Women in the World Summit
New York City St. Patrick's Day Parade
New York Auto Show
Architectural Digest Design Show

Figure II.4 Niwa no hanami, Women resting in a Park, Hosoda, Eishi

New York International Auto Show
GLAAD Media Awards
Who's Afraid of Virginia Woolf?
All the Broadway openings
New York Pride Parade (except for a few splinter events)
Puerto Rican Day
Celebrate Israel Parade
The Mermaid Parade – Coney Island
Graduation ceremonies at Columbia, NYU, Yeshiva, Fordham, and City
    universities
Governor's Ball

The Season at the Metropolitan Opera
Intellectual Property Law & Policy Conference
The Met Gala
About Time – exhibition at the Met
Record Store Day
Irish Arts Center Book Day
Studio 54: Night Magic – at the Brooklyn Museum
Major League Baseball Opening Day
Smithsonian Museum Day
"The Art of Impermanence" at the Asia Society

This minute sample of what didn't happen during the pandemic is a catalogue of trashed plans and shattered aspirations. But here is what did happen in New York during roughly the same period (through spring 2020):

Over 200,000 infected with COVID-19
Over 20,000 dead
Over a million jobs lost
90%+ drop in MTA ridership
Nightly demonstrations against police brutality
A City budget deficit of $9 billion
Thousands of stores closed

What all these have in common – what didn't happen, and what did – is the suddenness of their occurrence. During February, we were still told to "go about our business," while some cases appeared on the West Coast. Then on March 1, the first case was confirmed in New York City. Two weeks later, the lockdown began. Suddenly, everything stopped, except for massive efforts to contain the virus. Store shelves emptied of toilet paper. The stay-at-home routine kicked into gear.

As I talk with patients now, as the City inches towards reopening, I realize that all the suddenness had a cumulative, traumatic effect; the suddenness itself was the problem, even apart from any single closure or cancellation. There were supposed to be parades and shows, and then (BOOM!) there wasn't. Patients ask why, if everything good just collapsed and everything bad just exploded, they can expect any stable progress towards normality. That is, won't we be in for more shocks – for example, a second wave that we won't even see coming? There's no way to answer such concerns.

But at a deeper level, my patients project the jagged trajectory of our recent experience into a *weltanschauung*. They worry that the sudden massive failure of normal expectations, manifest in the sudden onset of epidemiological/economic/social catastrophe, suggests that so much of what we plan for and expect is illusory. A mirage. Anna, a 30-something programmer who lost her job at a downtown start-up, wondered "Why did I bother to move here, when I could have been unemployed back home? I feel so pointless and fragile." The idea that nothing is as it seems – that we are all wisps in the wind as things topple about us – is existentially terrifying.

Is it also legitimate? That is, do our understandable anxieties after a sudden intense trauma reflect a *papier mâché* reality that (up until now) we have failed to acknowledge? After all, if you add climate change, overpopulation, and a ballooning national debt to a pernicious virus, then it's not hard to believe that there is no point in counting on anything. Anna used the word "fragile" to describe herself, as if she could be broken into pieces.

As I spoke with Anna, I understood how the suddenness of all the closures and cancellations segued into specific disappointments – *this* closed, *that* was cancelled – and gave a particular, personal shape to her despair. Anna loved the rallies, parties, workshops, and lectures associated with New York's Pride Month. She loved the parade, which stopped traffic for a day in Greenwich Village. She had signed up to be a volunteer, and had hoped to start networking. Her goal was to become a speaker, maybe next year. She knew already what she would say ("Midwestern conformist breaks out in full color").

But suddenly, her plans vaporized. "I feel frail," she said again, "because I think that everything has been exposed as frail. We were so naïve." For Anna, her own disappointment was an emblem of the human condition. It stood in for how we think we know what's going to happen; how we confidently make plans; but the universe mindlessly cancels it all.

I said "But hey, you're here now. You can't just give up." She indicated that, of course, she knew that, but that her heart wasn't in it. "I'm afraid to want anything too much now." She spoke about love, and how she left the Midwest to recover from a failed relationship. "But that was just a relationship," she said. "This seems different, like it's the whole world." She was arguing, in effect, that there was nowhere to go, and that relative to a "whole world" of disappointment she was incommensurately fragile.

I told her that one element of resilience is accepting that one is not alone, and that other people comprehend our feelings. We can, at the very least, proceed on the assumption that we can share our feelings – even if that requires finding new groups who will listen, provide support, even demonstrate how to carry on. Disappointment is not new, and leads to creativity.

As evidence, I cited an exhibit at the Asia Society that had been cancelled, "The Art of Impermanence." It included Japanese calligraphy, painting, sculpture, ceramics, and textiles that referenced transience over the past several thousand years. In some commentary, a scholar said that "Although cultures have decried the impending end of civilization through the ages . . . impermanence takes on a poignancy – and particular irony – in today's world." I found these claims very moving. I also found them, in a way, to be an antidote to the shock that we felt when everything we'd planned on was so easily crumpled.

"You see," I told Anna, "people have lived with the realization that things fall apart. They have survived. Think of striving within impermanence as our steady state from now on." It may be that at least for the near term, we cannot rely on science and technology to obscure the human condition – and maybe even make it go away. Life is going to be iffy. Of course, we shouldn't live only for the moment and never make plans, but neither should we be so invested in our plans that we see no way to be happy except through their explicit realization. Happiness may become the support we receive from others. It may be more about community, less about ourselves.

In this sense, the new normal should be characterized more by reliance than will. For fulfillment, we should draw on people – and the commitments they make based on the strength of their character – rather than on the timely mani-festation of our personal projects.

Timelines and certainty are suspended. Happiness may come as a surprise; it may be fleeting.

If one good thing comes out of this pandemic, therefore, it may be that we fall back on friendship, and on the support of people who think like we do and share our fears and concerns. If we feel fragile, they can help keep us together.

GARDENING

Some of my patients who once had trouble relaxing, now look for ways to keep busy. It's a remarkable turnaround, as if staying home – and relaxing non-stop with no purpose or structure – feels suddenly decadent. One of my patients, Andrea, formerly spent her days teaching music to children on the autism spectrum. It exhausted her physically and emotionally, and we'd talked about whether she should try deep breathing. But now since the pandemic, where her school is closed least until fall, she needs something to do. "I actually like feeling that I've accomplished something," she said. "Otherwise, I dwell on myself too much and I feel like a dud."

But Andrea is a resourceful woman and, like several of my patients, she has taken up gardening. She bought tomato, pepper, zucchini, and eggplant seedlings at the local nursery (curbside pick-up, of course), which came with instructions on caring for them. "I'm growing all my own pizza toppings," she announced. "Maybe I'll even make room for some basil." So, every week, we talk about the progress of her garden; the weather; mulching; the acidity of the soil. It's an education for both of us as Andrea dives into what is now a challenge and, in fact, a time-consuming project as she reads up on each of the plants. "I don't want to sound weird," she said, "but they each have personalities."

As I speak to Andrea and my other patients about gardening, I realize why it has become so popular now; Andrew Keshner (2020), cites a gardening uptick, and a professor who opines that "plants are not judgmental" and are "grounding" in unstable times. But forget the unintended pun. People want to be outside, while still in a protected space not exposed to crowds. They want to pull off their masks and not feel guilty. For the more thoughtful, the real draw, I think, is that they want to produce something tangible. They want to make stuff with heft, that represents effort, and that other people can use. The pandemic has taught us to value certain types of workers – check-out clerks, package delivery guys, immigrants in meat-packing plants – whose vital functions once passed beneath our radar. But they don't anymore. These people keep us alive. We don't do what they do, because we don't have to; but we can't just let them do it, while we look for ways to soak up the day. Growing a tomato (how elementary can you get?) is one way to deliberately share the burden.

Andrea told me that while it's still too early in the season, she looks forward to bringing in her "harvest." She'll have to keep the bugs away, and maybe even the deer, but she thinks she can manage. One feature of gardening that appeals to her is that it softens the boundary between home and the outdoors. "If I cook with something I've grown," she says, "I feel integrated with the world. I don't feel like I'm just a post-industrial artifact." Her thought is profoundly resonant – even if there is a whiff of back-to-the-land utopianism. It's so easy to feel we've literally been manufactured by offshore clothing makers, bottlers of ketchup, the conglomerate that sells us shoes, and the other conglomerate that sells deodorant, toothpaste, and skin emollient. Our sense of separation from the natural world, and from the sources of everything that clothes and feeds us, is not unlike our sense that we've discounted the people who sustain us. Especially in this time when everything seems so precarious, we don't want to feel remote from what actually matters.

So, Andrea has started what she calls her real-life conversations. I don't often talk with my patients about their plans for vegetables, but Andrea has been thinking about tomato chutney. According to a recipe that she found online, it's made with garlic, onions, ginger, vinegar, raisins, sugar, and lime. You boil it up, then you can it. It can keep for a couple of years. But you can also give it away. To Andrea, however, it represents not just an effort to integrate with nature, and a bid to be that much more self-sufficient, but also a gesture to beat post-industrialism at its own game. "If I am vertically integrated, and grow the stuff that I can and then consume, I am recreating industry on a human scale. I am not letting them manufacture me." Her throw-back '60s utopia may be right at home, so to speak, in the world of COVID-19. We are rethinking our relation to globalism, which clearly has affected our health and our preparedness for the pandemic. We are bringing some vital industries home. On a human scale, so is Andrea.

There is a long tradition of thinking about why we garden. We take pride in what we produce. The routine of the garden – keeping it watered, pulling out weeds, making sure that the grubs don't eat it first – can give structure to our lives. A garden is a perpetual contest between us and nature, always calling us back to first principles: what is it like to try to survive, how much is luck and how much is work or brains or just timing? Gardens allow us to think about our place in the world, and in nature, without actually making us take risks. We can imagine the effort that's required to survive without the large-scale effort actually required. In this sense, gardens are a great metaphor for the times that we live in. I think we are drawn to them because they force us back onto our own resources without posing the existential risks that we may easily encounter if we step outside them.

One of my patients said that "my garden makes me stronger." I thought she meant that she was lifting bags of soil but, in fact, she meant that she was becoming resilient, quick-thinking, able to recover a situation when it defied expectations. "I think there is going to be a second wave," she said, "and if I can raise a patch of cantaloupe, I will be better prepared." My patients sense that they can use this time that they are off from work to work at becoming prepared for what may result in the future. It's funny to think of oneself as out-witting a cantaloupe but, in fact, the cantaloupe is part of the grand scheme of things of which we are a part. It's like COVID-19. We will have to learn to live in the world where it lives too, ideally coming out ahead by dint of the skills we develop.

As I talk with patients, I think about how we create gardens in our own image, overflowing with flowers or mapped out in neat rows of melons. What's the right kind of garden for right now? Either is fine. It's okay to plant a gorgeous garden, just as a utilitarian one will also work. Just so long as we actively engage in gardening. In medieval times, people resorted to a *hortus conclusus* (a secluded garden) for privacy and contemplation. Maybe even a tryst. To have such a luxury now, however, would be unusual. For most of us in this moment, "to garden" – the verb form of the word – holds out real possibilities.

SELF-CONFIDENCE

I am working with physicians and first responders burned out by the pandemic.

"Burnout" cannot readily be measured – like blood pressure – but it is a real medical condition. We see it in the emotional, physical, and mental exhaustion caused by protracted stress. A person may feel overwhelmed; unable to meet the constant demands on their time and capabilities; unable to endure expectations that they place on themselves in response to those demands. About 40 percent of physicians suffer burnout during their careers; nurses, paramedics, and other health care workers are similarly affected. The tiredness, lack of concentration, and decreased motivation can interfere with the quality of care they provide.

A physician who'd been consulting me, Daniel, described having a tidal wave of burnout wash over him. "It's like I'm still gasping," he said, grabbing a meta-phor that was, perhaps, impertinent given the effects of COVID-19. His lan-guage was an extension of life in the ICU.

Daniel was fit, in his 30s, and worked at a local medical center. For weeks, he had been doing 12-hour shifts with only a rare day off. He'd felt unable to cope with the endless admissions, lack of PPE, and the deaths that he was unable to prevent. "They don't train you for this," he said.

As the pandemic progressed, he'd stopped seeing his girlfriend and family, afraid that he might infect them. He'd become lonely and isolated. On his days off, he was so physically and emotionally drained that he could barely get out of bed. But he was barely sleeping anyway.

Even after the supplies and support staff increased, he still had difficulty coping. We'd talk about his diminished confidence, and whether the treatments that he gave even affected his patients' outcomes. "Why do I still keep going there," he asked of no one in particular, "if they just die anyway?" I've noticed that a grim rhetorical question is one sure sign of burnout: no one can answer it, there is no right answer, and it just hangs there – a mocking, surly reminder of one's worst apprehensions.

Worse still, Daniel's girlfriend couldn't deal with the intensity, and broke off the relationship. She called him a hero (and seemed to mean it) but found that his stress was just too much for her to bear. "There's no room to breathe," she complained, in a stunning example of how Daniel's absorption into the ICU had inflected *her* language and her view of how they got on (or didn't).

Daniel thought maybe the break-up was for the best, in part because he felt unable to argue against it. He couldn't see how his life was going to change at least for several months, and then he'd need several more to recover. "I'll be damaged goods by then," he suggested. "I won't have the strength for a real commitment. I'm not even sure I'll know how to have fun."

Yikes. Burnout often segues into depression, and I could see where Daniel was headed. The same lack of confidence that he felt towards his patients had seeped into his personal life – or what was left of it.

I considered starting him on medication to reduce his depressive symptoms. A low dose of an SSRI (serotonergic reuptake inhibitor) like Prozac, Paxil, or Zoloft can help lessen their severity. These medications act quickly, with only mild side-effects. Another possibility was a sleep medication to help him feel more rested during the workday. Finally, I recommended a course of psycho-therapy to help him work through the issues that he had with self-confidence.

It was crucial, I thought, for Daniel to begin to think well of himself again, and to realize that what was happening in the ICU – and was happening in ICUs everywhere – was not his fault. "Without you, these people would have no chance. You're increasing the odds that they'll survive." He could appreciate the math. He could appreciate that his rhetorical question (what "if they just die anyway?") could elicit a more nuanced, even more favorable response that reflected better on his capability and his reason for still showing up.

Ultimately, I thought that if Daniel recovered some of his self-confidence, he'd be less vulnerable to burnout. Burnout often occurs when we don't see why we are working up to and beyond our limitations. When, however, we can tell ourselves that we matter, that our contributions are changing things for the better, we feel energized – inspired to keep on keeping on. Probably, Daniel's girlfriend lacked sufficient self-confidence in her own ability to stick with Daniel and build a meaningful relationship. I didn't say that to Daniel, but I thought that he'd come to see it over time as he made progress on his own.

Self-confidence is a version of hope. It allows us to imagine ourselves beyond the immediate present, and it suggests that we'll get there – somehow.

In medicine there is a Latin saying, "Dum Spiro Spero" ("Where there's breath, there's life"). It applied to Daniel as much as to his patients!

Admittedly, his situation was tough – he was overtaxed at work, stressed out emotionally, and chronically tired. He would have a hard time seeing beyond the present. He'd even told me about a physician at Columbia who'd recently committed suicide in part because she was overwhelmed by the onslaught of coronavirus patients. The *New York Times* had quoted her father as saying "She tried to do her job, and it killed her." She lacked hope.

Daniel was not suicidal, but still. His dreams were haunted by patients unable to breathe, and by his need to choose who should get a ventilator. Such scenes had affected his language, the unconscious patterns of his thought. So, I reminded him of "Dum Spiro Spero" which, I suggested, could serve as a motto, not just for his patients but for him.

That gave him pause. Daniel reflected on how his situation at work was now easing off. "We'll probably have a second wave," he said, but he thought he could use the present to develop some perspective. He was sure that sooner or later, he'd have a chance for a meaningful relationship. He recognized that even though he was still confronted by troubling scenes of dying patients, he was beginning to distance himself from thoughts that he could have done more, and feelings of guilt about making the wrong clinical choices. He even made a joke: "I don't feel incompetent anymore, but neither do I feel like I have to play God." He was sort of in the middle, like most human beings with normal human prospects.

This gave Daniel hope. As it did me. I feel these physicians' challenges at one remove, but they still represent my own anxieties about coping with all my patients' concerns not to fall into despondency. I don't want to offer Pollyanna platitudes, but I do want to give advice that will keep my patients able to function. We have to find the right advice for each patient, and when we get lucky they do too.

TOUGH CHOICES

My patient Bethany runs a small nonprofit that may not survive the pandemic. It's vulnerable because its focus is on refugee camps – where healthcare has largely collapsed – and because it brings together people in physical activities that could easily spread the virus. So, even as the lockdown gradually loosens, who'll want to shout and sweat and exacerbate the risk? And even if people show an interest, governments will likely resist until any risk is remote (when could that be?).

"You know," said Bethany, "I just don't see how our work can continue. I would hate if we got anyone sick."

To Bethany, the pandemic is an existential threat. If her work can't resume, then everything she's built disappears. "I would disappear," she suggests, "this is who I am." She's given her life to her work. There's no daylight between them.

About 15 years ago, she gave up PR to help the thousands of people – especially children – displaced because of genocide, natural disaster, and encroaching drought. Her goal was to promote their sense of continuity by teaching them songs, dances, and games from their traditional past. "They have to remember who they are," she explained. "If they do, they won't become alienated. They'll have a culture to hold onto as they recreate their lives."

But now what? The mentors, educators, and elders that Bethany normally commissioned still won't enter the camps. Her fundraising has fallen off a cliff. Her small staff had to be furloughed and, besides, they couldn't travel anyway without going into quarantine.

It was a total bust.

When Bethany came to me, she felt as though she was not unlike the people that she helped. "We're all displaced. I don't know what to do any more than they do."

When Bethany left her career in PR, she was in her early 40s, and at the top of her game. Her specialty was product rollouts. She knew how to excite retailers and attract consumers. She was sure that she had the connections and skills to be a social entrepreneur. Fundraising would be easy. Who doesn't want to help refugees? (Even the more cynical would rush in to help, if only to stem immigration.) As it turned out, international celebrities offered their support and, over the years, the organization acquired cachet.

When the pandemic hit, she was blindsided. "Maybe if I had been in the crisis management side of PR – like with Tylenol – I'd know what to do. But I just don't see any options," she said. The worst part was that now, in her late 50s, she felt too old to start anything else but too young just to retire. It might be possible to wait things out, but she just couldn't handle protracted uncertainty. "Am I supposed to sit around and wait for five years?"

Yet while Bethany was uncomfortable with inaction, she felt that action was also fraught with uncertainty. "If I undertake a new project in one of the camps, and I make commitments that we can't keep, I'll feel like my ego got the best of my integrity – people would be right for writing me off." Since the virus could hang around for years, she felt that acting unrealistically would be seen as tempting fate, a kind of deluded vanity.

I was moved by Bethany. She wanted to do what was right for her organization, for herself, and for people whom she cared about deeply. But she was paralyzed, in part because she feared that whatever she did to preserve her organization could as likely tarnish it, as well as her own reputation.

As we spoke about what she could do (a far cry from what she *should* do), I realized how much the pandemic had thrown people's identities into disarray. These were solid, high-functioning people who, under most circumstances, would not have consulted a mental health professional. But now they were suffering acute stress. All of a sudden, seemingly out of nowhere, their reason to get up in the morning – their reason to throw themselves into work they believed in and that defined them – had seemingly vanished. They were unprepared, even somewhat flustered because they couldn't just get up and say "Okay, now here's what we'll do."

Their moxie was suddenly gone. They were unaccustomed to being unable to rise to the occasion.

So, the first thing I wanted to talk about with Bethany was that it was okay to feel bewildered. Most people feel bewildered in this pandemic. One of my patients told me that she had nowhere to buy shoes and nowhere to get her shoes fixed. It wasn't earth-shaking, but it was still indicative of the slow encroachment of powerlessness that everyone was feeling. "You have to recognize," I said, "that there may be no right answer. You may have to cobble together an answer from what scant information is out there." Life had become a maze. More specifically, the so-called re-opening was only tentative. You can't necessarily get from A to B without running into major problems.

I suggested that Bethany begin to address her prospects by talking with friends in the nonprofit sector. Did they think she should tough it out for the next year or so, and then make a decision? This wasn't just kicking the can down the road but, rather, it was taking advantage of the collective risk assessment. Nonprofits around the country were facing existential questions, and were beginning to formulate new approaches to salvaging their basic mission. I thought Bethany should join the conversation.

I also thought that by listening to the ideas of others, she would not be liable to turning her head into an echo chamber for her own ideas. Now more than ever, an intellectual community is necessary, even if only to keep us from convincing ourselves that we will never exit the maze intact. "You could look for Facebook groups, or maybe you could start one," I suggested. The point was that Bethany needed a way to retrieve some measure of confidence that there was a way forward. Without any sense of self-confidence, she would be unable even to evaluate advice. I reminded Bethany what it was like when she had lost her father in college. He had been her anchor, and she felt lost and confused without him. Yet she had found her way – worked hard, made good choices, built a life.

While it was a delicate subject, I also suggested that Bethany be prepared for the possibility of giving up her organization. After all the advice came in – and the funds perhaps didn't – that might be the best option. We talked about the existential problem of so entirely identifying one's life with one's work, that one cannot imagine oneself without it. Normally, most people don't face the need to give up on what they've worked for, but now that necessity is common. Small businesses are closing, professionals are being furloughed. "You are still smart, and you know a lot. Perhaps you could start another nonprofit that doesn't put people at risk." I suggested that she look around at what was likely to be a landscape full of need.

I am not sure what Bethany will do. My goal was to help her to raise her spirits – and her confidence – enough so that she didn't fall into inaction and despair. I felt that she would suffer terribly if, in the end, she had to close her organization. But I felt it was critical that she be receptive to new opportunities. "Our world has changed," I told her. "We need to be ready for it."

TO COMMUTE OR NOT?

Since March, I've worked from the attic in my home – Skyping, FaceTiming, Zooming, whatever suits my patients. I call the place my "office," in the sense that a turtle might refer to his shell: it follows him around, so he inhabits it. It's funny how wherever we do business becomes an office. Starbucks is some people's office, which suggests that the whole idea of professional space has diminished in gravitas since the digital revolution. It has certainly diminished during this pandemic, where the office is likely the living room table ten feet from the kids making videos on TikTok.

I spend a lot of time in my makeshift office, which is up three flights of stairs. It's smaller than my space in Manhattan, and a little claustrophobic. But interior dimensions are not the real issue – especially when your focus is confined to a screen that is orders of magnitude smaller than your office! It has emerged, after about a month or so, that the problem is the truncated commute between my personal and professional space. From Great Neck to Manhattan is 22.4 miles, 39 minutes on the Long Island Rail Road. I climb the stairs in 20 seconds.

Of course, nobody likes commuting *qua* commuting, but the transition that it provides has a certain appeal. You arrive at Grand Central, with all the other people making a transition, and voila, there is a collective sense that you're all professionals ready for work. This notion of collective cognition is no joke – you see it in birds and fish, for example, that suddenly veer off in sharply defined new directions. We don't know how they communicate, but they do. Yet when I'm at home, in my attic, I'm alone. I communicate (sort of) with myself. I assume the role of psychiatrist but it feels like a role – like I'm playing one until I convince myself that Yes! This is Me! I feel like a method actor applying Stanislavsky.

It's much easier when a bunch of stockbrokers, lawyers, and Madison Avenue types reinforce each other's commitment to the day.

So, I go upstairs maybe an hour before my first appointment so that I can ease into the role. By the time we're talking (through whatever medium), I'm fully Dr. Friedberg. But still, I'm not quite used to this makeshift transition period, a consequence of my makeshift office, and so I'm thinking of returning to work in Manhattan.

Several of my patients are starting to commute again, though we've talked about why. Do they also miss the transition? One of them said, "You know how at the end of the day you want to wind down? Well, on the train to work I wind up." He thinks about the stress that he's in for, and accommodates to it in advance. "It's like every day is a suicide mission, so I may as well be ready." This isn't exactly my rationale, but I get the point.

Yet I don't get it entirely, since these same people report that they've found a certain freedom in working from home: more family time, more leisure, more time to exercise (you can lift a lot of weights in the 90 minutes that you save every day). Why give this up, provided that you have the choice? Many of my patients do.

On balance, I think it's because for all the freedom that working from home confers (on the one hand), and all the psychic value of making perceptible transitions (on the other), we like to disappear for a while. Commuting *lets* us disappear. We are on our own. In charge of ourselves. It's primitive, but it's a thrill. Another of my patients said "When I get off the train in the morning, nobody who knows me sees me and I feel like I'm in the Foreign Legion." Yearning to get back to that is like yearning to go back to one's fantasy past. I get that.

Nevertheless, I admit that while (perversely) I miss the Long Island Rail Road, I like descending from the attic to spend time with my kids. I am more involved with their school work, and we have dinner every night. A few days ago, we got haircuts on the lawn. The spontaneity is great.

But there is just this feeling of La La Land that I can't shake. I think I need to get back to Manhattan. Maybe I feel a little guilty.

Patients benefit from their sessions with me. Several ask when they can "see" me again, which is odd because we stare at each other on a screen for the hour. But for them, sight is a shorthand term for an encompassing sensory experience – the physical sensation of sharing space with someone else. Psychiatry has always emphasized physicality, even though psychiatrists are among the few physicians who don't normally touch their patients. In this regard, Freud once observed that we leak what we feel through our pores. Less of that primary physicality emerges onscreen. We need intimate modes of connection to communicate.

If anything, we need this more after a protracted lockdown.

I go into my Manhattan office weekly now, mostly for paperwork or picking up mail. I drive alone in my car. Recently, I had an initial consultation with a young man in college who, like most students, was now studying at home. He's had trouble adapting to online courses, and was in danger of failing. As it turned out, he had a history of inattentiveness, difficulty with focus, concentration, and motivation. These symptoms of Attention Deficit Disorder had gone undiagnosed. So, I felt confident that with a low dose of a psycho-stimulant, his condition would improve.

The family appreciated my seeing him in person since he also has difficulty connecting with others and was emotionally distant from his father. As we talked, I wondered whether his social anxiety might benefit from a course of Cognitive Behavioral Therapy, or whether insight-oriented psychotherapy could help with underlying Oedipal issues. Such work would take time, and I wasn't sure how it would work if it were mediated through a screen. Could we continue talking in person? Perhaps, assuming that he was prepared to make the commitment. In the meantime, we kept a safe social distance and both of us had tested negative for COVID-19. I wore a mask, just to be on the safe side.

But I still have not decided whether to go back to my office full-time.

Yesterday, I ran into a physician who lives down the block. From across the street, we made eye contact and paused. I asked how he and his family were doing. His wife is a psychiatrist and works at one of the local hospitals. Even from across the street, I could see tears in his eyes as he told me his wife was now off the ventilator and recovering from COVID-19. I was shocked since she is healthy and under 60. Apparently, she had gotten it from a patient she was treating in the outpatient clinic. Concerned, I stepped closer. I said I was sorry that they had been through such a difficult time and relieved she was now recovering. I asked him to let me know if I could help. He thanked me and we walked off.

The danger is still real.

HIERONYMUS BOSCH

"I've come to a decision," said my patient Bernadine as we Skyped this past week. "I'm going to write a biography of Hieronymus Bosch."

I am accustomed to patients declaring ostensible intentions. They hope that if I'm impressed, they can muster the will to follow through.

Of course, I oblige if I can – especially now, when harmless distractions are a good idea. But in this case, I was stumped. If I remembered Art History from college, Bosch died over 500 years ago in the Netherlands. "How can you do any research? Nobody can travel anywhere," I said. "Who needs research," she replied (no doubt amused at my grave literality). "I'm going to make it all up."

Oh.

Sometimes, psychiatrists miss the obvious and contrive the absurd. To be literal with Bernardine (a biography! footnotes! traveling to the archives!) was to be *quite* absurd. How could I not have realized that Bernardine, a very smart young woman, was embarking on a mental adventure? Writing a biography was her way to compensate for what seemed like intractable loneliness. She would create a companion. The more of a stretch, the better.

As we talked, the picture (so to speak) became clear. As people were tentatively stepping out after weeks indoors, Bernadine felt her loneliness even more keenly. "The *Times* has all these spreads of people sitting around, having fun. I'm envious." If she could immerse herself in another human being . . . well, at least in her mind, she could (as she claimed) "get to know him."

I saw the point. Until I didn't. I don't normally encourage patients' fantasies. In an effort to raise that issue, however gently, I asked whether her reasoning was kind of circular, since creating a "Bosch" from her own imagination might still just be sort of a trick on herself. "Wouldn't he just be a version of you," I asked. Again, I was obtuse to the workings of the creative mind. "Of course not. Novelists create human beings, and they feel like they live with them." Okay, I accepted that. But then why not just write a novel? Why a pseudo-biography?

Here is where I learned something about how COVID-19 is playing out. Bernardine explained that since no one knew anything about the future – even whether they'd be alive, or whether our culture would be recognizable – there was a kind of new liberation. "We're making things up as we go along. If I want to write a biography without facts, I can will into being anyone I want." This was a startling, surreal approach to reality. COVID-19 was a license, as it were, to manipulate reality; maybe just to ignore it; you could redefine so-called factual genres, and fill them with people who had never existed. Conventions didn't matter. It was like nothing mattered. The projections of your mind were commensurate with verifiable fact.

I have been counseling patients to be resilient, and willing to adapt as the world morphs around them. Bernardine's take on my advice was new – a radical divergence – and I found it unsettling. It was a form of letting go, I thought, and of not doing the hard work that was necessary to come out ahead of the

Figure II.5 Death and the Miser, Hieronymus Bosch

curve. "How can you just let yourself live in a dream world – I mean, just give up?" I asked. But Bernardine was serious. She saw this "biography" as in sync with the world of COVID-19. "Go back and look at Bosch," she ordered. "He knew about humanity. He's diagnosed us." Since Bosch left no writings like, say, Michelangelo, no one knows what he thought. But that's why he was perfect for Bernardine. She was on a mission to create "Bosch," whose life signified what she believed he was saying. A very odd mouthpiece, to be sure, but I could see that this fantasy life (hers and his) ultimately linked up to a tangible objective.

We talked about some of the famous pictures: "The Garden of Earthly Delights," "The Hay Wain," "Death and the Miser," "The Last Judgment." To Bernardine, they conveyed a view of human nature as profoundly irrational and deeply unkind. Undeniably, there were scenes of monstrous apocalypse, chaos, nightmare. There was a mixture of fantasy and reality – in effect, they were surreal. In "The Hay Wain," for example, humanity is goaded by greed, led on by devils to destruction. "Can you imagine the life he must have led to think this stuff up? That's what's going in my biography."

To Bernardine, Bosch had crossed over into a world like ours which, she suggested, had given him license to create what he wanted without reference to natural forms. Bosch was already one of us – applying his extraordinary powers to fantasize, to break free of history and the conventions of perception. He had to engage with the surreal if he was to render how irrational, greedy, and unkind we had become. "If he landed back in New York, or maybe Washington, you'd get 'The Hay Wain' of maybe 'Death and the Miser' all over again."

I thought about my conversation with Bernardine after the session. Here was someone going up against my typical, straightforward advice, and still coming out with a plan to achieve a kind of resilience. She thought to write a book that, however slyly, would speak to her fellow humans about the world in which COVID-19 was taking a horrific toll. There was irrationality (look at how we delayed responding to the virus, look at how we politicized the wearing of masks); there was immense unkindness in how resources to fight the disease were allocated. A major factor in maintaining resilience is to have a purpose. Bernardine had found one.

Certainly, she affected me. I find myself haunted by Bosch. There was a time when I thought he was a religious fanatic. But as we try to dig ourselves out of COVID-19, I am returning to visionary artists like Blake, Bosch, and even Dalí, who saw the world from a personal perspective that did not always jibe with everyone else's. They found truths around corners. For Bosch especially, the world was deluding itself. In "The Hay Wain," for example, nobody knows that they're about to topple into catastrophe. The picture seems to be shouting from five centuries in the rear, telling us about ourselves.

So, I am inclined to give Bernardine a pass. I wonder whether she will ever try to publish her "biography," although she seems convinced that she should. But it hardly matters. She is creating a way to cope. As the pandemic winds through the culture, more people may feel liberated – to use her term – to adopt unconventional means to build resilience. They may feel intense indignation at how we allowed COVID-19 to wreak havoc. Their anger may take new forms.

In this sense, Bernardine may be a bellwether. It's either exciting or scary. Given the pace of change, we'll know pretty fast.

FATHER'S DAY

I feel like a vicarious mourner. In between sessions, patients send me grim emails about loved ones who have died. This past weekend, one patient's father died in a nursing home. His father was with a nurse at the time, with my patient on the phone. The nurse held his father's hand so that he could whisper something unintelligible – and then he was gone. Because of COVID-19, my patient was not allowed to see his father for the past three months.

So, what do you say? "I'm sorry, I understand" is often not helpful in situations of extreme grief. People assume that you cannot understand how they feel, especially when a lifetime's experience comes roaring back to remind them of why they feel the way they do. I usually just say "I'm sorry for your loss," and listen.

But still. I cannot help thinking how I would feel if I lost my father. This Father's Day, I had to think about that inevitability. But I was grateful that I didn't directly have to confront it.

So far, neither of my patents have become infected with COVID-19. My father is almost 90 and is slowing down. My mother had a bout with cancer. Both are especially vulnerable. But when you look at your parents, you tend to see them through your own life – what would I be but for them? What do I owe them? How can I show it?

My father is also a psychiatrist, and has been a tremendous influence on my life. We wrote a book together about life lessons. Sometimes, when I am talking with a patient, I wonder "Now what would my father say?" My brother and sister, in their own ways, feel the same way.

So, this Father's Day, we wanted to be there for my parents. They were staying with my brother on Long Island, and it was their first real outing. They hadn't left their home in three months (fortunately, they have help). But in beginning to venture out, they had to be careful. We found a reliable driver; my parents sat in the back with the windows open; everyone wore masks.

At my brother's, we sat around outside. We kept our masks on. In venturing out, I sometimes let my mask slip down beneath my chin . . . but not with my parents. We compromised on the social distancing (we were maybe three feet apart), but there were no hugs. I thought about my patient who had been miles from his father when he died, and I was grateful that we were together. The hugs could wait (maybe Chanukah?).

When we finally left, I told my wife about how grateful I was that my father was still alive and that I could see him. "Yes, but to whom?" she asked. But in fact, we don't have to be grateful *to* someone. Gratefulness can be impersonal. We can just be grateful *for* something: we can stop to realize how empty we would feel if something or someone weren't there. We can picture our life as if now we were mourning that emptiness.

In other words, gratefulness is the state of appreciating our own good fortune, made possible by the right concatenation of circumstances. I love my father and he is still here. In a way, that's just luck.

Of course, we can be grateful *to* our parents for being who they are, which is why in large measure we are who we are. I was in the right place at the right time – I am grateful to them but also, in some universal way, to the randomness of things that sorts people into their lives. Gratefulness is a complex emotion. We tend to address our gratefulness to people ("I am grateful to [insert a name]"), but I think we need to situate it in all the swirling circumstances that make up our fate.

Without being religious, gratefulness can evoke quasi-religious feelings.

Studies have shown that being grateful for the positive aspects of a challenging situation can help one to cope. The Harvard University Health Service, in its *Managing Fears and Anxiety around the Coronavirus*, suggested: "Practice a mindset of gratitude. Spend time each day thinking about three things you are grateful for. Picture holding these things in your open hands." Notice how Harvard does not suggest being grateful *to* anyone (although that's not ruled out). Rather, the idea is to find "things" – i.e., circumstances – whose existence helps to quell fear and anxiety. In my own case, I consider these circumstances: (i) knowing that I don't have to endure my parents' death (at least for now), and (ii) knowing how lucky I am that I had these parents.

During this time of COVID-19, and especially on Father's Day, I'm grateful for a situation that's allowed me to spend more time with my own children. Because I am working from home, I can steal a few minutes to help my kids with schoolwork or to work on a puzzle. We take walks or ride our bikes. It's a thrill. My own father had limited time for such spontaneity, but I do! In fact, a recent article in the *New York Times* bore the headline "The Pandemic has Reshaped American Fatherhood," although it asked "Can it last?" (Gelin, 2020). Clearly, there has been at least a provisional change, as fathers rediscover their families. The article was uncertain whether our society could ultimately accommodate these changes, but it observed that even short stints of time at home can have lasting consequences.

So perhaps Father's Day is on its way to becoming a day to reflect on one's own status as a father, as much as on how lucky it is to still have a father – let alone, such a great one. I am grateful that, so far, I don't feel the guilt that most parents do as they think about what they could have done, and didn't. I think that going forward, however, I will try to put myself in my kids' shoes, and ask (ventriloquizing their pre-adolescent voices) about what matters to them. What do they expect of me? What do they really need?

They know only in part. The real answer has to come from me, refracted through their still-developing brains and personalities. My job is to get to know them better, so that I can figure out what they need. Of course, for this I will have to talk with them. I will have to treat them as individuals. Above all, I will have to resist projecting myself onto them ("I'm a doctor, so you should be too"). I will have to avoid what comes easily. I will have to remember that I will never be as modern as my kids or see the world entirely as they see it.

At some point, however, I will just have to accept their ideas about themselves which, in the end, will be what they expect of me and what they need.

WHO NEEDS ANXIETY?

It's only the third week of June, but my patient Lara is already concerned that her university may require her to teach in person in the fall. Lara just completed a semester's teaching online and, while she disliked the technology, she acknowledged its virtues. "At least no flying droplets can get you in cyberspace," she sighed. Lara is obsessed with her health. She is finicky in general (nothing quite pleases her when she goes out to eat). She finds this period trying, and can't stop worrying. When she solves one problem – like getting through the semester on an awkward techy platform – she finds another, even if it is way in the future and still largely conjectural.

The problem with the pandemic is that it's one long field-day for worrywarts. While they're isolated at home, they imagine the worst; when it's time to re-enter the world, they perceive the worst out to infinity. There is no discontinuity in the trajectory of their concern. Once embarked on a rationale for worry, they're unstoppable. It can be debilitating.

I asked Lara "Has the university made any plans yet about how to reopen?" No, she said, but it was enough that it was "floating options." One of those "options" might endanger her. There might be a Hybrid Curriculum, where some courses could be moved online while others – where students actually needed to talk – would be taught in real time around a table. "I'm sure," she said, "that French would be one of the latter. I just can't imagine Zooming with someone who thinks he understands Proust."

So, here's the issue: even though nothing is definite, and everything could change overnight (we might get a second wave), how can I convince Lara that it's pointless to assume an outcome that could threaten her life or her livelihood? How, in other words, can I persuade her that there is a difference between prudence – i.e., ensuring that we're prepared for likely adversity – and constant anxiety that never allows for anything but the worst?

"No sense spinning your wheels at this point," I suggested. "It's too far out, and you don't know what will happen." But Lara calculates the way Napoleon might have. "I don't think in terms of what they may want to do. I think in terms of what they could do." They could do anything. Nothing is foreclosed. The potential damage is endless.

I decided on another approach which, I hoped, would make Lara conscious of what seemed to me a self-fulfilling anxiety. At the beginning of the pandemic, as universities sent everyone home, they tried to keep galloping dystopian visions from torturing the chronically well-read. In *Managing Fears and*

Anxiety around the Coronavirus, Harvard University Health Service warned against runaway anxiety. It sought to get into the heads of people exhibiting it, and suggest a way to stop:

> Anxiety is an emotion that tends to seek out confirmation. While at times this can be validating, it can also intensify the emotion, leaving you feeling helpless and overwhelmed. Acknowledge your emotion with understanding, and then turn your mind to other things:
> *"It's understandable I am concerned about the current situation, AND I understand that worry is not an effective way to respond."*

In other words, worry can lead to more worry, and you need to break the cycle. You do so by telling yourself to stop. You enforce a renovated regime of rationality; you short-circuit your propensity to perpetuate worry when you see that there's no basis for worry except your pre-existing worry.

I suggested that Lara come up with a sort of internal questionnaire that she could administer to herself every day, and that would test the rational basis for her continuing to worry. For example: what objectively verifiable reasons justify my worrying today? How much time is this worry worth, if I am just going to linger on the same reasons for worry? Since I tend to worry about what I don't know, how can I find out some answers (and until that time, I promise to stop worrying)? The point, I said, was to confront her own pernicious mental processes – and reverse them. Thus, if she could allow herself to proliferate anxiety, she could allow an equal and opposite rational discourse to issue in common sense.

I also suggested that Lara felt anxious because she was being so passive. If returning to in-person teaching seemed like a scary prospect, then why hadn't she spoken up? Lara was a tenured professor. She could write a letter to the university administration, telling them that if enough people were concerned about in-person teaching, then it would likely be ineffective. Why shouldn't the university test the waters before deciding which classes should be taught in person? Maybe they could let each professor decide. "You know," I said, "challenging times are a license to speak when normally you wouldn't. The people in charge want to hear from you." If nothing else, they want reassurance that their actions are appropriate. Thus, what may come out of this pandemic is that stakeholders are newly welcomed to the table, and are more inclined to speak up.

The great antidotes to fear – rationality and action – should make us confident to undertake *rational action* to ward off potential trouble down the road. We don't know for sure what will happen, but we can act now to prevent anxiety from stifling our access to a favorable likely outcome.

So, I advised Lara to literally rehearse what she'd say to the administration – assuming they asked to consult her – and experience herself as her own best advocate. She could get a sense of herself as competent, even before she acted. Mastery is a potent rejoinder to fear, even if no one knows yet how good we are. The point is that *we* know. We can *anticipate* rational action, plan for it in many dimensions – what we would say, to whom, and whom we would recruit as support. After a while, anxiety will seem boring.

Finally, I suggested that Lara take up something that comes naturally to her, that's reinforcing, that can take up the mental energy that she devotes to worrying. After all, she has the whole summer! We talked about what that might be. French cooking? A blog about French literature in translation? The *nouvelle vague* in film? If she could engage with other people, remotely or even at a discrete distance, that would be terrific.

She couldn't resist. She committed to starting a Facebook group for lovers of vintage French fashion. Not the runway stuff that is still trying to grab fashionistas' attention, but the hip stuff that you ferret out by knowing where to look.

Voila!

I suggested that we keep talking, since we both acknowledged that it would be easy to backslide in the daily onslaught of bad news. I don't believe in ignoring news as a way of controlling anxiety. Rather, I think we should learn to keep it in perspective, in part by strengthening our defenses against it. "Our" refers to ourselves and to the community that, ideally, we develop to help us.

Of course, after a while we can readmit our fears, since some fears are legitimate. The point is to know when they are.

Part III: The new normal

As the pandemic lumbers on, new patterns of life emerge – so unsettled that "pattern" seems like the wrong term, too optimistic, too discernible. In some cases, we hardly recognize ourselves. Thus, Part III is about getting used to change – new ways of dating; elder care; shopping; pursuing a career.

While some of these altered activities are stressful enough, our getting used to them – that is, making the transition – can call into question our judgment, even pitch us into guilt. We may worry, for example, that our resistance (or simple ineptitude) makes it harder for others to get on with their lives. On the other hand, we may resent those who accommodate more easily. We may *really* resent those with the wherewithal to ignore what's troubling everyone else (as they depart the City for second homes, do business remotely, and school their kids in protected "pods"). In Part III, I counsel people struggling with change, and help them develop skills to deal with alterations that (deep down) they do not want to accept.

We hear the term, New Normal. But I almost rejected it as the title of this Part because, in most people's minds, it suggests a phalanx of settled (usually disheartening) conditions that we have to accept and adjust to. In my experience, this is a misperception. As it is depicted here, the New Normal is shifting terrain, hard to accept or adjust to because we can barely make out what it is. The contours are blurry, and may change from one day to the next. People's frustration comes from not knowing where to start, and having no clear end-point in sight. We wonder what may be possible as the world's parameters shift, change their shapes, and startle us with a fluidity that suggests a kaleidoscope.

Forget assumptions.

The New Normal is continuous uncertainty . . . except that now we're getting used to *that*, and trying to discern provisional fixes. Our horizons have become shorter. Why make plans when you'll just have to alter them tomorrow?

Yet we still have to live, and make do with resources and choices that we have. The one bad option is to stand still, awaiting clarity (which could be a long time coming). So, we use our judgment, and realize that we're cannier than we've ever known ourselves to be. We contrive what we need *right now* to live with reasonable degrees of dignity, self-respect, and hope. We learn how not to cut off options, even as we make provisional choices.

Some essays in Part III talk about money since, even if we haven't physically handled it in months, our finances still influence what we can do and expect. How we use money in this pandemic determines how we think of – or want to think of – ourselves. Thus, one patient decides that Retail Therapy is no longer proper as a way to spend an ordinary day. A kind of empathic austerity feels somehow more appropriate. But some of my patients think it's perfectly fine to leave the City, physically and emotionally, in order to avoid the mere thought of other people's struggle (let alone risk any part of it themselves). All these people think they are caring for themselves, and I wonder: how far can I (or anyone) go in second-guessing them? I try not to be judgmental; it's not my job; but sometimes I just can't help it.

Judging has consequences. Whenever we think about someone's choices, let alone give them advice, we have to confront our own choices. So sometimes, we just suspend judgment on everyone, if only to avoid passing judgment on ourselves. Judgment seems so burdensome now, when our real business is just deciding how to get on with things.

Yet amidst so much uncertainty, things go on whether we do or don't encourage them. Thus, one essay in Part III involves having a baby during the pandemic: Are hospitals safe? How can family pitch in when nobody can travel? Is the risk of depression increased? The choices are unnerving, but the predicament itself is somehow reassuring. Having a baby when you want one is great! It tells the pandemic: You're Not Winning. Of course, family finances become a factor, but the somehow-factor (as in somehow, life goes on) encourages new parents to find new ways to cope.

Likewise, with having sex in the first place. Plenty of people still want to couple up. Desperately in some cases, since coupledom has become a safe haven when so much else seems scary (it's just getting past the scary parts of incipient coupledom that poses a challenge). One essay tackles the issue of the new Safe Sex. When it was first published in *Psychology Today*, the Editor cited it as an essential read. Apparently, uncertainty or no, sex marches on – the question is what's left of it in the New Normal (enough, probably, provided one attends to the flashing yellow lights).

So, this Part is more about the New than the Normal. Very little feels normal, and we're reluctant to acknowledge the normality of anything because, in many instances, we wish it were something else. But it's not. These essays are about learning to live with what we have and, ideally, make the most of it. I thought it would be interesting to start with an essay discussing an earlier transition to a New Normal when, in the 19th century, women lost their role as the family pharmacist and go-to nurturer of good health. The professional physician displaced them.

Part of our own new normality consists in feeling that – like those 19th century women – we are no longer in charge of our health or that of our family. Not long ago, we'd go to the doctor, we'd likely get fixed. But now we are dependent. Waiting. Actually, we're waiting for some vaccine that has yet to emerge. Our New Normal feels like one long meantime.

GENDER

During the early 1720s, Britain was terrified that the Plague, raging across the Channel in Marseilles, would break out at home. Daniel Defoe's brilliant recreation of the Great Plague of 1665, *A Journal of the Plague Year* (1722), was timed to coincide with Britain's fear – a spot-on commercial move that was also admonitory, reflecting the popular angst that prevailed until the threat subsided. Defoe was a master of timing, a journalist as well as novelist who understood what stories people craved. During our own pandemic, sales of *A Journal* have shot up over 700 percent, with the Penguin edition selling out on Amazon.

But while we look to *A Journal* for its uncanny resonance with COVID-19 – the tardiness of government's initial response, the people sequestered at home, masses of bodies piled up unburied – we may be unaware of how other, less vivid, but perhaps no less timely, texts responded to the plague. I am thinking of 18th century cookbooks. Yes, cookbooks, aimed at women who sought to avoid quack remedies, but provide their families with what seemed like reasonable protection available from traditional herbal medicine. In the 18th century, many

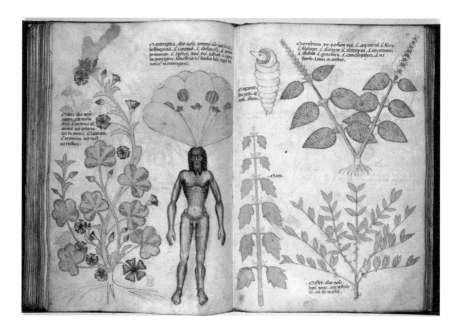

Figure III.1 Miniature with man and mandrake plant

cookbooks (still not devoted entirely to food preparation) recognized women's role in the still room, and bootstrapped that role into teaching them how to make home remedies for everything from bug repellants and cures for mad dog-bite, to medications for hair loss and – yes – resisting the plague.

Of course, when we read these remedies, which I will discuss in a moment, we have to get into the spirit of them, and consider them in the way that an 18th century homemaker would have. In context with her role as preserver of her family's health, these recipes were a valuable addition to her armamentarium. They made her feel competent, resourceful, prepared. Before the professionalization of medicine, when anyone could be a doctor, it frequently fell to women to respond when a member of her family fell ill. Accordingly, women kept personal manuscripts filled with recipes for food and "physick." When printed cookbooks began to compete with and overtake these private compilations, they earned women's trust by emulating the format of these compilations – there were recipes for food, but also for medicines, often accompanied by assurances that these offerings were well-sourced.

Eighteenth century cookbooks recognized that women maintained the kitchen garden, which grew a variety of edibles but also an astonishing array of herbs less used for cooking than healing. Cookbooks like Martha Bradley's *The British Housewife: Or, the Cook, Housekeeper's, and Gardiner's Companion* (1756), viewed the household as an integrated amalgam of kitchen, kitchen garden, still room, dairy, and poultry yard, with the "housewife" ensuring that the elements functioned well together. It was assumed that women would grow herbs that would then be distilled into useful remedies.

It's hard to imagine feeling so potent today. As individuals, we are at once more sophisticated in our understanding of medicine, but also more aware of our helplessness. We *know* that until science develops a treatment for COVID-19 and, ultimately, a vaccine, we cannot help ourselves much beyond wearing a mask and staying apart from each other. But in the 18th century, it was still possible to believe in home-made remedies. It is clear from their inclusion in mass-market texts that many people did. As a consequence, it is clear that while we consider ourselves vastly more advanced regarding the role of women, their early role as healers conferred considerable power at a time when few other sources offered any better remedies against disease.

The first place I turned for advice on herbal remedies for the Plague was Hannah Glasse's *The Art of Cookery Made Plain and Easy* (1745), an 18th century blockbuster that was reprinted dozens of times into the following century. As assurance that her "Receipt against the Plague" will work, Glasse refers to its provenance in the Great Plague:

> They write, that our Malefactors (who had robbed the infested Houses, and murdered the People during the Course of the Plague) owned, when they came to the Gallows, that they had preserved themselves from the

Contagion, by using the above Medicine only; and that they went the whole time from House to House, without any fear of the distemper.

(p. 166)

Glasse's reader might believe this recommendation just because the remedy's initial beneficiaries were so unsavory – a saint might survive because of his saintliness, but Malefactors probably needed some real knowledge. Here is the recipe that Glasse says they followed:

Take of Rue, Sage, Mint, Rosemary, Wormwood and Lavender, a Handful of each, infuse them together in a Gallon of White Wine-Vinegar, put the whole into a Stone-pot closely covered up, upon warm Wood Ashes for four Days: After which draw off (or strain through fine Flannel) the Liquid, and put it into Bottles well corked; and into every Quart Bottle, put a Quarter of an Ounce of Camphire. With this Preparation, wash your Mouth, and rub your Loins and your Temples every Day; snuff a little up your Nostrils when you go into the Air, and carry about you a bit of Spunge dipped in the same, in order to smell to upon all Occasions, especially when you are near any Place or Person that is infected.

(p. 166)

In an era that had seen microorganisms under a microscope but had no idea that they caused disease, this sort of recipe – backed up by a long tradition of herbal remedies and the extraordinary provenance ascribed to it here – could have made sense. Accordingly, it provides evidence of a domestic role for women that transcends the cramped domesticity apparent in 19th century novels. As medicine became professionalized and male, women's healing role receded. We see the kind of highly trained, male doctors such as Tertius Lydgate in George Eliot's *Middlemarch* (1871–1872, set in 1829–1832).

There are similar recipes to Glasse's – or, rather, recipes in the same spirit – all over 18th century cookbooks. *The British Housewife* has one for Plague Water that uses many of the same ingredients as Glasse's, but adds Angelica Root, Virginian Snakeroot, "Melasses Spirit," and Sugar (sugar was itself thought of as medicinal – until it wasn't). This, however, was only the simple version. A more complex version later on was composed of almost three dozen herbs, seeds, and flowers, and could also be used as general protection "when a Person is going into a Room where any Person is ill of a contagious Disorder, or otherwise into a bad Air" (p. 273). What woman would not want to have this on hand?

The *Complete Family-Piece* (1736), composed by a committee, as well as Eliza Smith's *The Compleat Housewife; or, Accomplished Gentlewoman's Companion* (1728), also had recipes to ward off Plague. Like other fiercely marketed texts in the genre, they responded to a concern that plague could come again.

Today, we know this concern is true, though we would shrink from concocting home remedies, even assuming that we had a garden with dozens of herbs. The difference between now and then is science and its professionaliza-tion. But what we learn from these old cookbooks is that, not too long ago, the household was the locus of defense against disease. We have lost that ethos to a considerable degree and, with it, the healing role of women.

As a psychotherapist, I see women who feel guilty about not doing enough to keep their families safe during this pandemic. I counsel them that there is still much that we can do to help others, not least by maintaining the family's spirit during isolation. This is less tangible than the help offered by 18th century women, but it is no less real and certainly more efficacious in the long run.

DO WE STILL WANT TO BUY STUFF?

The plywood has come down off the windows of Madison Avenue shops. It went up after night-time looting marred the Black Lives Matter protests. Before the looting, you could walk down the Avenue and see no more indication of anything amiss than the signs wishing us good health. But that all changed with the plywood. The Avenue seemed defeated, somehow, or perhaps in retreat from its haughty self-satisfaction. The boarded-up windows sent an updated message: we're not sure how to present ourselves once we reopen (if we do).

Now that the shops are slowly reopening, they'll have to decide how to renovate their personae. Act as if nothing happened? Act as if the world has changed? The answer could be a moving target, based on how the returning foot traffic ultimately responds.

That traffic does not represent that of most American retailers, or even most stores in New York City. Madison, which runs parallel between 5th and Park Avenues, is the shopping corridor of the City's One Percent. Shoes can cost $1200 (each). A watch is the price of a decent new car. So how these

Figure III.2 Coin purse

shops act reflects on how high-end retail envisions its future. (Ironically, since most of Manhattan's Gold Coast has vacated to homes in the Hamptons, the Adirondacks, or Spain, nobody's around to notice.)

Except my patient Grace. She stayed and, at first, was delighted to see the new activity. It was a hopeful sign after so much shuttered silence. "The only place that stayed open throughout was the caviar store," she laughed. "Well, caviar is food, so I guess it's a 'necessity'."

But now, after thinking about the imminent reopening, Grace is puzzled by her reaction: she doesn't want to buy anything. "I thought I'd be one of those people who drove all that pent-up demand," she said, "but I think the economists misjudged – or at least they misjudged me." So, the issue was whether Grace's loss of interest was anything to worry about (depression, maybe?), and whether anyone *should* regret their losing an interest in buying fancy stuff. (It's not like losing your sense of smell or taste.)

This pandemic has pushed people to re-evaluate their priorities. For some, thinking about their priorities was never a priority in the first place. They're surprised, therefore, when now suddenly they've turned on themselves, questioning attitudes that had seemed ordinary, normal, certainly okay. If you're not conscious of your priorities, you have trouble balancing the demands of society on your time and resources.

Grace now discovered that she had that problem. "I'm not sure what I'm supposed to be doing now," she said "I feel kind of weird."

Thinking about her role in society never seemed terribly important to Grace. She didn't think she *had* much of a role. She and her family lived in a building on Park Avenue, not far from my office. She made sure that the van picked up her kids in the morning, when they went off to day-school, and made sure to be home in the late afternoon when it delivered them. In between, she arranged dinner with the maid, volunteered a few hours a week to speak English with immigrant women, and otherwise shopped and had lunch with her friends. What's wrong with that?

Well, for starters, it no longer worked. As we spoke, I realized that Grace was not depressed so much as bewildered. It was like she had landed in a new moral environment which had invaded (and disrupted) the placid certainties of her mental space. Like everyone else, she had been pummeled by news of how some socio-economic strata had been more affected by the virus than others (namely, hers). She had seen how many Essential Workers had to use public transportation, exposing themselves to getting sick; she took Lyft if she had to travel. Moreover, she was able to turn to her friends, not just for company but for support as she tried to keep her kids occupied and safe. "I'm beginning to realize that I'm privileged to be comfortable," she said. "I'm beginning to realize how hard it is for so many people."

It emerged that Grace's loss of interest in the stuff newly on display was a result of her consciously adopting new priorities. There has been a vast amount of writing with regard to how, during the pandemic, we are turning inward – becoming more introspective – and turning more towards friends and family. As a consequence of isolation and deprivation, we are figuring out what we actually *need* to make us feel happy. Concomitantly, I think, we ae coming to see that some aspects of our previous existence represent a type of moral incoherence. Acquisitiveness, as in the case of Grace, represents a failure to see the world in its entirety, and the state of all the people in it. "It didn't feel like I was just focused on me," she said. "But I was."

All that stuff in the windows reminded Grace that while she could buy it, other people couldn't come close.

The paradox of this pandemic is that even while, in one sense, our world has narrowed to a sliver of its vibrant, roaring former self, in another sense it has vastly expanded. We have seen – or, rather, been made to see and consider – the lives of people whom we never thought we would ever encounter. Their realities have been riveting.

Grace did not say, as I had expected her to, that she now felt guilty buying a designer dress or a new, gorgeous handbag. She just felt that she didn't need them. "I have enough," she said. "I'll wait until I need something."

The pandemic has taught us that resources are finite and disproportionately accessible. It's hard to consume as if everything were infinitely available to everyone.

Grace had never put her head in the sand, deliberately evading the realities of privilege. It's just that she had never really had to think about such realities. She spoke to the immigrant women, of course, but mostly about their children, their extended families, their eagerness to find jobs and become citizens. It wasn't until Grace encountered images of body bags in cold storage – right here in New York – and hospitals closing their doors for lack of space in Pakistan, India, and Venezuela, that she began putting things together. "There's just not enough to go around," she said.

It may be that as we venture out after COVID-19's initial onslaught, Grace's example will stand in for many other people's reaction to this experience. We may never, at least not for a long time, return to spending the way we used to. More importantly, we may demand of ourselves a heightened consciousness regarding the materialism that has been ingrained in us since . . . well, forever. We may read different books, for example, about how to conserve what we have. All of this is totally fine.

In fact, such a paradigm shift could be expected during the challenging times that we are experiencing. In *The Structure of Scientific Revolutions* (1962), Thomas Kuhn suggested that "normal" models for approaching a question can sometimes change radically, all at once, when the need for a new direction suddenly becomes apparent. It is likely that as we step out into a world still reeling from the pandemic, we will see the need for a new direction.

THE BROOKLYN BRIDGE

Concepts in engineering do not ordinarily inform psychotherapy (do I hear muffled laughter?). But if you stop to think about it, the analogies are startling. Both fields are concerned with managing stress. Cables that support the

Brooklyn Bridge, for example, were designed to bear the weight of 35,400,000 pounds. That's a lot of cars, runners, and cyclists. New York City spends millions every year to keep the cables from rusting. That is, it tries to keep the bridge from sagging under all that traffic. Little wonder. The idea that stress can result in deformation is basic to engineering. Likewise, it is basic to psychotherapy where, as a result of Post-Traumatic Stress Disorder (PTSD), people walk around literally bent out of shape.

I've thought about applying basic engineering concepts to my patients under stress from COVID-19. In particular, I like the idea of "elasticity" vs. "plasticity," which every first-year engineering student learns. The NDT Resource Center describes the distinction as follows:

> When a sufficient load is applied to a metal or other structural material, it will cause the material to change shape. The change in shape is called deformation. A temporary shape change that is self-reversing after the force

Figure III.3 Brooklyn Bridge

is removed, so that the object returns to its original shape, is called elastic deformation. In other words, elastic deformation is a change in shape of a material at low stress that is recoverable after the stress is removed. . .

When the stress is sufficient to permanently deform the metal, it is called plastic deformation.

As we begin to emerge from lockdown, are we elastic or plastic? How, in other words, have we endured the stress, and are new types of stress keeping us from returning to our original mental shape? In this regard, questions regarding the psychological impact of COVID-19 are parallel to those involving its physical impact since, as we now know, affected individuals can have trouble walking, breathing, and eating even after they ostensibly recover. The difference is that while we still have little control over the virus' physical effects, we can (to a degree) manage how it affects us psychologically.

The point is to take charge as early as possible, and not allow stress to feed on itself and spiral out of control.

My patient Jeremy is a case in point. Jeremy is an Assistant Professor of Chemistry at a university in New York City. Before the pandemic, he was already under stress to publish enough peer-reviewed articles to get tenure. He was advising the chess team, and also coaching Pre-Med students on the Biochem portion of the MCAT. When the pandemic struck, and added the stress of online teaching, it felt like it was all just too much. "I still have to write those articles, the chess team is preparing to compete remotely, and my Pre-Med students are hysterical. I'm responsible for everyone, including myself – and now it all just got harder." I was concerned that Jeremy might give up on himself. Maybe quit coaching, or prepping the team. The risk of failing anyone who depended on him might cause him to duck out of the risk, and then hate himself.

So, my first response was to help Jeremy see that he could handle the stress. "Think back to graduate school," I suggested. "Wasn't that the hardest time of your life?" Jeremy had to complete his dissertation and interview for jobs. He actually won a two-year fellowship before taking his first teaching position. I reminded him of how well he did. "You can do that again," I said.

But then I realized that he didn't have to.

I told him that while he viewed himself as the Same Old Jeremy, always ready to juggle multiple responsibilities, everyone else saw him as Jeremy + A Pandemic. They understood the added stress that he was facing, and would obviously cut him some slack. "Won't the Tenure & Promotion Committee give you a few more months?" I asked. "If you asked the chess team to practice on their own a few times – maybe recommend Bobby Fischer's book, or Jeremy Silman, or Aron Nimzowitsch – that would be fine." I wanted Jeremy to realign his view of himself with how the rest of the world saw him. "You can sometimes be self-absorbed," I said, "and it's eroding your strength."

If Jeremy was to snap back after all this was over, he had to be strong enough to remain intact. In "elastic" materials, deformation occurs when atomic bonds stretch but do not break; the atoms do not, therefore, slip past each other, and the material can return to its original shape. On the other hand, "plastic" deformation occurs when some of the bonds do break, and the material cannot recover its shape. I suggested that Jeremy think of himself in terms of resisting the effects of intense, prolonged stress. "You need strength enough to push back against stress."

I've noticed over the years that sometimes it's useful for someone to abstract themselves from themselves, and reimagine themselves schematically – in this case, as a structure subject to lines of force. "If you were a cable on a bridge, wouldn't others ensure that you could bear the stress?" He could see that. People wanted him to succeed.

"I get it," he said.

In fact, Jeremy started lecturing *me* about materials science, about which he knew a great deal. We got into tensile strength – the maximum stress that a material can withstand while being stretched or pulled before breaking. It was fascinating. But the point was to allow him to realize that we all have our breaking points, and it's necessary to pull back from the brink. COVID-19 has made the load greater, so we have to be more attentive to its potential effects. We also have to acknowledge that if the stress is greater, so is everyone's understanding – they are stressed just like we are. "You know," I said, "there is sort of a new stress equation. If our stress-level seems like it's doubled, we can expect a doubling in how people make allowances for it."

I suggested that if we proceeded under the old rules – the rules before the pandemic – we would subject ourselves to a level of self-induced, self-magnified stress that would be highly destructive and leave us depleted. We had to live under a new set of rules, which required that we come out of our self-involved bubbles and situate ourselves in the world at large.

Jeremy was accustomed to setting his own standards without reference to any external allowances. He had to get over that. For this, he had to learn to open up to other people and ask for allowances, something that he had never done – or even wished to do. I suggested that if he imagined the situation in reverse, where other people asked him to cut them some slack, he certainly would. So, in the end it all came down to seeing himself within a community. "Look," I said, "you already do so much. Everybody knows." COVID-19 is forcing us out of ourselves which will, I think, allow us to recover ourselves in the long run.

HAVING A BABY

With a gallic shrug, the French have laid claim to the pandemic's basic principle: "*Plus ca change, plus la meme chose,*" the more things change, the more they stay the same. That is, while everything looks different, it really isn't. Life goes on, despite upheavals. Each new challenge collapses – more or less – back towards the center, and we never quite tumble into the unknown.

Traditionally, "...*plus la meme chose*" has been viewed as dispiriting (war with catapults is no less awful than with howitzers); but for the incidentals, the parade of horribles continues. But we can also flip the idea; continuity is comforting. Thus, while SARS-CoV-2 is technically the "new coronavirus," it is still a virus, and in the ballpark of medical knowledge. We know that we have to quarantine, cover our faces, ultimately find a vaccine. The virus is new but not so new that everything stops while we try to beat it. "*Plus la meme chose*" is no rationale for twiddling our thumbs.

In this weirdly upended time, markers of continuity emerge in the simplest things. For example, people are still having babies. As I write this in mid-July, these babies were obviously conceived before the pandemic. But here they are, or almost are, as some are due in the next few weeks. As my patient Audrey says, "I can't exactly postpone it."

Yet even while babies are a quintessential marker of the human life-cycle, and in that sense provide reassurance, the "*plus ca change*" half of the equation currently governs our reality. These are not normal times for babies or their parents. We have very little data about risks of COVID-19 during pregnancy, or to the infant as its immune system remains only partly developed. We don't know whether nursing provides advantages against contagion, as it would for many diseases. We think that maternity wards are safe, but are they? Is a home birth preferable? I am seeing several parents concerned that bringing a child into this mess is riskier than they had ever imagined. How do I remind them that life goes on, and that we are not entirely in *terra incognita*?

Not to say that we aren't there, somewhat. My patients display a new kind of bewilderment. Audrey said "I can't feel guilty, since I got pregnant before the pandemic. So, I don't know what to feel." When patients want to feel an emotion but can't define what it should be, it's hard to know where to begin. We are finding new ground together. I want to help patients to think through their concerns since, obviously, neither I nor anyone else has all the answers.

Audrey's case is probably not unusual. She was excited about finally getting pregnant at 36, and was reassured that her family would help her during the first few weeks. Her sister would come up from Florida, and her mother would follow when her sister went home. But not anymore. No one from Florida can travel to New York except if they undergo two weeks' quarantine. "I'm beginning to feel alone," Audrey said, "even before I am alone." Her husband is planning six weeks' parental leave, but he knows less about babies than she does.

So, I told Audrey, "It's natural to be anxious." The bottom has fallen out of her plans, and a joyous event has turned scary. As a psychiatrist, I never discount how people feel. They are where they are. To them, their feelings are legitimate. However, I don't want Audrey to become depressed, either before or after the birth. Depression is immobilizing. Now – while she still has some time – she needs to be proactive. To help women in her position, there is now a vast array of resources. "Check these out," I said. "They're excellent." For example, many hospitals offer weekly conversations with experts about what to expect. The

University of Virginia Hospital (n.d.) says "Get answers to your worries and concerns." The website assures parents that the hospital is doing everything possible to prevent the spread of COVID-19 to the delivery unit, and notes that home deliveries are far riskier. It answers questions about breast-feeding. Hospitals know what parents are feeling.

Another source of support is other women's experiences. In May, *Vogue* had a great article by Sadie Stein, "'You see Your Smallness': On Giving Birth in a Pandemic." The author's point is that even while giving birth in this period can be fraught, your own troubles shrink when you see the pain around you. In effect, you get a hold of yourself, you do what you have to. In fact, a vast literature has emerged, almost overnight, about how to cope with the New Childbirth. While some of it concerns how to mentally face this reality, much of it is simply practical. Either way, it's encouraging. I recommended that Audrey read it. "Maybe you'll have to bond with your baby while wearing a mask. Okay, it's possible."

We also talked about hiring a night nurse so that Audrey and her husband could get some sleep. "I'm not sure that I can afford that," she said. We had to restrict ourselves to the possible.

The problem with having a baby during a pandemic puts the "*plus la meme chose . . .*" front and center. In that truism, money has always made things easier.

For some of my patients, much has stayed the same. Take Samuel, a financier, and Linda, an accomplished artist. They're among the One Percent. During Linda's last trimester, they moved from their Manhattan townhouse into his family's guest house on their Greenwich estate. They hired help who agreed not to leave the property for at least six months. Recently, Linda gave birth to a beautiful healthy girl, and the baby was attended by parents, grandparents, and a nurse. The parents had full control of people's comings and goings, and could give their newborn the best of everything (and get ample sleep for themselves).

Sam and Linda don't feel guilty about their advantages, and don't feel guilty about not feeling guilty. While I could nudge our conversations into socio-economic brooding, that's the last thing they need. I ask myself whether my recusal is a cop-out, and I decide that (for now) it's not.

Another couple that I work with also just had a baby. Michael and Cristina live in a one-bedroom apartment in New York City. He works for the federal government, and she for a nonprofit. Michael moved his workspace into the bedroom, while they turned an alcove into a nursery. But now they're anxious.

Michael worries about how COVID has reshaped childhood: "Would you bring a baby to a Mommy and Me class? And what about school and play dates?"

His worries are existential. "What if my agency downsizes?" he asks. "How will I get insurance?" I can say something reassuring like "It'll work out," but that would seem facile. I don't know any better than anyone else what the future holds.

Money has always mattered when it comes to having children. This is not the time to fix that, but sooner or later we'll have to.

The way things are going, sooner always seems later.

DATING –WHO SAID IT WOULD BE EASY?

I am often the silent partner in relationships, counselling people on how to convey what they feel (or act on their feelings, or recover from them and move on). It's challenging, since I never want to project my own inclinations onto how someone else should proceed. Besides, the history and nuances of a relationship may be refracted through the stress of the moment; I'm never certain what the real story is – in any case, we are different human beings, and what seems right for me could be disastrous for them. So mostly I just listen, and encourage people to find their own correct response to an emotionally fraught situation. Until now.

Since the pandemic, my patients seem much less interested in upsetting the status quo of their relationships. They want stability at all costs, since so much else seems beyond their control. "The last thing I need," said one of them, "is to go looking for a new girlfriend." The consensus is that even if the relationship has lost much of its spark, there is comfort in continuity. "At least she's there. I know she cares about me, and would . . ." That failure to finish the thought conveys exactly the fear that keeps the two together. At least for now, maybe for the foreseeable future.

Figure III.4 Lovers from the *Romance of the Rose*

People in more or less stable relationships – however unexciting and even unfulfilling – count themselves lucky. With everyone social-distancing, and so few outlets for making even casual new friends, relationships are the new gold standard for how to keep your sanity. "Most of the time, we just talk on the phone," said one of my patients, "but we talk." The alternative is a world of business calls, nothing more. "It's like we have the same conversation every day, but we know each other. It's okay."

Sometimes people in relationships but not living together figure out how to see each other, even have sex. But they're more careful now. They take walks, in their masks. They hold hands. Now that outdoor dining has resumed in New York City, some have even ventured out for brunch. If it all feels artificial, it's way less so than if the people are just getting to know each other, and not sure how far to extend their trust. They may even be discovering that comfort is at least as worthwhile as excitement. They may even be growing up.

So, I'm concerned about a few of my patients who are struggling to *find* a relationship. These are people accustomed to jumping onto Hinge or Bumble, getting a date, maybe having sex, and making up their minds pretty fast. Usually, they just move on to next person. "I don't want to just settle," they say – a refrain that I hear from both men and women. But now that whole process has been radically skewed ("fu—ed," one of them said, not to put too fine a point on it). Yes, I know that online contacts have soared during the pandemic, with everyone cooped up at home, but how do you establish a relationship when you're scared (to death!) of meeting a stranger for any more than a walk in the park six feet apart with your faces covered by masks?

Even if we discount sex, intimacy involves sharing experiences; touching; the body language of affection. Most of us grasp this instinctively. We want to let go, to sink into a situation without formalities and safeguards – without the barriers – that separate the people we encounter from those towards whom we have feelings. But how is any of this possible now?

Well, it is. Sort of. But it takes a new level of imagination – not fantasy, precisely, but dedication to adopting the new protocols of dating and becoming close.

I am thinking of my patient Greg, a 40-year-old divorced guy who's been dating for the past two years. Normally, he meets a woman online, exchanges a few emails, talks on the phone once or twice, and sets up dinner if things seem pleasant enough. He really wants to establish a relationship, he said, not just find a series of sex partners. "But you know," he confessed, "I don't feel that I can really talk to a woman until we've had sex. Otherwise, I just can't open up." I've heard a version of this declaration more times than I can count, and I used to think it reflected the male ego. But now I hear it from women too. In the era of disposable online dates, sex has become a barrier-buster, a shortcut to reassurance of one's own attractiveness ("well, at least he/she will go to bed with me"). It's a source of self-confidence when you've met someone new. As Greg puts it, "I really want to tell someone about who I am, about the divorce. But . . ." (and here is the hitch) "I can't find the words until I've slept with them."

Greg's whole *modus operandi* has been upset. Actually, it's pitched into reverse. While there is no shortage of women, he doesn't know what to talk about. He can't even describe his usually frenetic days in pharmaceutical sales, since now most of the doctors he would normally visit – his territory is New York and New Jersey – are just reopening their practices and are way too busy for a long presentation. Maybe there is a phone call at the end of the day. Ho hum. Big deal. "Am I becoming boring?" he asked.

So, I talked with Greg about how he could break the ice. "You have to start from the assumption that, if you like each other, then you will finally meet in person. You can do things remotely to *start* liking each other."

Greg was skeptical, but I pointed out that there are tons of resources that could guide people in this new dating regime. One common practice is to watch a movie together on Netflix, and then talk about it. You could cook dinner together over Zoom, and then enjoy it with a glass of wine. Form a book club – of two – and talk about the book. In other words, get to know how each other thinks, approaches problems, approaches art. Of course, there isn't much body language on Zoom, and faces tend to be weird distortions. But cut each other some slack. The point is to gauge compatibility – could you have a conversation, at least about something? Is the other person funny? Do they have an interesting, spontaneous personality? Create situations, however remote (okay, artificial), to help you answer those questions.

Then comes the challenge. If you find yourself increasingly comfortable with this person, then take that walk in the park (for the first time, at least, six feet apart in a mask). If both of you have been tested, it's okay to hold hands, provided you wash them. If it's nice, do it again. Talk about having sex, or maybe just kissing. Get tested again. If you're both negative, see if it's possible to quarantine for two weeks. Then ask yourself whether it's worth becoming closer (Safe Sex just entered a whole new dimension).

In other words, weigh the risks. Not having a relationship during this awful time can make it feel much worse.

Greg knows that. But I'm not sure how he'll proceed. "It all sounds like a lot of work," he said. Welcome to the pandemic. We are reinventing the basics, like dating and human relationships – we have to relearn what we thought we knew.

Several of my patients in relationships feel smug right now, since it's one less thing to worry about. Getting into a relationship will be challenging. But human history is fraught with challenges. We're here because we have learned to adapt.

ELDERLY PARENTS

The pandemic is reconfiguring families. Children who are back from college are now bemused (if somewhat discomfited) that their old rooms were (in their absence) turned into memorials to their long-forgotten selves. Grandparents follow, afraid to be alone but (like their grandchildren) bewildered as to where exactly they will fit in. In the middle, parents manage everyone (sort of).

I'm thinking of my patient Bob, who – like many wealthy New Yorkers – has decamped with his family to the Hamptons. His elderly father, Dan, lives alone in Boston with a caregiver, and desperately wants to spend time with his grandchildren. At 93, he fears that he has little time left.

Bob drove to see Dan a couple weeks ago, but Dan yearns for the whole family. He survived the Holocaust and WWII, and his loneliness now contemplates the next world. "I hope Mildred is waiting for me," he told Bob. He misses his wife, whom he lost last year.

Yet while Bob and his family want to see Dan, and think that he'd like the Hamptons, they wonder whether such a visit is safe. Is permitting it even responsible? We spoke about finding a sensible approach, so that no one would feel guilty and no one would get hurt. My own complicated concerns about seeing my elderly parents lurked in the background. For the longest time, I struggled to live up to my father's example, and I knew how hard it was to engage with one's father objectively.

So, I wondered how anyone (namely me) could advise anyone else concerning elderly parents in a pandemic – the situation is so personal, so bound up with one's relationship to one's parents. The most I could do was to help Bob think through his feelings.

In fact, and as I suspected, Bob's feelings were not just about pandemic-based logistics. His attempt to assess his father's visit was not – and could not be – objective, based on his complicated feelings. These went deep into his history with his father. Though Bob was not initially aware of why he was having such trouble deciding, we finally discovered it: his real concern was whether he could trust his own judgment (and treat his father accordingly), or whether his judgment would be colored by this history.

Bob had joined the family real estate business – a modest, if successful operation – and had built it into a fiefdom. Though Dan remained its titular head until a few years ago, Bob had made the quiet, lucrative deals that paid off as the City gentrified. But the company was still Dan's. Until a formal reorganization transferred ownership of the business to Bob, everyone knew it was Dan's. Bob assumed that people wondered why the transfer took so long. "Maybe they think I got here by default." For a very long time, therefore, he felt that he had never "been the business," as he liked to say, and that he had never been allowed to receive the recognition he deserved. "Why couldn't my father just bow out gracefully?" he asked. "Why did he have to keep living his illusion – at my expense?"

In psychoanalysis there is the idea of the Oedipus Complex, which originates from Sophocles' tragedy, *Oedipus Rex*. In the play, Oedipus unwittingly murders his father, King of Thebes, at its crossroad into the City. He then unwittingly marries his mother. When he realizes his crime, he blinds himself, and pursues a life of solitude and reflection. According to Freud, conflict with his father is inherent in the psychological development of the male child; it is embedded, unconsciously, in a man's psychological structure. Accordingly, men always experience some competitive strivings with fathers and father figures for the love of a desired woman, their mothers.

I saw this pattern with Bob and his father. He was always a dutiful, respectful, even compliant son. But he harbored feelings of resentment about being under his father's thumb, which especially rankled after he had exceeded his father's accomplishments. I felt that these feelings inflected how he viewed his father's potential visit to the Hamptons.

For sure, there were legitimate health concerns. What if his father should get infected with COVID-19 and die (COVID is especially lethal to the elderly)? Would Bob be at fault, even though his father asked to come? (Bob was in charge now, and *his* decisions carried greater weight.) The children were beginning to socialize with other children. His wife owned a fashion store in town and (by appointment) came in contact with her clients. He occasionally met with clients, albeit out in the open.

Thus, the whole situation was complicated. While Bob had concerns that were reality-based, they were tied up with feelings of competition and resentment towards his father. When I told him so, he acknowledged that it was true. Such feelings had, in fact, surfaced during our years of working together, and had complicated other problems that he had faced. During the current crisis, people can rarely deal with health issues head-on; they are refracted through other issues that we carry around – indeed, that they have carried around for years.

In facing COVID-19, we face multiple issues simultaneously. Some seem acute – like how we care for elderly parents – while others have just never gone away, like how relationships with parents still bother us. All of these issues now appear to gang up on us, so that we can't deal with any of them on its own. In a perverse multi-dimensional matrix, each makes the other harder to isolate and individually solve.

The pattern is a classic example of stress, where one stressor aggravates others – sometimes it's impossible to tell which aggravates which and, in fact, it rarely matters. For Bob, the immediate present (what to do about Dan) and the lingering past (the Oedipal remnants of their relationship) converged, leaving him uncertain. He wanted to make his father happy, but he was afraid that his judgment was unreliable – even warped – to his father's detriment. "Can I trust my own judgment?" he asked.

At the very least, Bob understood his dilemma. He was self-aware . . . but for that very reason, feeling immobilized.

He also found humor in how his fantasy and quotidian lives merged like two images projected from opposite directions onto a screen. There was irony, he said, in how reality – the pandemic – had roused his Oedipal fantasies. "It's like science meets the Loch Ness Monster," he suggested. So how do you resolve this fix?

I found the dilemma fascinating. Often, it's hard to establish the contours of a patient's reality based solely on how they describe it. As we dug deeper, we had to disentangle objective reality – the dangers to the elderly from COVID-19 – from psychic, intersubjective reality. Once we did that, however, Bob thought he could put his Loch Ness Monster aside, and make a reasonable assessment of the risk. He plans to tell his father that the family will visit Boston very soon. It's not ideal, since it means less time with Dan, but it will be less stressful for everyone else. During this period, it's okay to act in the interest of stress reduction – especially, as in Bob's case, where the result makes everyone at least minimally happy.

THE PSYCHIATRIST AND THE GUITAR

Did Freud say "Everywhere I go I find a poet has been there before me"? Well, if he didn't, he should have. (Recall that other semi-apocryphal exchange between Oscar Wilde and James McNeill Whistler, where Wilde says "I wish I had said that," and Whistler replies "You will, Oscar, you will.") [See Quote Investigator, 2013.] In the spirit of what Freud might have said (and would have, had he thought to), I naturally turn to poetry as a signpost of where I'm going during this stressful period. How am I supposed to think about my experience of all the grief that presents to me, day after day?

Early in my career, I found Wallace Stevens' "The Man with the Blue Guitar" (1937) and lately I recalled its opening lines:

> The man bent over his guitar,
> A shearsman of sorts. The day was green.
> They said, "You have a blue guitar,
> You do not play things as they are."
>
> The man replied, "Things as they are
> Are changed upon the blue guitar."
>
> And they said then, "But play, you must,
> A tune beyond us, yet ourselves,
>
> A tune upon the blue guitar
> Of things exactly as they are."

Traditionally, the poem is read to involve the player's improvisations, the changes he creates – almost like riffs – as he interprets "things as they are." The audience wants him to play things straight, "a tune beyond us, yet ourselves." We drift into a display of the poetic imagination, a negotiation between the world and its attuned, yet not quite disciplined interpreter.

Psychiatrists are not poets. But we are somewhat like the guitarist/poet in that we play another person's reality back to them, interpreting it through our own experience and understanding. We seek a kind of enhanced clarity, a version of "things as they are" that goes beyond mere surface resemblance. We try to find the psychological truth, and make it more apparent.

This process often involves sharing the sources of a person's pain, then explaining how – even in their pain – they can find a way forward. In a sense, we ask our patients to be like the guitarist, indeed like the psychiatrist, by imagining reality as different (from how they see it) but still no less real.

This week Raul came to me after losing his only son. A Cuban-American, he had served his adopted country in the military and then worked his way up to responsible positions. He had instilled in his children the same work ethic. His son, Jesus, was an athlete and a leader at his school. For the past few months, they had sheltered in place, which had brought them even closer.

In May, Raul had given his son permission to visit family in Florida. But a week after Jesus arrived, he felt ill. A test for COVID-19 came back positive. No one knew where he had contracted the disease – did he pick it up in Florida, or bring it with him from New York? His aunt, worried for her own children, helped Jesus quarantine in the garage. He delayed seeking treatment because everyone thought he'd pull through.

Three days after he entered quarantine, he didn't wake up. By the time EMS arrived, his pupils were fixed and dilated; he had no pulse and could not be revived. It was assumed that he had died of the virus, but traces of opioids were found in his system. Did the drugs have something to do with his death? Had Jesus experimented once he'd left home? No one was sure, and it didn't matter. Now Raul's only son was dead. He felt that his life had no point.

Raul spoke of his love for his son. He had been looking forward to working together with Jesus in the family construction business. They had gone deep-sea fishing together earlier in the spring, and Jesus had shared his big plans for the company and his own life. But now those dreams were finished, forever.

Raul blamed himself. "Why did I let him go?" He felt irretrievably guilty. "I should have protected him. I should have known." Known what? Though nothing I could say would change anything, I did offer a reality check: in early May, the disease had not yet spiked in Florida. I did not have the heart to mention drugs.

Raul was inconsolable. He wished it had been him instead of Jesus. He said that his wife was so angry that he thought she would leave him except for the children remaining at home. He came from a culture where family was paramount to a man's sense of self. "You know," he said, "there is a special bond between a man and his son. When it breaks – when he allows it to break – who is he anymore?"

I had to respect that conviction, but I also had to present Raul with a reality that was not so unforgiving.

I thought of Stevens' line, later in the poem, "I cannot bring a world quite round, although I patch it as I can." So much of what I say is inadequate to address people's losses. It's a patch. Something. A lot of what I do during this pandemic is patch-work. But while the reality I offer is not good-as-new, it is a new reality. I ask people to dwell in it, to make do. I accepted that Raul felt he had failed in some deep cultural sense – he had not protected his family, as a man should – yet I wanted him to see that he still had value. "You did what seemed okay at the time," I said.

As a psychiatrist, I'm good at treating symptoms. Anxiety, depression, post-traumatic stress are treatable conditions. With medications, cognitive-behavioral and insight psychotherapies, and other treatment modalities people can feel better. But some losses don't respond to "treatment." They are so unfathomable that if we offer patches, they don't stick. They fall off, blow away in endless grief.

In these situations, I can listen. I can mourn. But I recognize how limited my words are. I cannot just tell someone to accept what's past, learn from it, and try to do better. In the case of Raul, who lost an only son, such advice would seem like mockery.

But as Stevens said, reality sometimes weaves in and out of our consciousness, giving us moments that stand in for joy:

> The stone will be
> Our bed and we shall sleep by night
> We shall forget by day, except
> The moments when we choose to play
> The imagined pine, the imagined jay.

I am convinced that eventually Raul will be able to situate himself in a willed reality which, if not the reality he had hoped for, will still provide him comfort – even joy.

As Raul and I spoke, I thought of other patients who had lost loved ones during this awful period. I've followed some of them and, while they are still grief-stricken, they are beginning to see that other people still depend on them. Severing one bond does not sever every bond. Raul's commitment to family, which was now torturing him, may yet be the means for pulling him through. I reminded Raul of his other children.

Like the guitarist, I offered an improvised reality – close enough, I hoped, to be sort of redeeming.

CAMPING

Actually, I'm on vacation. My family and I hitched a trailer to our SUV and are camping for a few days. I thought the kids could use a change, and I had visions of campfires, fireflies, and watching the stars come out. But now that we've settled in (and figured out how to assemble the tents), I realize why – this year of all years – I felt compelled to rough it. Okay, to play at roughing it, but still to work at the challenges posed by cutting the cord, living off-the-grid . . . maybe even catching a trout. In this time of COVID-19, where survival (mental and physical) is on everyone's mind, I wanted space to make conscious choices about elemental needs: where to sleep, how to keep busy, how to get back in tune with a natural world that's easy to forget.

I wanted to think about survival, not just have it happen to me. I hoped that my kids would realize that survival is not automatic — as it pretty much seems to be when everything else is automatic, from devices that play jazz (or rock, or soul, or reggae) on command to groceries that arrive in the Fresh Direct time-slot. If we view survival as contingent, we become strategic. Humble. Aware of what we still have to learn. We're not just affecting some primitive state. We're practicing a form of enlightened self-interest.

One of my patients, a lawyer for the government, took a six-week trek in the Himalayas to experience what it was like to consciously try to survive. "You see those gorgeous pictures?" she said. "The rest of the time, I was terrified." But she made it, and it changed how she thought about her life. "I realized that decisions have consequences. I'm more deliberate now."

Survival has been so easy in post-industrial America that we forgot — when the pressure is on — that we could still fall off a cliff because we never imagined we could. Having to work at survival would have seemed weird — like "what planet are you on?" Until now. Now the need stares us in the face. In the past few weeks, patients have said that besides taking the usual precautions — wearing masks, washing their hands, not going to parties — they're adopting rituals that instill notions that survival takes conscious effort. Like checking on the batteries. It's the moral equivalent of kids' hiding under desks in the '50s, when teachers warned them against Cold War bombs. One of my patients, a licensed clinical social worker, said "It's operant conditioning. I get a mental reward when I know I'm taking care."

Before I left on vacation, my patient Ben expressed disdain for how some people went camping: they barely left their double-wide trailers, and spent all day watching TV. At the time, I put it down to disgust, even condescension. But now — sitting in my relatively simple tent — I realize what he was trying to say.

Ben, I think, was annoyed at how people could waste the chance to challenge themselves — however briefly — to think about how to make do. Especially now.

Ben and his wife had rented a tent, driven to a national park, and met up with another couple. They were going to cook, watch birds, and rock-climb. But when they arrived, the scene was surreal. "I couldn't believe," said Ben, "how other 'campers' just replaced their houses with RVs . . . what's the point?" Summits, Renegades, and Commanders (Ben got lost counting the wheels) had full bathrooms, full kitchens, large flat-screen TVs, and fold-out patios the size of a badminton court. One gaudy number was a duplex, and reminded Ben of a double decker bus.

Without articulating what he had felt, Ben implied that he'd experienced a let-down — even despite his own ability to enjoy himself in relatively rustic circumstances. "I had to share the park with that crowd," he said. "I hate thinking that we're all going back to the same world." Translation: we're all in this together, so we'd all better act like it. Ben seemed to suggest that if he ever had to rely on such people, he'd be sunk.

Yet here's where it gets interesting. Ben also mentioned that he'd brought along the latest high-tech kayaks, a thousand-dollar fly fishing kit, and LED lights to illuminate the campsite. If he was looking for the simpler life, even for a whiff of the survivalist experience, he was going to do it in style. The perfect kayak? Gimme a break. Ben felt superior to the yahoos in Summits because he had good taste.

But okay, I cut Ben some slack. It's hard to let go of our comforts. It's even harder, when we do, not to compensate by ramping up in other ways ("Let's see, I'll trade my TV for anything fiberglass"). We're still struggling with how far we want to go, or can go, in preparing ourselves to take on a world where existential threats are not obscure, and where we have to think about how we get out of this alive.

Still, Ben's venture into the wilderness had some redeeming value. He spoke about the first night when the moon was full, the stars were out, and he sat around the campfire with friends. A chipmunk ate some leftover sunflower seeds that they'd spilled. "I hadn't seen one of those little guys in years," he said. "I know it sounds corny, but I got to witness the economy of nature." (Okay, no chipmunk will ever let good trail-mix go to waste.)

But on a more serious note, Ben said that he was even moved to say an evening prayer. "You know," he recalled, "when I was growing up, we said prayers sometimes, especially when the news was bad or we were worried. My father led us." He felt that in that beautiful place, where he could forget about the troubles outside, it was his duty not to forget. In a way, it was like practicing survival in another key. It was like coupling an awareness that survival takes work, with an equal awareness that we have to hope.

Not a bad start, I thought.

In our current environment, as we seek to venture out, we have to think about where we venture to. The great outdoors offers a lot of potential. There's space to reflect on how much stuff we can readily let go of, and what is essential to life going forward. We can practice versions of simplicity – well, maybe not hyper-simplicity, but still a non-automated life that demands our full attention. We can practice being more deliberate.

Of course, those people who rarely climbed down from RVs may just have been scared. But more likely, they lacked imagination. As we adapt to this new normal – still a fast-moving target – we will need to develop the skills to adapt. We will need to develop the best-suited disposition. Ben sort of recognized that when he acknowledged that there was still lots of trouble . . . but that the will to handle it requires a degree of hope.

Sounds like a decent formula.

RETURNING TO THE OFFICE

Slowly, my patients are trickling back to their offices, and I thought perhaps I should do the same. Ronald, a hedge fund guy who's been sequestered in the Hamptons for the past four months ("Just me and a Bloomberg Anywhere connection") said, in effect, that the party was over. He was tired of never getting tired and, of what seemed to him, laying about with the liquor cabinet too close for comfort. "You know," he said, "I could use some stress. I miss all the shouting." He sounded like a character who'd dropped through my screen from a rerun of *Wall Street* (1987). But I got the point. I was feeling a little itchy myself.

Since March, I have been conducting my practice entirely remotely. I've been happy with the results, and even wrote approvingly that "Sometimes treatment can be more focused than is possible in an office visit; we get to the heart of an issue more quickly; we lock eyes . . ." I still stand by that assessment, but now, after the passage of time, I should factor in the effect of my prolonged separation from where I'm used to practicing. Like Ronald, I miss my home base – not the melee of a bunch of guys turning over options, but my office on Park Avenue where, I guess, I know who I am.

The space you are in defines you to a degree that I hadn't appreciated. In my "real" office, as opposed to the attic where I talk with my patients remotely, I am surrounded by artifacts that I've acquired because they're reassuring – they represent my growing into this profession after years of arduous training. There are the books. A collected edition of Freud that fills a whole shelf. Journals. Art. An old piano. Together, they soften the geometry of so many square feet, and make me feel like I belong, like I know what I'm doing, like I ought to be here doing it.

Okay, maybe that's irrational. I'm still Dr. Friedberg, wherever I go. But I deal with the irrational, and the concerns don't stop just because I'm personally involved. In fact, my reaction to being out-of-place is more than just "personal," since I'm beginning to think it's affecting how I treat patients. In recent weeks, I've noticed that I'm not as focused; my mind wanders; my responses are less attuned than they should be. In part, this could be due to the stress of the pandemic (I'm seeing more patients, and they're jumpier). But I think it's less specific, more of a general need on my part to be back in permanent digs (as opposed to the screamingly provisional).

The place where you feel you belong comes with a lot of reassuring ritual. Ronald told me that he likes to get to the office before 7 a.m., go to the kitchen, and make instant oatmeal from the little packets on the counter. "I use two of them. The hot water comes out of this machine, and it's so easy." A guy who earns millions of dollars a year likes to make his own oatmeal. But wait. It's the ritual, the easing into the day before all hell breaks loose. At home in the Hamptons, there was no hell, so there was no need for any comforting rituals . . . but then the whole day just seemed somehow unhinged. It never started, and you never knew when it had stopped.

In my case, the ritual starts when I say hello to the doorman at my Park Avenue building. We've known each other for years, and he calls me Doc. It continues when I make coffee in the antique kitchen that I share with two other physicians. I'm easing into the day, like Ronald, like the vast army of people who crowd into Manhattan to earn a living. I look at the mail. I skim a journal or two and mark the pages that I'll read on the way home. In point of fact, I am slowly waking up. By the time the first patient arrives, I'm with it. I hadn't realized (until now) how skipping these rituals would actually affect me. But now I see that they serve to focus my attention: be a psychiatrist (they insist), not a daddy, not the guy who walks the dog between patients. The rituals of the office set us up to perform.

So, this week, I started going in, two days out of five, enough at least to give me a sense that I'm back where I belong. I drove, rather than taking the train, which seemed like a sacrifice – dead time that I could have used for reading. But I'm still not confident about confined spaces and, I guess, I wanted my office badly enough to endure all the traffic. It didn't matter that I still spent most of my time treating patients remotely. I was back, and that's what counted. A couple of patients did actually want to see me in person, and I met with them. They and I had been tested for COVID, and we wore masks. We sat six feet apart. But there was a camaraderie, like old friends meeting, that was inescapable – and also astonishing, since we had talked by Skype just last week. I think it was because I felt energized.

One patient had been asking to see me in person for a couple of weeks, and I knew I'd be helping just by showing up (as Woody Allen said, "showing up is 80 percent of life," a precept I'm coming to appreciate) (Allen, n.d.). He was concerned about his dental practice, which had fallen off a cliff. Not only were patients too scared to get their teeth cleaned/filled/extracted or otherwise fixed but, if they did come in, he or she expected that the office be run like an isolation ward. No other patients in the waiting room. Everyone in protective gear, starting with the receptionist. "I can't afford this," he said. "There's no such thing as remote dentistry."

I cringed. I've been able to maintain my practice during the pandemic, while hands-on guys like dentists have seen their practices crumple. I didn't know what to say, but finally suggested that, if things stayed the same, he might consider joining a larger practice with the wherewithal to ride all this out. Of course, I could have said the same thing over Skype, but I could see that just talking (with a proximity that scared his own patients) made him feel better. He said he felt "touched" by my coming in to see him, conflating our near-physicality with his emotion.

So, for now, at least, I've decided to continue coming in two days a week, maybe upping it to three over the coming months. I probably won't go back to four days in Manhattan (I spend one in Great Neck) for some time, since some patients actually like not traveling to sessions. But I think that my sense of myself requires that I be in my "real" office. It has become real over time, but now it is and now I understand why I feel that so keenly.

TALKING TO THE KIDS

Victorian novels are readable again! And not just because we have time to plow through these triple-deckers. Rather, it's the melodrama, the sudden and extreme turns of fate that were possible then and now seem all too real in a post-COVID world. Think about it. The banks were unregulated; India and Africa beckoned, putting life and property at risk; women were dependent on men, whose pasts were kept well-hidden. In the space of one chapter, your savings disappeared, your railroad stock turned out to be worthless, and your husband's first career as a professional gambler upends his new perch as Bishop of London. Those old novels reflected contemporary expectations. Trouble is, the same maddening uncertainty has come around again.

I thought about that parallel universe when, recently, I picked up George Eliot's *Daniel Deronda* (1876). The flighty, selfish heroine, Gwendolyn Harleth, faces instant expulsion from polite society when her family loses its fortune and she contemplates the prospect of becoming a governess. A governess! A fate worse than death. Instead, she makes an injudicious marriage that saves her financially but plunges her into emotional distress. Hovering over Eliot's novel is the sense that pride goes before a fall but, worse still, who knows when a fall will occur? We can't get too comfortable. We can't be too self-satisfied. If we are (alas for Gwendolyn), we mishandle adversity, and take the desperate, unbecoming, self-destructive way out.

My patient Hillary might have been a Victorian heroine. Until she was furloughed this April, she was a highly paid auditor at an insurance company, with a staff of her own and an expense account. But the insurance industry is bracing for COVID-related losses – or, rather, for thousands of lawsuits relating to claims that will be denied. Her company had to cut costs. Hillary was a cost. She went from earning a respectable six figures to applying for unemployment (". . . from one end of the insurance spectrum to the other, all at once," she jokes). Like Gwendolyn, she didn't know what hit her. She had never thought about money. It was just there. Until it wasn't.

The worst part was that Hillary was a single mother of two children, 8 and 10. She did not receive alimony because she earned more than her ex did. She hadn't saved much either, since she had a great career (okay, there was the 401(k), but that was for years down the road). So, when she came to me, she said she felt uncomfortably humbled. "I never thought this could happen to me, and I feel like my kids will be angry when I can't give them everything they're accustomed to." She didn't know how to handle the situation. "I like spoiling my kids, and they like being spoiled. How can I face them?" she asked.

What I heard in her fear was a kind of self-regard, less about the kids than about what they would think of her. In this crazy time, I think a lot of parents – who are used to being their kids' heroes – are concerned about falling off their pedestals, and becoming lesser beings in their kids' estimation. They're worried about the potential discipline problems but, mostly, about becoming the agents of their kids' lowered expectations. As Hillary put it, "I've brought my kids up to think that I will always be there for them, that so long as they work hard, they'll have the support to do anything they want." That sounds like a concern for the kids, but it's still ego-driven – Hillary needs to feel that her kids see her as unfailingly benevolent, in their corner 1000 percent. If she can't be, she suffers.

When I pointed this out to her, she acknowledged that while she'd vaguely thought about it in the past, she'd never had to dwell on it. The money was always there. No big deal. But it was becoming a big deal now. The problem, she said, was that her own parents had been brutal. They actively resented her. Her father was in college at the same time she was, except that she'd gone "outta-town," as they derisively put it, while her father went to night-school, supporting the family. They were always threatening to yank her back home. They accused her of turning her back on her roots. They said that she wanted to be better than they were, that she had contempt for them, when all she really wanted was to succeed. They would have hobbled her to assuage their own sense of inferiority.

Hillary counted herself a survivor, but swore that her own kids would never suffer because of her own (potential) failure. She would succeed so they could succeed – but now that glide-path was disrupted.

I told Hillary that while the shadow of her parents was enormous, she shouldn't allow it to cloud her relationship with her children. "They know that you love them. But you've just been afraid to test that, so you've showered them with everything." Kids know stuff. I said that during this awful period, when she couldn't give them everything she wished to, she didn't have to worry about their loving her. Primarily, they looked to her for protection. So, it was important to let them know that they're safe, that she's still there for them with what really matters. I said that the best thing she could do for them now – the best way she could show her love – was to make sure they didn't become fearful, afraid to engage with the world because everything was not just as it had been. "You developed resilience," I said, "and it's time to see that they do too."

So, we talked about what she could tell them. First, I said that it was important to be honest, and not sugar-coat the loss of her position or the effect of the pandemic on the economy. "You can say things like 'Human beings are adaptable. We have to adjust, but we will.'" I said that it was important that they not feel ashamed if, for now, they were watching how they spent money. But I also said that it was okay to share their disappointment. Let them be unhappy, and show them that you understand. The emphasis should be on sharing, as a family, so that the children do not feel alone. As a young woman, Hillary had felt abandoned by her parents, and had at one point developed an eating disorder – common among young women whose mothers withhold love. She felt that she could empathize with her kids.

I also suggested that she explain the current situation – let them know that the country is fighting hard against a formidable virus. Let them know that the best doctors in the world are working on a solution. "You could say 'We don't know how long this will last, but it won't last forever.' Give them grounds for hope." The idea is to make sure that they do not think they're being talked down to, that the "real" story is being kept from them. "They look to you for credibility. You're their reality check."

Hillary's parents were never straight with her. They were manipulative, jealous, petty. Hillary had to rise above her own personal history now. She had to be her kids' bellwether. Once things turned around, assuming they ever do, she could go back to being extravagant – if that ever seems plausible again.

In the meantime, don't let the kids think that love is transactional. It's sustaining.

CLIMATE CHANGE

Things are opening up in the City but, in some quarters, that's cause for despair. My patient Claudia observed "I'm in mourning. New York is like London after the War." I see her point. Now that the chaos has subsided, it's possible to assess the damage – familiar shops are closed; Midtown is empty; so is Times Square. Nobody takes the subway. "You remember how they woke up when the war was over and they'd lost the Empire, and Austerity was in place, and whole areas of London were in ruins? Well, how are we different, practically speaking?"

We are different, but I understand her profound sense of loss. What's gone is the self-assurance, the Big Apple's shine. COVID-19, like a new Copernican revolution, robbed us of feeling like the center of anything (except perhaps of a pandemic that finally migrated south and west).

Claudia is upset because from now on, everyone's focus will be more local, intent on restoring personal finances, for example, rather than the overall economy. "Who's going to think about existential issues? Even Black Lives Matter is local – it's all about the police." Claudia advocates for population control and the climate, and sees the two as inextricably linked. As far as she's concerned, you can kiss these issues good-bye for a generation. "With so many

Figure III.5 Fire-stones

people dying . . . well, it's unseemly to talk about *fewer* people. And who's going to worry about carbon trading when industry is struggling and travel is limited?"

It was as if the work she'd devoted herself to had vaporized, becoming logically and morally impractical. She couldn't even raise the issues with her friends who'd been furloughed or, at least, seen their neighborhoods lose their glitter (not to mention all the people who'd decamped to the Hamptons/ Adirondacks/Vermont). For Claudia, the aftermath of the pandemic meant that just when you thought you were getting somewhere, you find out it was all a mirage. "What am I supposed to do now?" she asked plaintively.

Claudia had been very ambitious. After graduating with a degree in Environmental Engineering, she started an organization devoted to raising awareness about the link between population and climate change. In pretty raw terms, she reasoned that more people, equals fewer trees, means more carbon in the atmosphere. "If you want to get a handle on the climate," she said, "there has to be way fewer people." She could cite dozens of studies.

Until the pandemic, the organization was thriving. It had hired a couple of staffers, and had as many volunteers as it could handle. They were working on two major legislative initiatives which, though pie-in-the-sky, would – so Claudia believed – nudge the conversation in the right direction. One was to revoke the tax deduction for dependent children and, instead, impose a tax after the first child. "That'll make people think about having big families," she said. Maybe in 500 years, I thought . . . but still, she had a point. The second initiative was to allocate air miles and let people trade them, so there'd be a ceiling on total air travel. "You'd need a new bureaucracy for that," she acknowledged, "but think of the benefits!"

As the pandemic took hold, however, contributions dried up and both these initiatives shriveled. People turned inward. They were grateful for their families, and trying to protect them. Even if they were to limit their families now, they didn't want tax policy telling them not to have kids later on. It seemed too pessimistic when there was already pessimism enough. The air miles idea was also untimely – with the airline industry literally crashing, all the pressure was now towards reviving it. The government recently gave it $25 billion in aid.

But Claudia was convinced that people could not see past their immediate interests. "What kind of world do we want to leave to our kids?" she asked. "People think I'm anti-family and anti-pleasure, and that I have no empathy. But they miss the whole point." She was ready to give up; she was mad at the virus and mad at the world for not seeing past it. She complained that people felt entitled, after the virus, to live their lives in a way that made up for pain they'd endured and threats they still faced. "That's selfish and short-sighted," she insisted.

Of course, I wanted to help. But what do you say to someone whose life's work – and the organization they'd built to promote it – suddenly seems irrelevant? I've stopped telling people to just wait this out, that things will improve.

Nobody knows how long it will take for society to be interested in anything but rebuilding communities; getting kids back in school; and restoring some will-o'-the-wisp called Normality that will probably be forgotten before it's put back the way it was. So, I took another tack. I wanted Claudia to see that resilience requires that we look past the obvious and use our imaginations.

"Look," I said, you don't have to fold up your tents and go home. If your constituency is refocusing its interests, then consider meeting them where they're at." I suggested that she reframe her approach to take account of the virus, rather than arguing that people should look past it to a more regimented future. "What if you said that as population moves into areas that were previously animal habitat, the likelihood of viruses jumping from animals to humans increases exponentially? By controlling population, we limit that possibility." She thought about that idea, which was a hot topic in the literature. "If people came to accept it, then you wouldn't have to impose tax penalties that seem dispiriting and even possibly offensive."

In other words, I suggested that how she presented an idea was as important as its inherent logic. She could try the same approach with regard to her air miles proposal. "Okay, you hate people flying all around when they could use Skype or Zoom. But what about if they switched from planes to trains?" The idea was that she promote the kind of bullet trains that they have in Europe and Japan, which go 150 miles an hour and are replacing all but inter-continental plane trips. "These don't emit anywhere near the carbon that planes do, and city-to-city they're just as efficient." I also suggested that while she disdained local politics, she should get involved. "How about more congestion pricing to limit all those cars from entering cities? Or at least carpooling laws?"

Even when I'm neutral about people's choices, I try to help them maintain their commitments so that they don't fall into despair. In Claudia's case, I think that we do need to limit population if we're going to forestall the worst of climate change – though I'm not sure that I share her sense of overweening urgency. But of course, that's not the point. The point is, rather, to help her make sense of her life in a rapidly changing world. I want her to think her way out of feeling stuck – if she doesn't like some of my ideas, then she can choose others . . . but don't just assume that reality is resistant and won't respond. It responds if we can keep on going and keep an open mind.

THROWING POTS

According to the Partnership for New York City, as many as a third of the City's small businesses may never reopen. That's a lot of donut shops, coffee shops, bodegas, sneaker stores, optometrists . . . not to mention the vast number of ethnic restaurants in neighborhoods where English is the second language. Of course, none of these businesses wanted to close. But the virus gave them no choice. It was like the Mafia, whose demands for protection money had gone unheeded. The businesses just had to cave.

So, when Julie came to see me last week, intent on closing her successful ceramics business, it seemed like a counterfactual – it should only have happened under different circumstances. Julie had been making decorative ceramics for 20 years, and had a small Manhattan shop. On weekends, she taught pot-throwing, mostly to professionals who'd just discovered art after devoting themselves to being able to buy it. She'd studied classical Japanese glazes which, in fact, she never used but which sometimes brought appraisers to see her. She had a certain cachet, and was featured last year in a trade publication for interior designers. She had enough orders to last for years.

But then came the coronavirus.

In mid-March, Julie closed along with everyone else. But she opened up online. She gave demonstrations on Zoom, and showed her wares from dozens of angles in all kinds of settings. She partnered with a local caterer who was out of work, and together they created table settings with Julie's ceramics holding delicate quenelles, a Roquefort souffle, and perfect apple tarts. Again, the design publications got excited. So did the advertising sheets, which were starved for copy since their own clientele had gone dormant. "You know," Julie told me, "the virus has been good to me. I'm doing even better than I had been."

But now she thought that she ought to close. Why?

As Julie saw it, she was irrelevant. When she looked around and saw all the economic hardship, all the people whose lives had been upended – even shattered – by this virus, she felt like a not-so-innocent bystander, happily throwing pots in the midst of a catastrophe. She thought she ought to be doing something useful, like working in a food bank or teaching entrepreneurs how to open their businesses online. "It's not just that my products are decorative," she said, "*I'm* decorative." There's a time and place for everyone, she argued, and this was not her time.

She wanted to see what I could say in response – that is, whether I could convince her that staying in business was not an egregious display of vanity when the world needed everything-but.

Julie, it turned out, came from a family of thwarted bohemians who'd moved from rural Iowa to an intentional community in Arkansas. They'd come in search of a more egalitarian life. When they'd lived in Iowa, Julie's father had to participate in a cooperative that assigned quotas to individual farmers in order to maintain prices. But it meant that he had to take orders from someone who thought they knew better than he did what he should grow and how much he should charge for it. So, he sold the farm, packed up his family, and headed for the Ozarks. The only problem was that in Arkansas, the community was so disorganized that its finances suffered irreparably. After a few years, the group disbanded, and Julie's family was left with no resources. Her father went to work at a hardware store, and their life was seedy, boring, and without any trace of refinement. She fled as soon as she could.

Fortunately, artists had discovered Arkansas in the '60s. In the '80s and '90s, there were still pockets of weavers, potters, painters, and sculptors all around the state. Julie found some potters and, while she worked for a pittance, she learned a lot. In her mid-30s, she attended university on a work–study schol-arship, and majored in studio art. Ultimately, she got an MFA, and spent six months in Japan as an exchange student studying ancient glazes. When she returned, she would have stayed in Arkansas, except that she'd decided to become famous. "I thought I owed it to my parents, who never made me work and recognized that I had talent. Before he died, I promised my father that I'd make him proud."

It's just that now, she's become conflicted. That is, she believes that pursuing art when people are out of work and desperate is immoral. "At the least, I could be making life better for someone," she said. "Instead, I'm just helping con-sumers to consume even more." She acknowledges her promise to her father, but thinks he would understand. "Dad was very independent, and he'd want me to do what I thought was right."

Sometimes what people think is right, they ultimately regret. Like Julie's father, who uprooted the family and ended up in a situation that was even worse. So, I saw my job as counseling Julie based on her long-term best interests – not just what assuaged her immediate sense of guilt. I thought, in fact, that she'd feel guilty no matter what she did, since neither course was without emotional challenges.

So, I asked her, "Look, do you really want to give up everything you've worked so hard for, just to become an anonymous cog in the machine that tries to rebuild the City? Maybe the City *needs* people who add beauty to what could be a dreary phase in its history." But Julie had a retort. "The real need is now. I can contribute skill and compassion." Yes, so could we all. But that doesn't mean that we walk away from what we've built and loved and seen that other people love. Perhaps she could donate some of her profits – 10 percent? – to a group that's helping individuals recover. "It's not that money is a substitute for personal engagement. But engagement whose price is a significant personal loss, as well as the loss of a necessary beauty, is not a good trade-off."

Fundamentally, Julie wasn't sure that making art – making beauty – for its own sake had any place in our current environment. She felt guilty about it. She reduced herself to some marginal actor when, at the center of things, she saw people were cooking meals, teaching other people how to restart businesses, and going to bat with the government for increased aid to cities like New York. "I could become a lobbyist. I could work to get the right people elected." Sure, we can imagine all kinds of possibilities for ourselves that are noble, selfless, and possibly even draw on our last reserves of energy. But is any of this wise? "You don't even have a clear plan yet," I said. "You've got to think this through."

Finally, I suggested that putting herself out of business would just add to the City's troubles. "Maybe you do the most good by serving as an example – you're surviving, so other people can see that it's possible." "Yes," she said, "but I've got something to sell." Precisely. Maybe other people can do the same.

I'm not sure how Julie will resolve her dilemma. Decent people suffer in times of calamity, because they're torn over how best to help. In the end, the point is for Julie to be at peace with her decision – not just now, but in the long term.

WRITER'S BLOCK

"I've got writer's block," said my patient Geoff. "I can't imagine the future any-more." Geoff writes science fiction, and inhabits the future for a living. Cosmic wormholes, parallel universes, the Heat Death of the sun – he loves the stuff. He's there. He came in last week with "Hey, did you read *The End of Everything (Astrophysically Speaking)*? It blew me away." But it all went downhill after that. For Geoff, the virus makes the future unintelligible. It's opaque. "Who can say anything about tomorrow? It's a blur as far as the eye can see."

Think about that. According to a guy who imagines whole geospheres (or whatever he calls them), the prospects for humanity are so dicey that no specu-lation – however well-crafted – will allow a reader to suspend their disbe-lief. As Geoff observed, science fiction only works if it's plausible, if maybe it really could happen the way that an author suggests. "You know, like in *The Andromeda Strain*, or *Prey*, Crichton makes you believe it's possible." But Geoff doesn't think he can get anyone to take his plots seriously because the virus could muck us up for the next several generations. "Either the virus is the story, or I become a journalist and write about yesterday."

As a psychiatrist, my job is to listen to people and help them . . . not to listen and become so fascinated that I want to hear more just *because* it's fascinating. I have to be curious in a way that allows me to make sense of a person's story and help them see their situation clearly – then see a way forward. Geoff did not have an ordinary problem. He was depressed, in his way, and even debilitated. But I sensed something more complicated. He was afraid that nothing would be possible from here on out without accounting for the virus. He spoke as if it had parked here and, however much we went about our business, our "business" was only possible insofar as the virus permitted it. For Geoff, the virus was an occupying army.

Unless we kicked that army out, he couldn't imagine any future that wasn't controlled by the virus, and couldn't imagine a reader who didn't see the future the way he did. "If I write about SpaceX going to Mars, I have to put the virus onboard. You know, NASA is actually interested in how viruses behave in space."

When I finally got us back down to earth, I realized that if we were going to tackle his writer's block, we'd had to think about it as a form of despair. But I couldn't just say "Oh, come off it. We'll have a vaccine next year." Geoff didn't think so. He also claimed that the virus could mutate, maybe exchange genes with the flu and make the flu turn into a deadly killer. It was possible. Then he really threw me. "The real problem is the culture. I think it will be dystopian." Translation: Geoff didn't see people as venturing out much, let alone to Mars, and he thought we'd stay focused on the personal, the parochial, the immedi-ately gratifying. "The only plausible future is boring," he declared.

So how do you get around that? How do you even begin?

I asked if he'd talked with other science fiction writers. There were lots of Facebook clubs and dozens of dedicated organizations (how about Science

Fiction & Fantasy Writers of America?). He hadn't talked with anyone, in part he said because he saw no point. "I can't shake this. It's what I think."

In a way, being a psychiatrist requires Stanislavski-like preparation. In empathizing, you imagine yourself as your patient, you get into their head, think the way they would . . . so then you can think around them, and help them get past their impasse. I turned myself into a would-be science fiction writer, and asked: What would I do if I thought the virus would blight humanity for the foreseeable future? Answer: I wouldn't write about humanity. So, I asked if there were other places that he might write about.

He perked up.

After staring for maybe a lightyear, he said, "Look, I could write about the future on some other planet. Maybe they're checking us out; maybe they don't like what they see."

I never thought I'd suggest an idea for a plot to a blocked-up science fiction writer. But reality can be even stranger than (science) fiction. I decided to enjoy this . . . adventure.

But I also had another objective. I thought that if I could get him thinking in new directions, he'd experience himself again as creative. Maybe then he'd turn back to his natural subject: human beings. Maybe he'd see that he had a supple enough imagination so that if he could write about aliens eyeing us, he could write about us eyeing aliens. There would be a transition. He could, perhaps, get used to thinking about his own kind once again – and, in the process, find a way forward.

I was intrigued to know how Geoff would ultimately respond. A psychiatrist's worst fear is that you'll suggest a path that isn't right for the patient but that he'll follow it. (It's important for a patient to choose for himself and then own those choices.) I like when a patient second-guesses me, and penetrates my *modus operandi* for bringing him around. That is, maybe Geoff would take my suggestion but then fix it. After all, Geoff was a great inventor of plots, always thinking five moves ahead so that no character messed up any other (until they were supposed to).

In any case, something was happening. Maybe we were leaving gravity behind.

Sometimes being an amateur – or in this case, a total novice – has advantages. You approach a problem in ways that the pro would never hit on (they're so practiced doing one thing, that it never occurs to them to try something radically different). Geoff went for it. "You know," he said, "if I escaped earth's orbit for a while, maybe my head would clear out." He often spoke in cosmic terms, so I picked up on him: "A few light-years' perspective couldn't hurt." I was enjoying the ride.

What I was really enjoying, however, was seeing Geoff realize that in this crazy time, where all he could see was absurdity forever, he still had a sense of purpose, even a calling. We started talking about this plausible alien planet – their society, their technology, and whether they'd be so disappointed in us that they'd leave to await our Heat Death in a few billion years. "We don't have to settle that now," I suggested.

I'm cautiously optimistic that Geoff will get past his worst fears about the virus' long-term ravages. I hope he does; I hope that circumstances allow him to – or, at least, that he'll find some grounds for a plausible optimism. But that's not the point. During this period, where we are venturing out but unwilling to project too far into the future, we still have to remain effective – able to function as well as possible. Thus, my initial objective with Geoff was not, simplistically, to change his mind. Rather, it was to allow him to see possibility even amidst all his doubts and uncertainty. He was beginning to doubt himself, and if I could help turn that around I was doing my job.

A lot of our fixes feel provisional now. They're not, necessarily, aimed at the long haul and at who we are in some fundamental sense. They're aimed at getting us to the next day. You remember that old Kris Kristofferson song, "Help Me Make It Through the Night" (1969)? It offers a fitting time-frame. If Geoff can't imagine the future of humanity, he can – I hope – at least keep himself together and productive for now.

DRINKING

Several of my patients have put on weight during this pandemic – less exercise, less discipline, less distance to the fridge. Their jowls fill my screen a little more each week. We talk about sensible diets, but I'm not sure they really care. They prefer the pop psychology that counsels "Reward yourself. This is no time for deprivation. Keep up your spirits however you can." Short of telling people to go rob a bank ("You deserve it, honey!"), such advice can still do lots of damage. It lets people off the hook.

Of course, any decent advice would cite the difference between having fun – which is necessary for staying sane – and the unbridled self-indulgence that leads to grabbing at whatever one feels like. In the latter case, some self-restraint is required . . . but where is it when we're still working from home and barely socializing? That is, for many people such restraint as they experience is externally imposed: peer pressure ("Hey, are you pregnant?"), or maybe just the logistics of heating up a ramen cup on company time. Now that they're home, all bets are off.

I thought about the more pernicious temptations that come with sequestering when I spoke to my patient George. George was always a social drinker, and would knock back a few with the guys after work on Friday. But then he knew when to stop. He'd get home, sleep it off, and be himself again when it came to partying on Saturday. "I never thought I was an alcoholic," he said. "I never drank alone."

The pandemic, however, made him think about drinking in a different way. "I was feeling sorry for myself. I was so lonely." It would start after he signed off his computer around 5:30, wondering what to do with himself. "I got bored, so I drank." After a while, he'd nurse a beer, maybe starting around 4:00, and once he even had it by him during a late-afternoon Zoom meeting. It got so that he stopped making excuses for himself, and just drank starting after lunch. By dinnertime, he was sloshed – "and of course, I had to have wine with dinner." Usually, he'd finish the bottle.

So, we spoke about his increasing need for drink. Was it the effect of the pandemic (the loneliness, the boredom), or was there something else that the pandemic aggravated? It's often the case that a low-grade persistent stress can get much worse when we become more inward-directed – as we do when we're lonely – and then set off behaviors that (otherwise) we'd control because we're actively engaged with others.

As it turned out, George's isolation had aggravated fears that he'd been unwilling to face . . . fears that he was now trying to submerge in drink.

George was in his late 20s, and had a solid job as a computer programmer. Work from home? No problem. Flex-time? Choose your hours. It was great. But for the past couple of years, he'd wrestled with being gay. He'd always known it, actually, but now he hated it. In college, he could hang out with a small crowd of gay men, and nobody cared. But now, in New York and in a professional setting, he resisted the club scene ("I hate that whole Pride thing"); he resisted what he thought was a kinky aesthetic; and he didn't want to be hit on by other gay men at work. "I want to be a straight gay, if you know what I mean."

What he meant was that he wanted to live with someone like himself – quiet, conservative, just going about their business. He'd hoped to meet someone like that at the parties he went to, but he never did. "I never wanted to look gay, and I never gave off the right signals, I guess." The pandemic now just made that impossible, and he couldn't bear meeting anyone on a website. "Have you seen those websites for gays," he asked? "They're hardcore."

So, George just drank, with no one around to stop him or keep him from getting lonely. "I have all the problems of someone trying to date in this environment, with a whole bunch of added problems." I had to agree.

But I also wanted to help. I understood that eventually we'd have to deal with the underlying problem – George's need to express his sexuality on his own terms – but most immediately, we had to address the drinking. George didn't want to attend AA meetings on Zoom. "I'm not a spiritual person, and I'm not interested in other people's spiritual journeys," he said. So, I suggested that there were ways to deal with the loneliness, still short of intimate companionship but more along the lines of hanging out with the guys at work. Less loneliness, less drinking.

"I'm thinking," I said, "that you could join some online groups – maybe work towards something that you care about." I feared he was too deflated to care about anything, but you never know. So, I was surprised by the vehement response: "I'm interested in giving prisoners a fighting chance on their release." It turns out that during college, George had participated in a program that brought students into prisons to teach inmates marketable skills. The inmates loved the human contact, and learned much more quickly than they did online. George had become a convert.

More to the point, he realized that if he was an outsider – a semi-closeted gay – so were the guys he was teaching. He developed enormous empathy for them, and felt that he was "changing the world in advance." He said that he felt part of something important, and loved the team meetings where the students drafted lesson plans in coordination with a professor and the Deputy Warden. "I taught them programming, of course, but it was like I was in the army and we were planning an assault on some beach. There was great esprit de corps."

He might have gone on about his experience for half the session if I hadn't said "Okay, then let's see if you can do something like this again. Remotely, of course, but still in a group." We discussed how he might recruit a few of the guys from work, who were probably as bored as he was. "You'll have their company, at least on Zoom, and then you'll all be involved in the teaching." I pointed out that now, he could even give advice from the inside – "you can tell them what it's like to program, not just show them how it's done."

He said he'd give it a try.

So, my take-away from my conversation with George is that as we continue to emerge from this pandemic, part of the New Normal will consist of figuring out ways to recover from the pandemic's outrages. George felt imprisoned by the pandemic, until helping others who were literally imprisoned brought him some measure of relief. It wasn't going to be a perfect means of recovery since it wouldn't check all the boxes (sex being one of them). But we'll have to accept imperfect, provisional fixes that ameliorate vexing problems. If George stops drinking when he starts making lesson plans, that will be big progress.

Part IV: Life, simplified (not really)

The essays in Part IV are among the last that I published during 2020. They concern the apparent simplification of living on account of fewer choices – a situation that turns out to be just another complication. In this sense, they are about frustration, the short-circuiting of normal pathways. While the pandemic has not gone away (1000 people die in this country every day), it has already left in its wake a changed landscape with fewer roads and burnt-out destinations. It's hard to come to terms with all this. It happened so quickly, and is unlike anything that we've ever experienced. It's scary. Disheartening. It offers a vision of the future that no one wants to contemplate. But, of course, we have to.

My patients feel the effects of this narrowing (they might say harrowing) diminution of choice. The lack of child-care, for example, exacerbates tensions in a relationship and ultimately causes it to fracture. Children pick up notions of a cramped, grayscale future without the bursting primary colors that, until recently, they thought would surround them forever. Single people sink into a sea of regrets, blaming themselves for mistakes that have led to unbearable loneliness. The pandemic has exposed feelings that, once hidden or repressed, are now raw and rampant.

Amidst all the resulting disorientation, I experience my own stress. More patients, more grief – it feels so unrelenting. I force myself to stay focused, I worry that my patients will start worrying about *me*. We're all in this together, I keep thinking, psychiatrists included.

But still, there are times when it's one-step-backward, two-steps-ahead. A parent is able to teach her child about the perils of zealotry, and of how not to take on the scofflaws of this world who do not wear masks and do not maintain social distancing. Children are learning about the world in ways that they might not have until many years later. Adults are learning how to speak to children about matters that are serious, sensitive, the kind of stuff from which they would normally have been shielded.

If the pandemic accelerates breakdown – as it did in some patients' relationships – it also accelerates maturation, awareness, what we might call the development of character. In Part IV, I have tried to illustrate some of this rapid, radical change.

During the period covered by these essays, I treated several patients who confronted change not just in one area of their lives but in the context of total transformation. With careers shut down because of the pandemic, they had to literally reinvent themselves. A multi-lingual events planner, for example, now has to draw on skills that used to be ancillary but may now come to define an entirely new career. At least for now. The possibility of a return to the *status quo ante* is always out there, but no one can count on it and it would be foolish to assume that we'll all just go back to our previous lives. In the process of making provisional changes, we become new people.

In the process of compensating for missed opportunities, we discover others. Thus, a painter whose first-ever solo show was postponed for several months, uses the time to perfect his technique and further define his artistic identity. The postponement is not exactly a blessing in disguise, but it is a chance to think, grow, and experiment against the day when he can re-enter the market. All is not lost. People find ways to be resilient even amidst the narrowing, even closure, of customary paths – and even if they suspect that the provisional may turn into a sort of New Permanent. Think of rivers that are dammed, and burst out in other directions.

Of course, some patients do better than others. A rabbi who has not held open services for months is deeply depressed. He is also wracked with guilt, concerned that he may have caused people to get sick by encouraging them to pray in small groups. All I can do is to help him to take this one day at a time – we are all in a learning mode.

As the stories in Part IV unfold, I do not mean them to be the "last word" on how this pandemic will play out. Rather, they offer a snapshot in time, a glimpse into people's fears and concerns as the pandemic lumbers on. By implication, Part IV exposes the advantages that some people have – those in stable relationships with secure jobs – over everyone else. I see the people with problems. I have thought hard about how the nature of these problems has changed from the beginning of the pandemic (say, mid-March) through to the autumn. At first, what I saw was generalized fear, founded on massive uncertainty. Now, however, as we have become accustomed to living in uncertainty, the problems are more nuanced. They involve trying to find ways through the maze of closures towards some sort of manageable existence. It's a difference in degree, really, but still a big difference.

One effect of trying to navigate around the closures, disappointments, and last year's obsolete detritus is that our horizons are foreshortened. We think in shorter segments of time – if I can just get through today (without strangling my kids); if I can just get through this month (and still maintain the semblance of a career). Plans look different now. They have a shorter duration; they're more fluid. Very little is cast in stone. As always, the point is to adjust, to go with the flow so that we don't drown. Not all, but many of the people in Part IV have figured out how. So here are their stories.

PARTING WAYS

COVID-19 has made bad situations worse. People with relationship problems became estranged. Beer drinkers graduated to gin. It's the result of more stress and fewer outlets for stress. And that's not all. Just as society (gingerly) reopens, and we expect things to improve (more or less), it's stressful just to realize that things aren't all that better. We're still wearing masks. The economy is still shaky. Nobody's rejoicing. "Wasn't the curve supposed to have an 'upswing'?" one of my patients asked. Dismay feeds on itself, and our feelings – about ourselves, about our world – keep spiraling downwards.

Such was the case with my patient Brett, a film producer I've worked with for years. He's married to a partner at a law firm, Karen, who works 80-hour weeks. One of their two boys is moderately autistic, and may never live independently. But when Brett worked on-site and the kids were in school, the family bumped along. He resented Karen's frequent nights at the office ("She actually has a convertible sofa!"), and her travel to client meetings ("Why can't lawyers just Zoom?"), but there was always help in the evenings. Always "was." The situation was just waiting for COVID to disrupt it.

In fact, since the lockdown, Brett has been stuck at home; the kids have no summer activities; and Karen is afraid to admit outside help. Brett's domestic duties have doubled. He refers to himself as a Child Custodian who happens to produce movies from home. Or tries to.

It's not that Karen is still at her office. It's just that when the family moved to their country home in April, she took the office with her. She now spends 12-hour days on the computer, and starts calling China at 6 a.m. Shortly after the move, Brett thought things would improve ("Well, at least she can't travel"), but they didn't. "If anything, they're worse," he said. "She's here but she isn't." He feels like she's snubbing him. The resentment has grown.

When Brett came to see me recently (on Zoom), he'd ramped up his drinking. He said he'd always enjoyed a drink, like when he huddled with the writers on a script. So what? But now, without the usual professional constraints, it had become a problem. At first it was just a beer when the kids went to bed; then he added one while they were having supper; then when they were having lunch and supper; then there was the night-cap – a few shots of scotch. Karen was incensed. She warned that she'd throw him out of the house and divorce him if the drinking didn't stop. He really tried to stop. But when Karen was away on travel a couple of weeks ago (yes, during the pandemic), he relapsed. When she called one night, he was passed out on the couch. The younger boy, around 10 years old, answered and described the situation. When she returned, she insisted that he leave. He returned to their apartment in the City.

Now they've been separated for a couple weeks. He speaks on FaceTime with the boys every day, and he visited them one of the weekends. He's sobered up and joined AA (virtually). But AA was not a great fit for his binge drinking and, even though he's committed to sobriety, he envisions the inevitable relapse. "Look," he said, "I had too much of the kids, and now I don't have enough. Either way, it's stress."

Worse still, when he'd visited over the weekend, his wife rejected his affection. Sex with Karen had been lackluster for several years, but Brett told himself that was due to her punishing schedule. But now, she made clear that they'd drifted apart for good. "She said, 'Maybe it's my fault. But I don't have the time or the interest to work on it.'" When he got back to Manhattan that evening, predictably he drank three scotches in an hour.

When we next spoke, I asked about what he hoped might happen. He said that he loves his kids, which he clearly does, and thought it was better that they all be together. He even reaffirmed his commitment not to drink. But then he paused, and said, "You know, it's hard when your wife doesn't want you. I'm actually sort of stuck."

Indeed, he was. Marriage is hard enough when you're raising conventionally abled children. Disabled kids add a whole new dimension of responsibility and commitment. So, we spoke about whether Karen's obsession with work might have been her response to (retreat from) the stress of her son's disability. We spoke about whether her rejection of Brett was a type of displaced guilt, since Brett had accepted the responsibility of raising their son, however imperfectly. I said that since the pandemic, with the usual buffers now removed, all of this is out in the open. "The stress and guilt have been there for a while, but now they're greater. They're out in the open when, before, they were kind of repressed."

That made sense to him. He asked, with a hint of absurdity, "So, you think a vaccine will get us back to where our pathologies are just simmering?"

No, actually. What wasn't said, now has been.

So, Brett is living apart from his wife and kids. He spoke with his wife a couple of times, but she was indifferent to patching things up. "She doesn't want me back," he acknowledged. He said that even though they loved each other, it was – at least for her – an "abstraction," a memory of how they once were. "That was before the kids and the partnership." He said that had the virus not hit, they might have continued a while longer. "But I guess this has crystallized everything. She basically wants a lover, not a family with responsibility."

So, at least in Brett's mind, the virus accelerated what would have happened anyway. He said he'd probably known about Karen's feelings for years, but hadn't wanted to face it. "Maybe that's another reason I started to drink – the kids, of course, but also that growing sense that we were finally breaking up."

"Did Karen know too?" I asked. "Maybe," he said, "but she was too busy to care, and I made it easy for her." The problem, I thought, was that Karen never knew how to set boundaries. She was all-in or absent. She chose absence, if just to protect herself.

Over the years, I'd met with them a few times as a couple, and it helped – for a while. But Brett was now pretty sure that nothing would help, and that it was probably just as well. I asked if he thought this was okay for the kids. "No, but what's the choice? Kids pick up on a bad marriage, and I can't put them through that." He thought maybe she'd find someone else once the pandemic was over.

In this time of COVID, a lot of relationships are experiencing external stresses that exacerbate the stress that already exists. You could say that people are finding themselves in the process. But they are also losing what has mattered to them for a long time. There will never be a vaccine against that.

TEACHING THE PANDEMIC

In a few posh enclaves on Long Island, like where I live, neighbors have pulled their kids out of school for the semester to study in "pods" – face-to-face with teachers and classmates, no contaminated buildings, no distractions at the edge of a screen. These alternate-reality schools try to impart a sense of normalcy: sports, drama classes, lots of spontaneous interaction. My patient Leah came out of retirement to teach in one. "I thought it would be fun," she said. "I miss the kids." Until about three years ago, Leah taught English at a local middle school. She started seeing me now, however, because things haven't turned out as she expected.

The students are privileged, articulate, and eager to learn. There are no discipline problems. But Leah has never taught kids as obviously troubled, and she is not sure how to respond. Since mid-August, when the semester began, the level of stress among her students has only increased. "I can tell from what they write," she said. "They're worried about the future. They think they'll fall behind and never catch up."

Figure IV.1 Dish with sailing ship

Leah feels stunned by what the kids express, paralyzed, out of her element. She wants to understand her responsibility, whether she's just an innocent by-stander or something more – a designated Good Samaritan, perhaps, who cares and gets personally involved. "I'm a grandma, you know. I can listen." She wonders whether the kids are reaching out to her, indirectly, in carefully constructed essays that nonetheless scream for help. She wonders whether the kids are conscious of how they're reacting, and whether their parents even know. "Should I tell the parents," she asks?

Leah began to sense something wrong when she assigned *Billy Budd*, a middle school classic about a teen-age sailor who is hung for striking an officer on a British warship. Herman Melville left it unfinished at his death in 1891, and it quickly assumed a status in his oeuvre second only to *Moby Dick*. "I've taught that book for years," she said. "The kids always read it as a morality tale – you know, about duty, injustice, the big issues that you want them to think about." Except this year, when they started taking it personally. "They identify with Billy. They feel they're caught in an upheaval, like he was in the mutiny, and that they're just as helpless."

Here are kids from affluent homes, and they worry, figuratively speaking, that their lives are being cut short. Leah showed me the essay of one boy, Ian, who is 14. In part, he wrote:

> Billy wasn't far from my age. He was the victim of circumstances beyond his control. He never wanted to be in the British navy. But they got him. Then he had no way to defend himself, even though almost everyone loved him. In the end, there was no way out of the inevitable. You see it coming. I feel that Billy could have been somebody if they hadn't got hold of him. Now I'm in the same situation. So are all the people around my age. Instead of the navy, it's the virus. But it's the same thing. We started out thinking we were going somewhere. But we are going somewhere else, and it won't be as good.

Ian's fears were typical, said Leah. Despite their parents' cossetting, the kids had picked up on news about the economy, job losses, colleges closing, and a general contraction of opportunity. They seem to have taken it personally. They seem to have assumed that they were part of a developing story – a developing catastrophe – that would hang them up. Like Billy. More or less forever, since the kids coming after them would not suffer the same disabilities. "In their minds," said Leah, "they're competing with kids they'll never even meet, since they'll never catch them."

As a psychiatrist, I could see depression in the works – a feeling of being had by "circumstances." Leah, a literary type, saw irony – that being in a "pod" made the kids see everything outside as dysfunctional, a threat from which they're artificially protected. One kid even wrote, "Our parents just outsmarted themselves." It was as if their parents' money, and admittedly good intentions, couldn't change anything. They saw Billy as the future.

Before she had come to me, however, Leah had tried to change the subject. She assigned parts of Ben Franklin's *Autobiography* (1790), the classic paean to

American opportunity. "I thought it would be the counterpoint to *Billy Budd*. America isn't the British navy." But it didn't work. The kids' basic take was that nobody needed a college education in the 18th century because the country was wide open. All you needed was to be smart, like Franklin. And even Franklin started out with good connections. "He had a letter of recommendation," wrote one girl. It was as if they were determined to write themselves out of the American Dream.

Leah wondered whether this was adolescent hysteria, which they'd grow out of by the time they got to high school and reconnected with all their friends. But she worried. She wasn't sure. Earlier in her career, if a child seemed troubled, she'd suggest a visit to the school counselor. The counselor could decide whether to involve the parents. But this pop-up pod had no counselors, just a few teachers with no real training in adolescent psychology.

"So, what should I do?" she asked. "I'm afraid that if I offer some advice, I'll say something wrong. The parents might become upset." Tough question. I wondered about my own kids, who were somewhat younger than Ian but very aware – what are they thinking? Are they telling me?

As we spoke, I realized that Leah had come to care about these kids, not least because she saw them as articulate representatives of millions of others. She said she'd feel guilty if she did nothing. Indeed, I thought it was good to take on their fears, so long as she didn't transgress their parents' expectations (which, according to her contract, was to teach them American literature). So, I suggested, "Why not have a few lessons on young people who've overcome adversity? Helen Keller's autobiography, *The Story of My Life* [1903], would be a great place to start." In other words, have the kids think about, and talk openly about how the worst disabilities imaginable – being deaf and blind – couldn't keep a smart person from becoming world-class.

Up until now, the kids had been open about their fears in their written work, while in class they discussed the books and characters in conventional terms. It was as if they didn't want their peers to know how they felt – how the books reflected how they felt. I suggested that urging the kids to be open, to share their feelings, while appreciating Helen Keller's success, might give them some perspective. "If they can see adversity as part of the human condition – part of what they share right now – but see people who've found a way through it, that could help." Helen Keller had a devoted teacher, Anne Sullivan, and they have teachers who care about them.

Of course, the kids felt anxious. But Leah said she would try to meet them where they are, under cover of their peers' added support. "At least I don't want them to feel like nobody knows and nobody cares." It was somewhere to start.

GERMAPHOBIA

"I think I've become a germaphobe," said my patient Derek. "I've been wearing gloves when it's 90 degrees outside." Even before the pandemic, Derek showed signs of obsessiveness – he never stopped checking up on manuscripts

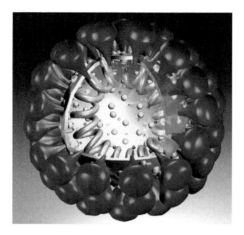

Figure IV.2 Coronavirus

he'd submitted to journals ("Did you receive it?" "Is it in the queue?" "Have reviewers been assigned?"), and he kept rearranging mice in their lab cages so they wouldn't get bored with their cage-mates ("You can't take the mouse-mind for granted," he'd muse). Derek was a scientist at a local university, specializing in behavioral research. But increasingly, he'd become concerned about his own behavior. He kept worrying about germs everywhere.

The pandemic has sharpened a lot of our worries. If we were financially stressed, we're now petrified. If the rent seemed confiscatory, now we dread eviction. In the case of ever-present germs (justifiably menacing if we take the subway), we now feel their nasty receptors binding onto us to death. COVID-19 has only heightened our awareness of microscopic trouble-makers.

In Derek's case, the cause for alarm hasn't stopped with the new coronavirus. Now he worries over every germ he might meet. The other night, for example, when he took some chicken out of the freezer, he first checked the FDA website to find out if bacteria are killed when food is stored at 0^0. When he found out that they were only deactivated, and could reproduce again once the food was thawed, he panicked. "I cooked that chicken 'til it was like concrete," he said. He's stopped eating salads ("you've heard about that spinach scare . . . and then there was the lettuce!"), and he thought about washing fruit in Clorox.

You wouldn't know about Derek's germaphobia just watching him resist COVID-19. He's sensible about the virus, and wears a mask wherever he goes. His university has partially reopened, and mandates masks on campus. It urges frequent hand washing and, for personnel who work in labs, it requires weekly tests ("they don't want us killing off the postdocs – bad for business," he jokes).

But what has started Derek worrying is how his obsessions, which we've been working on for years, now seem to have burgeoned into looming hysteria. He's tried to keep what he calls his "germ-craze" from other lab-members by getting in early to clean, but it's begun interfering with ongoing experiments. "I threw out an open beaker of nutrient," he said, "because it could have been contaminated. The person who was using it spent hours getting the titer just right again."

So, the question became: how do you deal with excessive obsessions when, in principle, the motivation is reasonable but the person has begun taking it to extremes? When symptoms such as obsessions interfere with functioning, they rise to the level of a disorder. So obsessive traits burgeon into Obsessive Compulsive Disorder (OCD). Derek became a successful scientist by paying attention to detail, and checking and rechecking his work for error. He's trained a generation of postdocs to be scrupulous, and working in his lab is considered a smart career move. It's just that now, what was by-the-book has become conspicuously nuts.

Over the past several years, Derek and I have spoken about his father's inability to hold a job. One year, his father worked as an office manager in an electronics company, making sure that orders were processed. But he was fired when there were missed deliveries. Then he worked at a gym, putting out towels and re-shelving equipment. That went bust too, and he ended up in construction until he was hit by falling sheetrock and fell backwards – hurting his back. He retired on disability, and Derek's mother had to go out to work. She resented working while taking care of the family, and Derek thought she cut corners. Once, when Derek's sister was selling Girl Scout cookies, Derek's mother handed in all the order slips without counting who had ordered what. When 76 boxes of Chocolate Mint arrived, and half the people had wanted the Shortbread, that did it for Derek. "I swore that I'd never be like them."

It's common for children, who find fault in their parents, to want to be different. So, Derek became a stickler. Everything had to be just right. He'd sometimes arrange the food on his plate so that vegetables didn't touch meat. He liked order and predictability. He hated anything messy . . . which may account for why he still lives alone. He has a girlfriend, but they've never been able to find a place together. The issue is her casual house-keeping. "I actually think it's disgusting," he says, "but around her I just complain about the dust."

Except now. The relationship has taken a dramatic turn. Before the pandemic and Derek's germaphobia, they'd have sex maybe twice a week. Derek would stay over and then leave for work early the next morning. Now Derek is reluctant to have sex unless his girlfriend has changed the sheets in the morning. He insists that they both scrub up before they get into bed, and then he jumps into the shower as soon as they're finished. "I know that's not exactly romantic," he said, "but I just can't stop worrying about germs." His girlfriend thinks he sees her as dirty. He won't even share breakfast with her anymore ("she has no dishwasher"), and he's afraid that she'll get sick – or at least sick of him.

The psychological effects of COVID-19 can splay off in extreme directions. Derek is not afraid that his girlfriend will infect him with it, so much as that she might have something else that is lurking in the biome. The same is true for all his other contacts. For the first time in ages, he said, he feels like that kid in his parents' house, afraid that trouble is everywhere. "You don't know when to expect something, so you have to be vigilant." His girlfriend resents being lumped in with everyone else.

Obsessive compulsive symptoms can be deeply embedded in a person's behavior. Sometimes they don't even notice. Derek is aware enough, at least, to notice the outcroppings of his condition. He recognizes that a stressor like COVID-19 can kick his condition into overdrive. So, we've talked about how he can deal with this latest manifestation. Even though, ultimately, we want to work through the fundamental causes of why he reacts so obsessively, I recently suggested starting a serotonergic reuptake inhibitor (SSRI) like Prozac, which can help with symptomatic relief.

We also discussed other approaches that touch on exposure therapy. Like the next time Derek visits his girlfriend, he should try being more relaxed and maybe stay for breakfast. If he remains healthy (as I was sure he would) then he can relax a little more. He could try getting into the lab a little later, permitting the postdocs to clean up their own spaces as they see fit. I teased, "If there is no contamination, and the experiments work out, then maybe you've found a new protocol!"

One way to address OCD is to allow the person some exposure to what stimulates their undesired reaction, and then let them realize that they've survived. Then they can move on, exposing themselves a little more until the obsessive reaction is manageable.

Of course, COVID-19 is no joke. We can't become complacent. But neither can we permit it to become a universal stressor that aggravates every corner of our complex mental environment. We have to stay sane, despite it. Or perhaps, paraphrasing Friedrich Nietzsche, "What does not kill me (ought to make) me (at least a little) stronger."

PAINTING THE PANDEMIC

"I'm so damn frustrated," said my patient Paul. He actually wanted to talk in person because, he insisted, "all this virtual stuff is ruining my life." Paul was an artist whose first gallery show was postponed from May to November. The gallery that represents him was closed from March to August and, on reopening, had reassigned his show's place in the queue. In the interim, some of his work was posted online but, according to Paul, "no one buys an artist they don't know from just looking at digital images." What Paul hoped would be his breakthrough was, in his mind, a dud.

The pandemic has postponed a lot of events like, for example, big splashy weddings. But in Paul's case, this show was to be a coming out, an affirmation of his identity as a legitimate, practicing artist. "It's on a par with when I came out as gay," he said. "It's my identity." He thought that when people saw his work – and bought it – they'd be affirming that identity. In his view, being an artist wasn't just painting *per se*; it was interacting with people who love you and love what you do. "I've been waiting so long for this moment, and now I have to wait six months more."

The wait was especially significant to Paul because he'd waited so long to start painting in the first place. Now in his mid-30s, he'd started off as a Civil Engineer. "I built bridges and highways," he said. "Big stuff." He'd always loved lines and precision – the way pieces fit together and click into place. Civil engineering seemed like a good fit. But as he began to practice, and joined a firm, he'd felt isolated. "It's a very macho profession. The guys who design the bridges have this affinity for the guys who build them." As a gay man, he didn't feel part of the culture. He began wondering what else he could do.

In his late 20s, he started taking classes at the Art Students League, the storied West Side institution whose alumni include Winslow Homer, Thomas Hart Benton, Maurice Sendak, Helen Frankenthaler, Thomas Hoving, Mark Rothko, Peter Max . . . towering figures in American art. It was instant acceptance all around. "After about a week, I knew that I belonged. I couldn't get enough." By the time he'd finished studying, he'd begun to develop a distinctive style. "I wasn't just abstract or figurative. I was somewhere in the middle, but with very clear outlines."

Paul's training in math and engineering had set him apart from the other students and, right away, he'd set off on a personal adventure. His teachers didn't always know what to do with him, but they saw that he had talent and they let him develop it. "The great thing about the League," he said, "is that they don't straightjacket you." Paul's been on his own now for a couple of years, so when he finally got the gallery show he was ecstatic.

"I know I'm good," he told me. "I don't need validation. What I do need is to get known." Paul wanted to become part of the art world, with his works auctioned at Christie's. He wanted his work to be photographed, discussed, featured in *Artforum*. He had fantasies of Chinese billionaires giving him commissions. "Maybe when John Grisham writes his next novel about some killer law firm, they'll have my work on the walls." While I suppressed a smile, I realized quickly that Paul was not an egotist. Rather, he felt that he'd built an identity – sort of the way he'd carefully design a bridge – and he wanted to live that identity to the max.

The delay was a delay in making his identity manifest.

It was also having collateral, more pernicious effects. Paul said that during this period of protracted waiting – to which he now added the year or so of waiting until he'd found a gallery to represent him – he'd been unable to paint with the same intensity that he'd displayed while at the League. "You know," he said, "other people are part of who you are, and if they're not around to encourage you then you can't be all of who you are." He cited Andy Warhol and The Factory, the group with Andy at the center that revolutionized art in the '60s. "I'm not fully inhabiting my identity," he said.

So, the question was how to tide Paul over from late August to November when, he was sure, his show would bring sales, commissions, and the buzz that he needed.

I reassured him that his was a common predicament. Creative people frequently run out of energy when they're isolated. Their logical minds can taunt them – "hey, why bother if nobody knows and nobody cares?" We can be our own worst enemies, questioning our place in a vast Rubik's Cube that's perpetually under construction. So, I told him "Look, you've waited this long, you can wait a few months longer. In the meantime, try to think of yourself as preparing for a great reception." I thought that if he looked forward to being recognized (rather than backwards at all the down-time), he'd rev himself up and paint furiously. "Don't you want to be ready?" I asked.

The pandemic is a study in delay and postponement. One patient told me, "I feel six months younger than I am. The past six months didn't happen."

But we can't just suspend who we are. We have to act *as if* the world is coming to meet us – sooner or later, but eventually. In Paul's case, at least he has a pretty firm date.

I suggested that instead of fretting, he could further develop his technique. I've seen photos of Paul's work, and I was impressed. There is an intriguing tension between figurative and abstract elements that seemed to waver – sometimes one element seemed to dominate, sometimes the other. "Does this represent a tension in how you want to represent the world?" I asked. "Maybe it's something to work out on canvas."

Paul said that every painting was its own unique take on the world, and that maybe he really hadn't worked out some larger vision. "Maybe I need to think about that. I know that I like outline, but I should probably figure out how I approach shape." That sounded interesting, and like a useful way to fill up his time. I pointed out that theorizing one's work is often a late development, after one has enough actual work to think about. "Sounds like this is a good time to start," I said.

As we emerge from the first acute stages of this pandemic, and try to recapture some sense of living in a present that actually does "happen," it's important to figure out what we can actually do to make it happen and to connect with the future. Paul's initial option – waiting for the other shoe to drop – wasn't much of an option at all, and seemed in practice to be self-defeating. If we are going to look to the future, we have to be ready for it. We have to make ourselves ready for it.

BACK TO SCHOOL

"I'm not sure if I'm in school or I'm not," said Beth, whom I treat for moderate ADD and an array of teenage anxieties. For many kids, the new hybrid schedules – one week in class, the next week on Zoom – can be disorienting. "As soon as I become familiar with my environment," Beth complained, "they change it." She understands that on/off attendance is supposed to protect her, but she thinks it reflects a homogenizing tendency that overlooks how some people learn. "Maybe most kids don't need steadiness, but I do," she insists.

She's afraid that she'll fall behind. She's resentful (of the virus? of her school? of her own limitations?), and calls the alternate weeks of in-person and remote instruction an "alternate reality," a departure from school as it should be.

Beth attends a toney private school on the Upper East Side of Manhattan. She's precocious, and into the petty politics of her classmates, teachers, and the school administration. She and her clique think the school is trying to keep students from worrying because, otherwise, the parents will become worried. "You know," she says, "worry is contagious – like the virus. And if the parents get worried, they could send us somewhere else." Beth feels that the on/off attendance regime, which she dislikes, is really aimed at the parents. She knows that other schools have it too, but that hasn't changed her mind. Her sense of grievance has colored how she thinks about the virus and its impact on her routine.

It's not as if Beth hasn't spoken to her parents about the school's efforts to keep students safe. "I asked my mother whether the on/off stuff isn't just primarily for show. I mean they could have let everyone make their own decisions." According to Beth, she's old enough to make such decisions. But her mother disagrees. She told Beth that the school was acting prudently. She suggested that Beth put up with the "alternate reality," since years from now she'd be grateful that she did. But Beth was disinclined. When she said that maybe other kids would be grateful, but that on/off didn't work for her, her mother said that it was still better than contracting a horrible disease and spreading it to everyone in the family.

Beth heard her mother's comments as selfish, and unwilling to take account of Beth's particular needs. She told me that when we spoke last week. "I had expected her to take my side, and ask the school to make an exception for me." She was disappointed that her mother had not stood up for her. In fact, she was surprised, since her mother was active in the Parents Association and was always going to bat for more school trips, increased pre-college counseling, and ethnic food options that would introduce the kids to cuisines from around the world ("They had someone from Queens come in and teach us to make Moroccan mint tea," she told me).

Essentially, Beth thought that her mother didn't understand the virus. According to Beth, young people were rarely infected and recovered quickly. "She's willing to trade away my long-term success in school for maybe a mild infection. She wouldn't do that if she thought about it, instead of buying the school's line."

It's amazing what information kids pick up, and how they interpret it to reinforce their own preconceptions – a sort of adolescent confirmation bias. Because Beth didn't like the school's safety protocols, she heard what she wanted to hear in order to oppose them.

I was afraid that if I told Beth that she was mistaken – that she could get a mild case and make everyone else extremely sick – she would say "Well, you would say that. My mother is paying you too!" But I had to try. If she could accept the school's precautions, she'd have less trouble adjusting to them.

She'd do better work. So, I said "Look, we don't know that much about the virus yet. But we do know that kids can bring it home." Her father, one of these Wall Street Alpha Males, has high blood pressure. Her older brother has asthma. Moreover, her grandparents were visiting from Maine. I told her that they were all especially susceptible to severe symptoms. "Think of it this way," I said. "You're a special case, but so are they."

That gave her pause. Until that point, she had been entirely focused on herself and her own perceived needs. She saw no reason why the world couldn't revolve around her, at least insofar as allowing her to attend school full-time when everyone else was alternating in-person and remote attendance. She had not thought through the consequences of her position, if only because she heard what she wanted to hear about the virus. But now she started to listen.

We spoke about the nature of the virus, and how it could be passed from one person to another in confined spaces. "That's why they have you attending alternate weeks. They can seat everyone further apart." She understood. I wanted her to appreciate that she'd allowed herself to process information selectively, so that it wouldn't conflict with desires that she had for herself. This troubled her.

"I'm not selfish, you know. I love my parents and my brother and my grandparents." She started to cry.

I explained that no one was accusing her of being selfish. Rather, she should regard her failure to think through the consequences of her behavior as a learning experience. "You thought you were looking out for yourself, like anyone would. You just didn't appreciate all the information that was out there, and how it could affect your thinking." She replied, "So, I guess I just have to make the best of this on/off for a while. I hope it doesn't hurt me academically."

I suggested that there was no reason to weigh her concern for her own health, and that of others, against her ability to perform. "Now that you know you're doing the right thing you'll accept the new schedule and get on with your schoolwork. At least give it a fair chance." Giving it a "chance" was key. No one was telling her that she *had* to accept anything. I wanted her to know that she could make the effort; that she could use good judgment; that everyone around her wanted the best for her.

During this difficult period, adolescents can chafe at what they see as needless, adult-imposed restrictions. Beth's mother had made her wash her hands constantly. She bought Beth "fashion" masks that Beth thought were supposed to make her think that masks look cool. "They're dumb-looking, no matter the color." Well, maybe. But that's not the point. Once adolescents understand the reason for these requirements, they can take pride in (or at least commit to) adopting them. They can feel part of a community, and become less focused on their personal, immediate desires.

Beth told me that her school requires everyone to wear a mask indoors. I explained that masks are really a protection for others, so that if we each wear one, we protect someone else. "Think of it as doing your part. Like going to class on/off." I hope she got the point.

VIGILANTISM

Kayleigh came to see me after her daughter, Trix, caused an uproar after returning to school. Trix is in 10th grade, "going on 21st," according to her mother. Apparently, and without Kayleigh's knowledge, Trix had organized some of her friends into what she called the Infection Brigade, whose members followed various students after school, watching to see if they adhered to the Governor's rules on mask-wearing and social distancing. When students were seen at a park or congregating at someone's house without observing the rules, their names were posted on a Facebook page. Their parents were called out for not requiring them to behave. "The blowback was horrific," Kayleigh told me. "Of course, I was blamed."

Trix attends a private day school on Long Island. The school makes a point of emphasizing its social consciousness, and has classes in sustainability, diversity, and microfinance of Third World enterprise. The kitchen is solar-powered. Parents of students, many of whom have ties to nonprofit organizations, regularly give lectures on serving the community. Citizenship is drummed into the kids, whose families are activist, money-where-their-mouth is, and unabashedly concerned for the human race.

It's just that this time, it all went awry.

Kayleigh said that Trix had been complaining for weeks that many students, while observing the rules at school, were quick to abandon them once off campus. Trix even wrote a letter to the school newspaper – not naming names, but arguing that these students were endangering others, who could then spread the virus. Trix told Kayleigh, "If I do my part, why shouldn't everybody? That's the school's ethos!" Kayleigh told me that she'd never imagined that Trix would – or could – do anything about these students since, after all, their off-campus actions were beyond the school's jurisdiction.

But then it happened. First the phone calls started to Kayleigh's home. Parents of the named students were incensed. Then students themselves started posting messages about Trix and her parents – even students who were not named, but who thought that the naming-and-shaming was a violation of students' privacy. A few parents, who were lawyers, and whose judgment had been called into question, threatened to sue Kayleigh and her husband for defamation (Trix's parents were legally responsible for her actions because she was a minor). Finally, the school principal sent a letter to Kayleigh asking that the Facebook page be deleted. "This posting has been problematic for the school, its students and our community" it asserted, "and reflects poorly on the values of tolerance and understanding that we seek to instill." The Parents Association asked Kayleigh for an explanation.

Trix stayed home from school for a few days after the uproar (classes were half-remote anyway, so it wasn't that great a sacrifice). But when she did show her face again, some people wouldn't speak to her. Students who'd been part of the Brigade were also shunned, at least to an extent and insofar as they were known. Trix herself was stunned by the response, since she thought she'd acted courageously (actually, she'd expected to be thanked). She took the posting down, but only because there was so much pressure. As she told her mother, "I did what I thought was right. Now those kids will just keep ignoring the rules – and we could suffer."

The question, like many we encounter during the pandemic, is where do we draw the line? There is so much that's gray and uncertain, it's often hard to know.

By the time she came to see me, Kayleigh was mending fences with the school administration, the parents, and the Parents Association (in which she was an active member). Not everyone believed that Trix had acted on her own, and they saw the posting as a betrayal on Kayleigh's part. "I have to defend myself by pointing to Trix, which I hate. And Trix will hate me for it." She really wanted to defend Trix, but wasn't sure who would listen. I could see her dilemma.

But Kayleigh was most concerned about how to talk with Trix regarding what she had done, and the fallout it had produced. "The school teaches social responsibility – do I tell her that only goes so far, and stops when the school or someone you know is disgruntled?" In other words, is all the talk about responsibility just a line? Is it hypocrisy?

I suggested that it wasn't hypocritical not to believe in absolutes. The problem with Trix's action was that she had not understood that social change, to be effective, has to take into account how people will react. "Trix didn't intend to hurt anyone. She really thought that if people were embarrassed, they'd shape up – a naïve assumption, probably based on her own sense of responsibility." Under the circumstances, I thought it unwise to discipline Trix, who clearly had the makings of an idealist. Rather, it would be better to explain to her that actions have to be calibrated to their likely outcomes. If Trix had realized the reaction that the post would provoke, she would have realized that it would be ineffective, and that other means would be better.

We talked about teaching Trix the art of the possible. During this period of immense stress, young people feel that many adults are failing them, and that many of their peers are indifferent. They feel justified in doing whatever they can to defeat the pandemic. Trix is one of these young people. Her mother saw her in a Fauci/Gupta shirt, not-so-silently rebuking the Washington establishment. Certainly, Trix felt that her school, which strives to be progressive, should guarantee that its students were not vectors for the virus. But this just wasn't possible using the bludgeoning, blunt-instrument approach that Trix had adopted. I observed, "Maybe you could have a family discussion about how, while not compromising one's principles, it would be possible to reach the irresponsible students. Maybe the school needs to bring in speakers, offer a mini-course on epidemiology, show a documentary on the Flu outbreak of 1918."

Kayleigh told me that she had such mixed feelings about what Trix had done. On the one hand, of course, she was upset that so many people had been hurt. But on the other, she was proud of Trix. "I can't defend the way she behaved. But I'm proud that she saw a problem and tried to fix it – she has principles." Kayleigh didn't want to discourage Trix from acting on her principles in the future. So, we spoke about how to channel her principles into practical action. To clear the air, Trix wrote a letter to the school newspaper apologizing for what she'd done. But privately she felt this was unjust. "Greta Thunberg never apologized," she told her mother, "so why should I?" Trix then volunteered to organize a series of Zoom discussions about the importance of wearing masks and maintaining social distancing. Everyone was afraid of a Second Wave, her mother explained, and maybe Trix could get some modelers from Columbia to explain the potential.

In other words, there were ways around Kayleigh's dilemma. She could teach Trix about practicality, while still preserving her commitment to strong, principled action. I suggested that as the world changes over the course of this pandemic, people like Trix will have a lot to contribute, maybe even be invaluable with their clear-eyed focus on the human factor in any problem.

GETTING OLD

"I haven't worn a bra since March," said my patient Jean, who's in her mid-70s. "It's not that I don't care anymore – it's just that nothing matters." From Jean's perspective, the ties that bound her to this world were slipping away. Life was narrowing. She felt isolated. In the past month, two of her friends fell on the sidewalk, the result of twitches in their brains that doctors couldn't explain. "Old age, I guess. Nonspecific dilapidation." The events riveted her, making her think that maybe she was next. She came to me dragging a cargo of frightful potential scenarios. She felt that nothing made a difference anymore – except to make things worse. "If I get the virus, it'll be the last straw."

During this pandemic, older people living alone have suffered silently. If they are not sick, they are terrified of getting sick. They cannot see their friends, and the initial Zoom calls have petered out. If back in the spring there was this sense that we're all in this together, now in the fall there is the feeling that things are falling apart. "You know that idea that entropy is inevitable, that it's a slow-motion law of physics? Well, I think we're watching it in real time." Jean can hardly remember when she last had fun. She resents the At Home section of the *New York Times* with its cheery depictions of cooking, gardening, and what she calls the "basket-weaving" view of life. "That's for people with families," she said, "and younger people."

The pandemic has made Jean feel old. Up until it hit, she went to museums. She saw the latest films. She'd have breakfast or lunch with friends. But now nothing. Her married friends have turned inwards, worried about their own health and that of their spouses and grandchildren. Her unmarried friends are

Figure IV.3 Statue with no face

in her own position – basically scared, still sitting out a lockdown that has gradually lifted for other people. Jean wouldn't dare go to a museum, even though they're open now and have adopted social distancing rules. She walks around, but the people in outdoor cafes make her feel left out. "I could always cope with loneliness, maybe just because I had distractions. Now I don't have any," she said.

Last week, it was her birthday, and all these e-greetings arrived from dentists, her bank, her health insurance company, and the firm that manages her retirement account. "Oh, I just could have screamed," she complained. "Not one normal person." The greetings, all commercially motivated, felt dehumanizing. "I wrote to one of those dentists and told him to take me out of his computer – it gave me something to do. Besides, I don't see him anymore anyway." The idea that only a computer would remember your birthday seemed poignant. Jean said that she used to get funny downloadable e-cards from one of her friends, but that now she doesn't.

"You know," she said, "getting old is so impersonal. It's like you're watching yourself become a statistic." The worst part was that while she felt she was aging in other people's estimation (statistics have no individuality), she was also falling in line behind their estimation. Until recently, she hadn't thought of herself as old. But now she does. It's affected everything. She no longer bothers looking for men on Match or Ok Cupid, and Silver Singles makes her feel ancient – "All those 70-year-old guys think they can get 50-year-old women. I'd need some guy on his deathbed." Besides, she didn't think she wanted sex anymore, and all the men did.

Jean had broken up with her last boyfriend about eight years ago, and after that she'd stopped having sex. Now sex seemed like a foreign country. She desperately wanted affection, but didn't see how that was possible now – the virus, for one, and then the tricky position of offering friendship with no "benefits." "No guy wants that. Or at least, he'd never admit to himself that he did." So, the loneliness continues, exacerbated by the threat of getting sick.

Jean had maintained a connection with one old boyfriend who now lived in Boston and taught at a university. She always thought he should have married her, but their timing was out of sync. Now he lived with some wealthy woman. But he'd always come to New York for Jean's birthday – ostensibly for a conference and to see his kids, but he wouldn't have come at just this time if it weren't for her. But of course, this year he couldn't come. He was holed up at the country house that he and his partner owned in Maine, and he was getting ready to teach the semester remotely. Still, he set up a couple of Zoom calls with Jean.

"Oh, I felt so alive! We always have so much fun, and there's such electricity between us." Even on Zoom, which she said made her look ten years older.

But as always when she spoke with Jonathan, there was so much regret. And repressed anger. "I've forgiven him, but I guess I really haven't. Our timing was off because he was so unsettled back then." When she and Jonathan would get together after so many years, she always wanted to tell him how she felt. But she never could. "I know that I grasp at the fleeting revival of how we used to be. I feel like I never stand up for myself when I don't tell him how I feel." She wondered how he felt. But in the end, she said, it didn't matter. She wondered what did.

During this pandemic, we're all trying to define what matters, and jettisoning stuff – like pricey amusements – that seem less important than human connection. We're spending more time with family. Or, as Jean's hated At Home section recommends, taking up activities that provide some diversion. Great. But for some people, Jean among them, "priorities" have lost their meaning. They're unachievable, or at least they believe that they are. For Jean, there's no use trying for new goals when you've already blown past them and inhabit a desert.

Jean's tragedy, which she thinks is commonplace among her silent cohort, is that the pandemic has made her feel old before she was ready to be old. It's closed off outlets that she might have pursued – ephemeral, to be sure, but still energizing and fleetingly meaningful. We talked about what she could do. Her old boyfriend suggested that she write a novel. "You'd be in it," she told him. But she thought he couldn't even imagine how he'd hurt the heroine (herself, of course, though young and beautiful at the time). Still, she thought she might give it a try. The effort might force her even further into herself, and push her into even greater proximity with her demons . . . but it might also be cathartic. "Right now, I have no one to tell how I actually feel. I feel like I want to out myself."

The pandemic has not been easy for people who are aging but still alert, even vigorous. They feel out of sync with all the advice to "adapt" and "grow," but they understand that they have to nonetheless. Though Jean says that nothing matters anymore, she still has a sense of her own dignity. It may matter enough that she tries to preserve it.

SECOND CHANCES

"I've never seen a psychiatrist before," said Blaise in a crisp French accent. "I used to be everyone else's psychiatrist." Blaise was obviously discomfited by the situation, straightening his shirt, rearranging a wine glass and a plate on his desk. He glanced over at a parakeet, then got up to hand it something. Our appointment must have interrupted both their lunches. When our eyes finally met, Blaise's phone rang in his pocket. He moved to shut it off, but not without furtively checking the number. He was out of focus again. I'd learn later why the call might have been important but, for now, Blaise just seemed unable to sit still – i.e. to concentrate. The accent added an element of large-scale, global transitioning, a more long-standing version of his twitching in place.

As we finally began to speak (the parakeet chirping nonstop, as if he wanted in as well), I learned that Blaise had been in this country for ten years. He had emigrated from France, after having tried Montreal for a while and finding it "equally silly." Blaise found French culture grandiose and bizarrely self-obsessed. He wanted no part of it. "I came to the States," he said, "almost how I might have sought a sex reassignment. It was that profound, a flight from everything I was supposed to be." Blaise said that in America, he was finally among people with imagination, who looked to the future and didn't derive vicarious glory from a mythologized, literary past that was long gone if it had ever existed at all. "I'm finally home," he said. The only problem was that now Blaise's life was crumpling, a victim of the pandemic.

When Blaise arrived in the U.S., he saw at once how to build on his Canadian sojourn ("Never let a punk experience go to waste," he said). In Montreal, he'd met everyone in the Anglophone community, convinced that they'd be much more interesting than those whom he called "those stodgy French." He made *contacts* (for him, a new, more efficient word as opposed to *relations d'affaires*). He worked at a PR outfit for a couple of years, expanding his contacts. Then he set up on his own, promoting emerging Anglophone performing artists, writers, and entrepreneurs to wider Canadian audiences. He organized their events – everything from bookstore appearances to major gigs. It was great. For a while. But eventually, he realized that his sole *raison d'etre* (so to speak) was to help those who, like him, were English-speakers stuck in a predominantly

French-speaking province. It felt limited. He bit the bullet, moved to New York, and never looked back.

He started an international event-planning business, which did everything from finding venues to arranging for a/v, lighting, flowers, and catering. He arranged transportation (local and anywhere-to-anywhere) and booked hotel rooms. He found hard-to-find theater tickets. He made reservations at high-end restaurants with months-long waiting lists. Because he spoke French and English perfectly, as well as German and enough Italian to get by, his clientele was large and sophisticated. He got referrals. But mainly, he was just having a ball. "I was finally around people who did stuff. I felt alive, like there was no end in sight," he said. He had hired a staff of four, all recent immigrants from Europe looking for excitement.

But now, after ten years, Blaise had furloughed everyone. He checked his messages obsessively, hoping for an enquiry . . . but no one was traveling. There were no corporate events. Anywhere. He felt that everything he'd created had disappeared. "It's like I'm back in France again," he said. "In Provence, you'd stare out the window wishing for something to happen – and, of course, it never did." Blaise had grown up in Provence, an hour south of Nice. His father had wanted him to join the wine exporting busines that had been in the family for 100 years. "He told me it was safe. French wines were 'nonpareil'." But the whole idea repelled him. "I thought my father was old at 40. I refused to turn into him." So, after university, he left. He felt too energetic to remain stolidly French. He couldn't bear the type of static equilibrium that he equated with being French – and, ultimately, equated with premature death. "I need action," he said.

So now there was no action. He and his partner had moved to their house in the Hamptons, waiting for the world to revive. But he came to see me because the wait was excruciating, and brought back memories of looking out the window at, essentially, nothing. "I'm going crazy here. I want my old self back, and don't think I can reinvent myself again if it doesn't come back." Blaise felt stuck. He had enough funds to tide him over, perhaps for the rest of his life. But that wasn't the point. "I'm bored and I feel boring." He also felt unnecessary, that the world had fundamentally changed and needed other kinds of people offering other services. He wanted to know if I could advise him about coping with all this. "Do you know how," he asked, "to get through your sudden, complete, irreversible irrelevance?"

I told him that I disagreed with the last term. I didn't think his current setback was irreversible. Rather, I thought that fear of becoming his father was temporarily paralyzing, making him think there was nothing left except slowly, quietly, inevitably sinking into permanent somnolence. "You created an either/or world for yourself," I said, "where if you weren't in a constant state of extreme activity you'd turn into a lumpy old petit bourgeois. It's a false dichotomy."

So, I told him there were things he could do, right now, to keep busy and feel engaged. There were plenty of start-ups – from new plant-based food companies to new transportation options – that could use his help. Some of these even aspired to become international. "You could arrange the PR. In three or four languages." He could do the set-up for promotional videos – the lighting, the logistics, finding the venues. "You could help promote new at-home clothing lines. Since you don't need the money, you could help nonprofits – they surely need it."

The point was that in this period of transition, where change is kaleidoscopic and opportunity unstable, we have to be opportunistic. We have to do what we can, though it's not ideal. The alternative is just to sit everything out, looking out the window, feeling sorry for ourselves. In Blaise's case, he could do things – even if they were not highly remunerated – that were allied with what he'd been doing, even if there was no direct match. "Keep in the public eye, let people know you're still here. Then when this is over, you'll be poised to return to what you were doing."

At this point, he was ready to try anything. "I guess it beats climbing the walls," he said. We both knew that, in our lifetimes, the world might never look as it had in 2019. Many more "events" may be virtual. But it was important to stay nimble. "Giving up is the enemy," I remarked. If he could never redevelop his business, he would at least be ready for what might come next. "You reinvented yourself once, and you can do it again." In the meantime, he could at least play to his strengths.

REINVENTING YOURSELF?

"I'm so full of regret," Lainie told me. "It's like when the present disappears, you just want to live your life over so you end up in a different place." Lainie is 60, a writer, who came to me when she felt that all she had left were her mistakes. She'd always had regrets, she said, but until now they'd been airbrushed out – she'd had work, friends, and a knack for pulling rabbits out of seemingly bottomless hats. "I could always reinvent myself," she insisted, "but now I can't." The result was that she'd come face-to-face with a life that she felt she'd mismanaged. She had nothing to fall back on – no relationship, shaky finances, no kids or grandchildren. "I can only blame myself. My life's been a series of missed opportunities."

In the midst of the pandemic, Lainie saw no way to jump-start her life again. She spent hours every day blaming herself for everything she could have done differently. "If I'd managed better, I wouldn't feel so washed up." It was as if Lainie had always kept one step ahead of confronting herself, until the virus made any new effort seem futile. "It forced me to withdraw," she said. Her past had returned with a vengeance, mocking her in weird, demeaning ways. Late at night, when she couldn't stand watching another *Columbo* or *Morse*, she'd troll her old boyfriends – maybe their wives had died. She saw who was still at the companies she'd left – maybe they'd been kicked upstairs. She looked up recipes, imagining how she'd make them for the guy she should have married. "How stupid can you get?" she implored.

The pandemic left Lainie feeling stuck inside her head, while her head was full of a debilitating past. She wanted me to help her get past her past, since she didn't see how she could on her own. Her tried-and-true method – just execute some radical change – didn't seem like it would work anymore. "Who can do anything in this environment," she asked, "let alone something life-changing?" She really thought she'd go crazy feeling sorry for herself, like Cate Blanchett's character in *Blue Jasmine*. "You're someone for a while, and then you're no one. Everyone forgets you and you live in the past."

I always want to help patients, but I try to remain pretty neutral. If I got too involved emotionally, I'd be less able to be objective. Yet Lainie's case was a challenge to this approach. I was moved by this woman, who herself seemed so overwhelmed with grief. I didn't want her to think I was worried about her, but I was. She seemed like a lot of people who were precarious before the pandemic but who now, seemingly, had run out of options to stay afloat.

Lainie had been an account executive in a PR firm that specialized in book promotions. They worked with authors and publishers, and turned decent books into best-sellers. It was interesting for a while, but the fun was vicarious. "Everyone wants to meet the author," she said. So Lainie decided to write her own books. She'd learned a lot on the job, and figured she had nothing to lose. Even better, she could *be* one of those creative types that everyone wants to meet. So, she left the firm to start writing. It was harder than she'd imagined, but she finally got a contract for a Young Adult novel about a teenage botanist whose studies of plant respiration catch the eye of NASA scientists planning to colonize exoplanet Kepler 186f (considered potentially habitable).

Wow (sort of).

Lainie continued to write, but so did the competition. It was tough. She wasn't sure if she should have left PR, and she tried some promotions on the side. She also picked up writing gigs at start-ups, and for a while she taught at a community college. In her mid-40s, she'd begun to feel scattered. But then her luck turned. She found a job as an acquisition editor at a major publisher, who wanted her to start a Young Adult imprint. Everyone said "you've landed on your feet." But after six months, she chafed at the company's guidelines and left. "I thought I knew better than they did," she told me. She went back to writing and sold another book, this time about a teenage colonist on Mars. It was modestly successful. But the market was moving in other directions, since space travel had progressed too slowly to sustain the kids' interest.

Of course, Lainie had met people. She'd had several boyfriends, at least one of whom had loved her. But he was too skittish to get married. So, she lost interest. By the time he was ready, she'd become involved with the literary editor of a major publication, who promised to leave his wife but didn't. She repeated that mistake with a rival author (he wrote books on teenage super-heroes), and ended up hating herself. When her old skittish boyfriend came around again, she rebuffed him.

So, about ten years ago Lainie seemed stalled. She took stock of every-thing – her career, her messed-up romances – and decided that she needed a reset. "I couldn't stand looking at myself. I had to get out." She found a job at a Midwest radio station which wanted to attract a younger audience. She started a call-in program that drew important advertisers, and for a while she thought she'd found her niche. She even dated the station owner. But then the station was sold to a large investor which, in a move to cut costs, changed the format to music, traffic, and weather. Lainie moved back to New York, and six months later the pandemic hit.

"I've run out of options. I'm too old to keep trying," she said. Instead, she keeps thinking about why she left PR – vanity, naivete, a young woman's search for fulfillment? "I was stupid. I just should have stayed put." Her friends told her not to act precipitously, but she thought they didn't understand her. One friend said that you never succeed at anything unless you do it for a long time. "But he started out teaching at Harvard, so I thought 'what did he know?'" She also regretted having left the publisher. "I was restless. I was unhappy over those men – I just should have followed the guidelines, which really weren't so bad anyway." She thought she should have married the guy who'd finally come around again. "He was really very sweet." In other words, she thought she should have done everything differently than she had.

So, what could I say to a woman swimming in regrets, too disheartened by history and by the present to move beyond regret towards something that might still make her happy?

"Look," I said. "I can't sugarcoat this. People are losing jobs. Relationships are a huge challenge. And then there's agism." She knew all this. "But you can't give in to despair – it's immobilizing." She knew that too. Her problem was how to get past despair. I said that the only way was to keep on trying. "You have to be practical. Instead of stalking all those people you know, call them up – make as many contacts as you can." Perhaps they knew of something she could do. Perhaps they'd even try to help. Of course, she'd have to update her resume, emphasizing everything she'd learned. "I've learned that I make poor choices," she said. "Well, you still have a sense of humor," I said. "Even if it's at your expense."

But I really wanted her to understand that since she couldn't change her past, there was no point berating herself for it. Rather, she could use it – the people, the experience, the know-how that had kept her going after so many set-backs. I told her that nothing would be easy, and that the pandemic would slow things down. But she had to start somewhere. I said not to lose heart if, as we start digging out of all this, other people seem to dig out somewhat faster. "Just don't give in to despair," I said. "You need to keep trying." ."

I'm not sure how Lainie will do. She carries a lot of baggage. She's afraid of believing in herself. But during this challenging time, she really has no other choice.

IN THE LIGHT OF ETERNITY

In a sense, psychiatrists are clergy with medical degrees. We comfort, we provide emotional support, much more than we write prescriptions. When we meet with clergy, we can speak the same language; when we comfort them, we're comforting the comforters. I've experienced this similarity first-hand, since some of my patients are clergy. During this pandemic, they're as stressed out as I am – but I have to be there to help them cope, get a grip, keep going when their congregants need nonstop empathy.

One of my patients is a rabbi. When he first presented years ago, he was a forensic accountant who worked for the local DA. He uncovered white collar crime, and helped lock up the perpetrators. Now, looking back on that radical transformation, he refers to himself kind of jokingly – "Did you hear the one about the guy who'd send you up the river and then pray for your soul?" But back before he was Rabbi Dave, he had a serious problem. He hated his job. We'd talk about alternatives to criminal prosecution – maybe corporate accounting or academe – but they didn't seem right. He wanted to be part of people's lives, to help them at ground-level on a human scale. For a while, he volunteered to provide tax advice to non-English speakers, and thought he saw his future. But the pay was near nothing, and he couldn't do it. So, after more

Figure IV.4 Rabbis at Benei Braq

discussion, followed by intense soul-searching and even conversations with his old Sunday School teacher, he became a rabbi.

Rabbi Dave loves his work, and regards his second act as a privilege. He leads a prominent congregation, teaches the sacred texts, and is a recognized community leader. Until the pandemic, he looked forward to celebrating life-cycle events: naming babies, conducting bar mitzvahs, marrying people. The funerals were hard to bear, but even those were part of life and its seasons.

Now, however, Rabbi Dave's experience has changed. The sanctuary is closed, except for Zoom services where he's alone on the bimah with the cantor. Maybe someone's in front of a computer. Maybe someone has a prayer book and is singing along. It's so dismaying. He feels diminished − a rabbi whose congregation is a mini-Diaspora. There's no energy; people can't hold hands, sway, sing together. "I'm officiating, but over what?" After the service, no handshakes, hugs, wine and cake downstairs. "Five thousand years, and now this? Hey, I could try stand-up next − I'll never know if they're not laughing."

It's so Jewish to laugh through your tears. But it's not funny. This year's fundraising has nearly collapsed. When everyone saw everyone else make a pledge, it was easy. But the effect can't be duplicated on Zoom or by email. Besides, people are focused on their immediate families. Rabbi Dave tried to raise funds for COVID relief but, when you're struggling yourself, you're not inclined to be as generous.

Even scarier, the High Holy Days are approaching. Normally, the whole congregation turns out − but where are they going to put 500 people? Nowhere, actually. "It tests your faith," said the rabbi. Early in the pandemic, like a lot of clergy, he thought that religious observance would somehow go on. He'd even encouraged members to meet in small groups for prayer and study. "Oh, how naïve can you be?" he asked. "Jews are supposed to believe in science." He was sure he'd made things worse. He was sure he'd made things even *more* awful when he'd admitted a couple of mourners to a funeral and, a week later, they were admitted to a hospital with the virus. "This is magical thinking, not religion," he said.

He named a dozen of his congregants who had suffered or died. One of those, a man named Robert, had recovered, but was sure he'd infected his older brother and his father − both of whom had died. "He's inconsolable. I should send him to you." I'm feeling a bit burnt out, and my own father just had a medical issue, but I agreed to talk.

The stories kept coming. Here's a sample: "I went to the hospital to visit a patient in our congregation. He was returning to work after the virus, and was still weak. On the stairs in his office, he fell and hit his head. Blood everywhere. He almost broke his back." Apparently, the man will get better, but may walk with a cane for the rest of his life. Punishment on top of punishment − and for what?

My problem is how to deal with someone whose existence is so consumed with others' grief that his own grief becomes overwhelming. How, especially, do you help someone see that they're doing the best they can when the grief all around them keeps escaping their capacity to address it? All I could say was that we're all in this together, and that no person can be expected to bear more than their fair share of the burden.

Clergy believe that in times of great stress, it is their job to ensure that people remember to hold onto their faith, to view their predicament in the light of eternity. We are just passing through. Stuff happens. It will all work out – whether in life or in death. But how can you carry on with that job when people are living day to day, trying to hold it all together before it all flies apart in a million directions? Rabbi Dave didn't know whether to include himself among the comforters or those needing comfort (no doubt both). He believed in some kind of Divinity, but he had a hard time seeing a divine purpose in any of this. He kept on going, but it felt rote, programmed, the product of a will not to let go rather than of a purposeful endeavor.

Okay, so eternity is far away. I reminded him that, therefore, every day is precious and he should try to make the most of it. "Think of the people whom you've comforted. They needed you." I wasn't sure that he even heard me. He kept staring. "There are so many people. I can't keep abreast of them." So, we talked about what he should reasonably expect of himself. What can anyone reasonably expect of anyone now? Only to do their jobs, one day at a time, as seems best. I acknowledged that his guilt over encouraging people to worship in small groups, or admitting them to a funeral, was a real problem. "You were perhaps too zealous, too intent on being a good steward of the faith. Now you've learned that less can be more." I added that we are all learning.

It's hard for laypeople to understand what clergy are experiencing just now. We don't live in a time when plagues are thought to come from God, and to be sent as punishment for our sins. They just happen. Often, they result because of human indifference to the natural world – to animal habitats, to the places where diseases are hatched and spread. They result because we mismanage laboratories and hospitals. So, the clergy's role is less defined. It is more that of talking people through their grief than of explaining why such a calamity has occurred. In this sense, their role is not clear-cut. It varies from day to day, from person to person. It requires empathy, grit, and a willingness to acknowledge that one does not have all the answers.

Like the rest of us, Rabbi Dave can only hope that, in the light of eternity, this too shall pass.

YEATS AND THE "SECOND COMING"

I'm supposed to help patients develop resilience, but now two of its major components – hope and optimism – are eluding me. Maybe it's because I threw my back out, and have been in bed all weekend. I'm sure it's stress-related.

But for solace, I'm reading old magazines and rediscovering books. I own a copy of the *Norton Anthology of Modern Poetry*, which has followed me around since college. I picked it up again, and found William Butler Yeats' poem, "The

Figure IV.5 Beast and Dragon

Second Coming" (1920), whose opening lines jumped out at me – actually, they'd been swirling in my head for days:

> Turning and turning in the widening gyre
> The falcon cannot hear the falconer;
> Things fall apart; the centre cannot hold;
> Mere anarchy is loosed upon the world…

The famous metaphor for disorder ("the centre cannot hold") was in my head, I think, because maybe it's us that's losing control. Okay, I know the infection rate has dropped in New York; we're contact tracing; more people wear masks than do not; the hospitals are no longer at capacity. But still. Just look around.

Health care professionals are burning out (just look at me). Colleges and schools are closing, after a brief reopening. Hunger is rising. The initial spurt in rehiring has slowed. There is a lot of pain.

There is a lot of anger. New York's top business executives wrote to the mayor to clean up the streets. Drug makers wrote to the public, assuring them that there would be no caving in to political pressure on the timing of a vaccine. There are calls to reconfigure American capitalism so that not just shareholders reap the benefits.

It's like you feel things are shifting under your feet.

Yeats' title invokes Apocalyptic imagery to describe the atmosphere in post-war Europe. In the aftermath of the Great War, there was civil unrest and dis-illusionment. In Ireland, the British had sent Black and Tan troops to quell an uprising. Now there are riots in America – Portland, Seattle, Kenosha – as police and the military try to quell them. There's an eerie similarity between then and now.

And then there's climate change. Wildfires in Washington, Oregon, and California. Local residents unable to breathe. Mass evacuations. The balance between nature and humans is fraying, with dire consequences. We learn that viruses jump from animals to humans because humans are invading their habitats. How can all this continue? More significantly, how will it all end?

In the poem, a "rough beast" "slouches towards Bethlehem to be born." Who is this monster in our time? Terrorists (foreign or domestic)? A cadre of hackers that turns off the lights and cuts off the water supply? Fires, hurricanes . . . or some crafty virus? It all sounds too real to be science fiction, and too off-the-charts to be real. I try to be optimistic, but my head keeps drumming Second Coming. Second Coming.

Yeats' poem was specifically connected to the flu pandemic of 1918–19. His pregnant wife had caught the virus and was close to death. That pandemic had death rates up to 70 percent for pregnant women. Now, COVID is more deadly for the elderly and the ill. At the current death rate, more Americans will die from the infection than were killed during World War II. But just as insidious, the pandemic has caused us to wonder whether our institutions are willing to protect us. I didn't say "able," I said "willing." Just this week, it emerged that CDC reports about the virus are being doctored to help the President min-imize the risk. His so-called "cheer-leading," on the other hand, has unleashed intense skepticism towards any potential vaccine.

The protests in the street are, I think, only a small part of what people would say if they had the nerve to say it. Or the time. Or the resources. They're just trying to keep things together.

Of course, every generation has its challenges, social unrest, and tragedies. However, even with the progress we've made in combating COVID, there is a sense that the worst may be yet to come: poverty and homelessness on the rise; education becoming harder; a likely second wave of morbidity and mortality when flu season starts, intensifying the effects of the pandemic. Second Coming indeed.

Our biggest challenge right now is to look ourselves squarely in the face (masks pulled up). We have to acknowledge the fault lines in our society that the pandemic has exposed. The rich are by no means immune from this pan-demic, but the poorer you are the worse you are hit. That is just a fact. When all of this is finally past, and we pick up the pieces, will we try to put them back in the same places that they were? I don't think we can. We've seen too much to even dare try. The "centre" is now in a different place and, if it is going to hold, we're going to have to think about a new kind of structure that's much more inclusive. A lot of people are already thinking.

I have to acknowledge that it's taken me a while to see what this pandemic has done to our society, and the weaknesses that it's exposed. For a while, maybe early this summer, I thought that we'd turned the corner. My patients seemed to be getting on with their lives, returning (more or less) to their routines. Kids were preparing for school. Parents were thinking of returning to the office. But then it hit me. My patients, for all their problems, are not homeless. They are not hungry, or poor, or living in a part of the country ravaged by fires. They have not been the victims of systemic racism. They think they'll be able to vote. I mistook them for the world.

When I realized that these people are but a sliver of the world, it was eye opening. I looked around, and was horrified. Yeats' poem started banging around in my head. It's important, I think, that we look outside our cozy frame of reference which, finally, I did. There is a temptation to circle the wagons during crises, and to shut the world out. But, as Yeats knew, the world is coming for us. We can't shut it out forever so we might as well face it.

In practical terms, what does this mean? It means that we have to be more active in our kids' education. It means that we understand that the environment is not some place "out there" – it's everywhere, and how we treat it affects our health. It means that we cultivate empathy, and make conscious efforts to help people who are not just like us.

If the pandemic has taught us anything, it's that we've been basking in a sense of false security. We're vulnerable. All of us. We have to push back against a Second Coming . . . or it will come. Part of resilience is taking steps to prevent disaster, not just reacting once disaster has occurred. Start with a flu shot. Think of every day as a flu shot. Do something that builds the community – that rebuilds it in ways that make it stronger. Vote. Teach your kids that getting involved is better than just passively enjoying themselves. If they're privileged, explain how they can use their privilege to help others.

There doesn't have to be a Second Coming, at least in terms of all-out apocalypse. You can cultivate a kind of optimism. Think of Churchill's admonition: "This is not the beginning of the end, but it is perhaps the end of the beginning." If that's the best we can hope for, I'll take it.

FRAGILE EGOS

Astrophysics is all over the news. Venus' atmosphere may contain life! Front-page story in the *New York Times* (Stirone et al., 2020). Closer to home, three astrophysicists published extraordinary books – *The Smallest Lights in the Universe* (Seager, 2020), *The Sirens of Mars* (Johnson, 2020), and *The End of Everything (Astrophysically Speaking)* (Mack, 2020). All are by female academics, and all received great reviews. My patient April, who is home on furlough from her job, went out and read them. This was, she said, a mistake.

The mistake, apparently, is that they made her feel useless.

April works at an interior design firm, and specializes in antique textiles. She knows a lot about rugs and tapestries. It's nothing she actually studied, but after years of working with clients – who initially knew more than she did – she picked up the language and developed her taste. "You want an 18th century French Verdure Aubusson for your office?" she asked one day. "Oh, just kidding. I see you more as the Italian cut velvet type." Oh, dear. Don't ask.

April likes to show off (even though she pretended the display of erudition was really a joke on her). It's part of our relationship that I play along.

I've been treating April for a few years, mostly for feelings of rivalry with her older sister Marilyn, who runs a logistics firm that serves truckers in the South and Midwest. "We couldn't be more different," she told me. "And Marilyn never lets me forget it." Since they were children, in fact, Marilyn has made light of April's interests, and suggested that she wasn't good for much of anything. When they were growing up, Marilyn said "Someday, you'll furnish doll houses," and the taunt still troubles April. "I guess I do really play with dolls, except now they're grown up and live in big houses."

I've tried to help April see that helping wealthy people furnish their homes is not useless. It's not going to save the world, but neither is it anything to make fun of. "You're adding beauty to people's lives, you're probably alleviating stress," I told her. But we go round and round on this idea, with April claiming that the only stress on these people is when their friends have even more beautiful furnishings. She sees life in terms of competition. So, she sees herself as laughably insignificant – a loser who can toss around some museum–quality terms. "Actually," she said, "I always want to be someone else."

When April read the books by these astrophysicists, she felt devastated. Here were three brilliant women (one actually was a MacArthur Genius) who were doing amazing work. When the news came out about Venus, one had been on the research team, and was quoted in the *Times*. "I feel utterly frivolous by comparison," she said. It was that "by comparison" that struck me. April has a hard time thinking of herself except in relative terms – if it's not her sister, then it's some idea of a terrific woman whom she'll never be. During the pandemic, when she's stuck at home and her clients are hunkered down, she feels this sense of relative pointlessness even more acutely.

"You know," April told me, "it's not as bad when I'm busy. My clients seem to appreciate me, even if I think it's all such a joke." The pandemic has pried her away from her usual sources of ego enhancement, and from most sources of support beyond her friends (who are largely in the same line of work, and would be insulted if she revealed what was really on her mind). It created a perfect storm to undermine April: lots more time, no reinforcement, so lots more self-questioning. It allowed her to discover even more people of whom to be envious. "I don't even know why I read those books," she said. "They sounded so interesting, and I thought I'd learn something." They were, in fact, fantastically interesting, but so were the authors and that was her problem. "I could have predicted I'd feel bad, and I did."

So how was I going to help her when she had no work, her friends couldn't be any help, and there weren't a lot of obvious opportunities to go out and be of use? (I suppose I could have bought that Aubusson, but I wasn't going there.)

I thought to encourage April by suggesting that, first of all, the mere fact that she plowed through those books showed real intellectual curiosity. "They're great books, and I'm sure they're not beach reading. You have a mind." I pointed out how much she'd learned about textiles, even though she was dismissive of how she'd used her knowledge. "Maybe while you're waiting to get back to work, you could write something for one of those professional journals – textiles are hot." I wanted her to realize that the circle of people who valued what she did was wider than she thought. But even apart from any outside validation – which she craved – I wanted April to realize that intrinsically, apart from what people said, she had value.

A lot of people who are stuck at home during the pandemic, not doing much of anything, feel as though their paltry value has finally been exposed ("Look at all those Essential Workers – now they're doing something!"). If you're stuck at home, what do you do all day except eat, exercise (if you can), and try to stay sane? If your ego is fragile, you suffer, and question what you're doing with your life. You turn inward; you mine all your old anxieties. Boredom doesn't help. Even some innocuous activity, like reading a book by an astrophysicist, can set you off. It reminds you of what you haven't done, and of whom you'll never be.

April told me that she never compares herself with men. "I don't care what they do," she said. "It's the women who make me feel bad." She was, by her own admission, still fighting a rear-guard battle with her sister. In fact, during the pandemic it was going full blast, since Marilyn was still doing logistics for truckers, much of whose work was critical during this period. "Marilyn said that she designed some route to get PPE from hospitals in the Upper Midwest to ones in the South. She felt she was really helping." And she was. But should that diminish April? We spoke about what she could do.

In fact, April was very smart. We talked about how, as the schools on Long Island opened up online, she could offer to tutor kids. She could even offer classes on textiles – the kids could use something besides the usual fare to keep them interested. The point was not to sit home and sulk. "It helps to feel productive, and do things that you admire without anyone's reassurance." She said that maybe she could start her own YouTube channel, and teach people how to beautify their homes. Wow! If she could acknowledge the idea that beauty was not some frivolous pursuit – if she could put that idea into practice – then that was progress. "Do you realize what you just said?" I asked. "You just identified your own value."

April thought about that for a while, and then wondered whether anyone would want to learn. "Maybe they'll get bored," she said. I suggested that, more likely, they're bored already, and that she could add something to their lives. It was at least worth a try.

During this pandemic, as we try to hold things together, we have to start with ourselves. We have to begin to see how we matter, and how we can convince ourselves that we do. Even if we're not astrophysicists.

IN-PERSON MEETINGS

My patient Carly, who's in her 60s, was thrilled to land a job with an international nonprofit that helps disabled kids. It was spring of 2019, well before the pandemic, and she laughed "I'm finally doing what I should have been doing — just 40 years too late." We talked about her plans for rebuilding the organization's website and bringing local color to its high-minded videos. She was over the moon . . . until the moon crashed, along with most of the organization's activities. The website-building continued, but barely, with very little impetus to complete it. Instead of treating Carly for a sense of pre-COVID aimlessness, I was now treating her for post-COVID depression.

We'd talk over Zoom about how she kept busy. "I'm helping the Director write a book," she said. "I'm not sure when we'll get back to helping children." It looked like long-term doldrums ("I knew it was too good to last") until, one day in mid-September, the Director told her that things would pick up. Over the Labor Day weekend, he'd met (in person) with some supporters, who urged him to get out in front of the pandemic. They told him that "If you're looking for funds, you want to get the jump on everyone else." He'd understood, and suggested that Carly start working on some new videos.

But then things took a turn. The Director wanted everyone to resume weekly meetings. In person. He said that the group's camaraderie had disappeared and, along with it, the spontaneous exchange of ideas. "If things are going to pick up, then they have to open up," he said. He even invited the head videographer, who lived in India, to visit New York so that he could meet Carly. He scheduled some meetings for late October. Carly was stunned and terrified.

Although Carly had disliked not working on big, important projects, she understood that the lockdown was necessary. She also realized that in her case, as opposed to that of most other people on the staff, her health could seriously have been compromised by close, personal contact. "I'm in that age group," she sighed. Everyone else was in their 30s and 40s. So, her dilemma, which she presented during our most recent conversation, was whether to attend the meetings. In particular, she had doubts about meeting the head videographer when he arrived from India. "Under the circumstances," she asked, "can't we just Zoom?"

Apparently not. The Director, who was around Carly's age, had started going out more and felt that everyone could do so responsibly. His trip to meet the supporters, one of whom had opened his house in the Hamptons to accommodate everyone, had turned him around. He was now convinced that people could meet safely in person, and that it was undeniably more productive. "Just being around those people," he'd said, "generated so many ideas. I cleared my head out and then started up again." He thought everyone – including Carly – would have a similar experience.

His idea was that people could meet on the roof of his building on the Upper West Side. If it finally got too cold (or too noisy, this being New York), they'd move downstairs to his living room. Everyone could wear masks except, of course, when they broke for lunch which he'd have delivered. "I cringed," said Carly. "I knew we'd end up in that living room." She polled some of the other people who also weren't thrilled. But they didn't want to start a rebellion. She was on her own.

"So, I told the Director that I was reluctant," she said. "But he has this thing about everyone keeping up their spirits – and keeping up our momentum as we return to action." He insisted that she meet the videographer, since that was directly related to her job. "You two need to work together, and there's so much to talk about." In fact, he wanted the three of them to discuss how best to pick up the pieces. "We can meet three or four times while he's here," he said. Carly thought she'd have a fit. She'd been hyper-cautious since March, and saw no reason to take any gratuitous risks.

Couldn't he appreciate her concerns? Apparently, he couldn't. During a Zoom call among the three of them last week, he started talking about the videographer's meeting schedule. So, Carly felt she had to assert herself. "Look," she said, "I haven't met anyone face-to-face since March, and the risks aren't going away. Everybody knows that." She was surprised that the guy was even coming. But he was. She was also annoyed, since they'd laughed at what she'd said, making her feel prissy and old (which she saw as weird as well as insulting, since the videographer himself was almost 60).

She felt bullied; the victim of peer-pressure; misunderstood. This was her dream job, and she wanted to do everything to make it work. But was she supposed to risk her health when, in her opinion, there was no absolute necessity?

Many organizations have found that people work just as well from home as they do at the office. Carly knew that. But still. There are times when in-person collaboration really is better, even if it isn't crucial. In the Director's mind (and with the support of the videographer), this was one of those times. Making and editing videos is a frame-by-frame art, calling for a good eye and skilled judgment as to what is likely to appeal. The videographer had been at this for years, and had a lot to teach Carly about technique. Carly had a strong sense of the organization's mission, and could guide the videographer concerning subjects that he should go for. There were obvious synergies. Carly couldn't just put down the Director's newfound interest in face-to-face meetings as totally misguided.

Thus, in counseling Carly, we talked about whether the Director's desire (demand?) that she come out of her cocoon was fair. He clearly wanted what he saw as best for the organization (even if his interest in face-to-face meetings was somewhat over-the-top). So, I asked if she thought that her fear was exaggerated – after all, there were stories every day of people returning to their offices while taking proper precautions. Some companies were even requiring that people return. But Carly still felt queasy. She was in a risk-prone group, and she felt that her routine had kept her safe. "I hate having to upset the Director, whom I actually love, but I don't think he understands where I'm coming from."

In the end, we decided that she was not being over-cautious. She had to do what she felt was right for herself, and not allow herself to be pressured over something so personal as her own health. She remarked that when she was a child, her mother would insist that she eat everything on her plate whether or not she was hungry. "I developed this sense that one's body is nobody else's business." She was a big supporter of Pro-Choice groups. She felt that in this instance, she would have to stand her ground. "By October, we could be starting a second wave," she said, "why should I give it help?"

As we adjust to life with a pandemic ("there goes the neighborhood!"), different people will have different levels of tolerance for its exactions. If our own is stricter than someone else's, then we shouldn't feel as though we have to apologize. Life is too short. Literally.

PLAY

One feature of the pandemic is that it's knocked us back to the 20th century, even as it accelerates developments that have remade the 21st. Thus, if we're Zooming and Skyping like a planet full of futurists, we're playing Monopoly

Figure IV.6 Chess board

again. And Scrabble. Rubik's Cubes are in short supply. We've rediscovered games. We're playing like we used to – which is to say we're doing stuff that doesn't change the world, but that takes up time and makes us happy.

It's not that there aren't 21st century games. But somehow, maybe because they're so involved with technology, they don't feel like games. They feel more like the real world on speed, or on some mission to subdue a civilization that would like to replace us. You can disappear into these games, of course, but they're *so* consuming that you have to remind yourself that you can still return. They're maybe a little too trippy for when you're already bummed out on bad news.

So, the pandemic has made us appreciate nice, safe games that let you play at your own pace while perhaps even talking with someone. In a way, we want pure, distilled distraction with an option to put down the dice and walk away when we feel like it. Nothing with proto-existential crises that, because they're so real, are a little too real for comfort.

Okay, so why? I think I know. The pandemic is already like some uncanny version of a video game that's so totally, perversely, surreally absorbing that you can't see your way beyond it. It's like wherever you turn, there's the pandemic. No walking away. It might as well be Dead Space 2 or Resident Evil 7: Biohazard – so believable and in your face that you wonder: "Where is this leading? Will I get out alive?" In contradistinction to the pandemic, we want games that allow us maximum discretion. No commitment required.

The problem is that even while we crave the experience of uncomplicated play, there are fewer people who can join us. We can't just invite someone over for bridge or backgammon. We could play online, of course, but then you can't just break for pizza or stop everything to talk about the people you didn't invite. Online play is inevitably more structured; its often timed; it's invariably *all* about the game with no time for hanging out. So why bother?

In this environment, it's come down to playing games within your bubble, which in most cases is your family. Then you can relax. You control the game; it doesn't control you. The issue for kids, however, is recruitment: how do they get parents involved, and maybe snarky siblings? Everyone's on a different schedule, even amidst the pandemic. Everyone's maybe willing to play, but they want to play something else. In the end, one kid's desire for play – for pure, happy distraction from online school and universal worry – can become a source of frustration and family fights . . . and the worst way to fight the Pandemic Blues.

Of course, if a kid is resourceful, he or she can play by themselves. LEGO, maybe, or all the new brain games "for one" available on Amazon (heard of "Cat Crimes Brain Game and Brainteaser for Boys and Girls Age 8 and Up"?). Down the line towards tradition, there are always jigsaw puzzles, dolls, and coloring books. But wait. Like most things in life, play is more fun when it's shared. When we strike up a game together, it's an antidote to loneliness, and to all the creepy, morbid preoccupations that taunt us when we play games to avoid them. Coloring can feel like a boring second-class substitute for the real make-believe.

I was reminded of kids' need to play – *with* somebody – when I spoke with my patient Rachel. Rachel is in Middle School, which she currently attends remotely. She's doing fine, but desperately misses her friends, the Chess Club, and cheer-leading (no, brain games and organized screaming are not mutually exclusive, at least for a kid who aspires to be an organizer like her unlikely idol, Emma Goldman). When we spoke last week, Rachel showed me a photo of the castle she'd constructed from LEGO blocks, but then she began to tear up. "Nobody lives in that castle but the lady of Shalott," she said, referring to the famous, pining recluse (they're reading Tennyson's eponymous poem in English class). Rachel (a.k.a. The Lady) needed someone to share her fantasies.

We tend to think of fantasies as exceptionally private phenomena. But that's just the point, i.e. it's thrilling to share fantasies with someone we trust. It's like extending our private world into new, uncharted realms, while still keeping it private – sort of a conspiracy of the imagination. Rachel said that while LEGOs, puzzles, and even her decorator house provided some useful distractions, she needed some of the buzz of other people. Without that, she felt too exposed, vulnerable to all the bad stuff that was out there: the virus, of course, but also the nasty politics and the drought in New England where her parents had a second home. "Before it all burns down and blows away, I'd like to escape into maybe . . . parcheesi?"

Actually, Rachel had asked her mother to join her in building the LEGO castle, or maybe even in redecorating the decorator house. But she wasn't interested. She felt that Rachel should "act her age" and read books. "You can never read enough books," she said. "I've bought you all the Harry Potters." She'd also bought *To Kill a Mockingbird* and *Good Night Stories for Rebel Girls* (in honor of Rachel's fixation on Emma Goldman), and *The Perks of Being a Wallflower*. Rachel's mother meant well. But she didn't hear what Rachel was asking for. Rachel needed to share her fantasies. She needed to play, so to speak, with someone she loved and trusted. She couldn't possibly ask her brother Simon, who was five years younger and into electric trains.

We talked about what play meant to Rachel. It meant a lot: escape, but also a kind of practice for handling tough situations. "When you play with someone, spontaneously, you make it up as you go along. It's kind of give and take, like life." Rachel was nothing if not precocious. She understood, at a conscious level, what most people understand instinctively – that play has social and emotional benefits. It promotes skills like problem-solving, collaboration, and innovation. You learn how to learn. It's probably no coincidence that the President of LEGO Education, Esben Staerk Joergensen, has been publicizing the benefits of play. He wants to sell LEGOs, of course, but for the right reasons.

There is actually an academic discipline devoted to the study of play and its role in cognitive/social development. We all need to play and, I'd argue, the need doesn't diminish just because we've "aged out" of dodgeball and jump-rope in the school yard. Rachel's mother had a monthly bridge game before the pandemic, and it was one of the social highlights of her routine.

So, I suggested that Rachel take a different tack with her mother. "Why don't you explain that the pandemic has made ordinary play – with your friends, at your school – pretty impossible? Then explain that you have to fill up the quotient." I thought that her mother, who is a CPA, would understand a numerical analogy, even if she didn't quite get Rachel's yearning to share. I also thought that Rachel could explain why her school encouraged play, i.e. it's not just to burn off excess energy, but to get kids thinking in collaborative, innovative ways. I thought her mother would get that too.

In this period, when we're threading our way past microscopic enemies, play (believe it or not!) enhances our skills. It's not a waste of time. It could help save your life.

ACCEPTANCE

You know that old Pete Seeger song, with the line "God bless the grass that grows thru the crack"? I thought of it today when I walked down Park Avenue near my office. Throughout the pandemic, the buildings have kept up appearances. You wouldn't even know there was a pandemic – except for the scarcity of people. But, as in the song, there are little unstoppable outcrops of nature, blades of grass where the concrete sidewalk has pulled away from the buildings. There are even weeds (weeds!) on the median running down the center of the Avenue, butting heads with the manicured flower arrangements. In other words, no obstacle (not even concrete) is impermeable. As in the song, the concrete "breaks and . . . buckles," and the grass finds its way.

The metaphor, because that's what it is, drives home the message that there's some kind of eternal work-around that, after a while, just becomes inevitable. In the protest era of the '60s, that song – with its subtle, but by no means innocuous message – was the quieter counterpart of "We Shall Overcome." In the pandemic year of 2020, the song says Look Around You, people are finding their way.

It's not that anything is close to normal – not work, or schools, or sporting events. Midtown is silent. Even some Starbucks have closed. But energy, and more specifically inventiveness, are starting to return (poking through concrete, as it were). On September 23, the *Times* ran a story with the headline "How New Yorkers Found Resolve After 6 Months of Pandemic Hardship," with the lead "Small transformations have unfolded that reveal the gifts and grit of the City's people" (Knoll, 2020). It went on to describe women who lost their jobs, and began selling street food; a nurse who planted corn and sunflowers on the median of a closed-off street; outdoor Zumba classes; artists sketching murals; stores selling dresses with phone-images, and arranging home delivery. It was terrific. There were quotes from ordinary people, citing resurgent feelings of community. Some people said that New York was showing its true, indomitable self.

Finally. I think that the key to this article is the phrase "After 6 Months . . ." With no end to the pandemic in sight, and cases actually rising in some parts of the country, New Yorkers are tired of waiting for this to go away. But rather than just throw caution to the winds, we've started to learn to live with the virus. In other words, we've moved on to the fifth stage of grief: Acceptance. Once you finally get past the denial, anger, bargaining, and depression, you

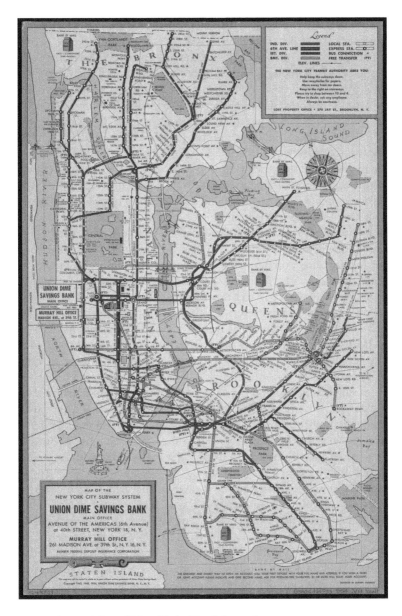

Figure IV.7 Vintage Map of New York City Subway System

move on. You figure out what to do. You work with other people who maybe can help. And as Reinhold Niebuhr (1932) said, "Grant me the serenity to accept the things I cannot change." That is, there's no point wasting energy when you could be trying to do what you can.

For some people, acceptance is difficult. They've always had everything their own way (more or less), and find it hard to adjust. It's an affront – so why even bother? In fact, those Park Avenue apartments are empty because their inhabitants *couldn't* be bothered. So, they just moved somewhere else. But I wonder how they'll manage when, finally, they return. Will they feel like Rip van Winkle, bewildered by all that's changed? Will they get with the program, or remain stuck in some stage of grief that is totally disabling? I guess we'll find out. But they're less interesting, for now, than the people cited by the *Times*. These are middle- and working-class people who've always had to elbow past concrete (!) and intangible obstacles in order to live here. They've always been scrappy. For them, growing through the cracks has been a way of life. Now, having accepted what's happened, they've returned to doing what they've always done, acting out plans to make life livable. It may be that everyone, eventually, will have to follow their lead.

Back in late August, Jerry Seinfeld wrote an Op-Ed in the *Times*, "So you think New York is 'Dead'?" (2020). It was a riposte to all the people who left and who, in his humble opinion, failed to appreciate the City's vitality: "We're going to keep going with New York City if that's alright with you. And it will sure as hell be back. Because of all the real, tough New Yorkers who, unlike you, loved it and understood it, stayed and rebuilt it." Seinfeld realized that there is a collective energy to the place that will – somehow – translate into new, revitalizing efforts. Of course, nobody sits down and says, "I'm going to rebuild this city." But people pick up cues, they sense other people's attempts to improve their lot, and then they try something too. Moreover, there are *so many* people, each with some reason for plowing ahead if for no other reason than they have to. They can't sit still, so they may as well get cracking . . . and after a while, it becomes contagious (not to give the virus any credit as a role model).

Of course, there are fewer options. Of course, it won't be easy. But people have come to terms with having to exploit the options that they have. They're figuring out ways to stretch those options.

We tend to think of Acceptance as a stage in the grieving process marked by withdrawal and calm. It's not happiness so much as repose, a kind of benign stasis. But I don't think that works here . . . and by "here" I mean post-pandemic New York City, and wherever else you want to apply the principle of getting on with life. Once we've reached the stage of accepting the virus, and the toll that it's taken (and is taking), we act in ways that are opposite to withdrawal and calm. We act in some kind of subliminal concert, even showing signs of excitement when things start to turn round. No, we're not really "bouncing back," but we *are* bouncing. We've summoned energy from somewhere to save what's left and, ideally, create new opportunities. We'll have to, since so much is gone.

The effort will be long-term. One of my patients, who stayed in the City, wondered if he'd "ever see some real kind of normal." I suggested that what exists now is just as real as what was previously "normal." It's just that the emphases are different. We have to try harder. We have to be nimbler. We have to accept what we can't change, but avoid accepting some comfortable, obsolete version of ourselves. We need to find new ways to sustain our lives when, in many ways, life feels diminished. Some people have already figured out how – or, at least, they're actively trying.

In this parlous period, when a second wave is possible, we can still hope that mere survival is too short of the goal. It's legitimate to want something more. But the onus is on us now. We have to hustle, New York style. Think of the grass, hard by the fancy buildings, sprouting pugnaciously.

Reflections

Initially, I did not intend to write a book about the pandemic during the pandemic. That's because as a psychiatrist, I tend to reflect on situations after they occur. My approach to healing is, in a sense, the medical equivalent of how Wordsworth describes poetry – "emotion recollected in tranquility" (1800). My profession is that of a healer: I help people repair their lives through insight and understanding.

But the pandemic startled me, as it did everyone. Every day, I was rivetted by statistics, by my patients, by the accelerating drama of heroism and lives lost. I could not *but* write about what I saw while I saw it. *Through a Screen Darkly* is the record of my experience. Since graduating from medical school more than half a lifetime ago, I have never been as intensely absorbed in an ongoing project as I have been in helping people navigate the pandemic and in recording their stories.

There were several reasons for my utter absorption. First, nobody on planet Earth could escape the pandemic's gravitational pull. How could you not think about COVID-19 whenever you touched something, or breathed, or woke up wondering if you could *still* breathe? The pandemic was (and still is) everywhere, all the time. But second, and more specific to me as a psychiatrist, I found that the vast majority of my patients had been touched by the pandemic – they'd been laid off, their kids were struggling with remote learning, someone they knew had died. I was literally talking about the pandemic from the moment I started my day to the moment it ended. Also, there were the adjustments I had to make, not least conducting my practice entirely through a screen. And then finally, after the therapeutic work with each patient, I tried to see how their stories might represent some facet of this pandemic that should be remembered.

Because the pandemic will ultimately be a saga of statistics – how many infections, how many deaths, how many unemployed – I wanted to record on a personalized, human scale the way that people suffered and the way they persevered: some endured loss and loneliness; others dealt with doubt and uncertainty; doctors, mental health professionals, and clergy were on the frontlines trying to help. As a psychiatrist, my practice was a window into how people articulated their experience of the pandemic.

But in writing, I still had to perform a balancing act. I had to think about each person in the present but also in terms of what we might want to know about the human experience once we looked back on this period. So, I had to maintain a double perspective: I was outside the present while I was in it, I was in the future and also right here. People's experiences were all so different, but I trusted that they would fit together in a common attempt to cope with the pandemic, forming a mosaic of pandemic-related experiences.

So, *Through a Screen Darkly* emerged. It's not exactly a narrative of the past several months, but I've sought to provide a sense of time and a developing trajectory – an overall arc, still coming into focus. The acute crisis was clear and present; then most people tried to go back out to work and into their communities; but we are still settling into a New Normal; and we are still discovering that it's hardly normal. Most things are still fraught. If we're more hopeful in some ways, it's mainly because we are tired of despair.

My clinical work during this period, and the writing that accompanied it, were sometimes exhausting. Like many doctors and mental health professional, I felt "burned out" from the work. In my previous book, *Psychotherapy and Personal Change: Two Minds in a Mirror*, I was more detached, i.e. I wrote up my patients' stories without trying to imagine how they'd be read months or years later when we tried to make sense of an exasperating, devastating time in our history. *A Screen* demanded that I situate myself in a future that, at times, I could hardly bear to confront. My friends and family members picked up on my sense of sometimes hitting a wall.

But I did my best and tried to be resilient, which is part of the story that I tell. Like most other people in this book, I had to find my way. When I felt exhausted, I had to bounce back. I hoped that this type of resilience, of putting one foot in front of another even in times of stress, would become an important dimension of the pandemic when, finally, we found time to study it.

While this was never intended to be a book about resilience *per se*, the theme emerged with increasing clarity as this book progressed. Even in Part I, in the depths of the pandemic, my patients find ways to stay upright, alert, even imaginative as they struggle with their particular challenges. I am thinking of the doctors that I treated, and the lonely people who nonetheless find outlets. I think that experiencing resilience changes us: it boosts our self-confidence, and it boosts our self-esteem. We won't go back to being who we were before the pandemic. We'll be stronger, better able to cope – though we may have frightening flashbacks. Whenever I write about resilience in this period, I worry that sequelae of chronic stress and even PTSD may result down the road. We get through today, yet we still may shudder at what that effort took out of us.

The point, however, is that we've learned something and, hopefully, are continuing to. Each of us now knows what it feels like to experience burnout; intense grief; fear; utter bewilderment. As I read over the stories in *A Screen*, I realized that they represent a degree of emotion that many of my patients had never experienced before. They represent a degree of self-questioning that had never been called for before. The intensity seems new and different. As I came to realize, COVID-19 intensified experience and accelerated events that might not have happened until years from now. It totally prevented us from procrastinating, or from shoving some uncomfortable feeling under an emotional rug. The pandemic was here and now, and we had to respond.

As a consequence, we redirected our lives (however provisionally), and we knew (or know now) that they'll be different when we entirely resume them. We're not sure how, but giving up our routines has been eye-opening. Many people now want to keep working from home; many find that they need far less stuff. So, here's the rub: what will the economy look like when downtowns are empty and last year's clothes seem just fine? What will become of whole industries, like fashion and hotels, that withered while we quarantined and may come back as mere ghosts of their former selves? We're waiting for the other shoe to drop, wondering how it will fit when it does. The uncertainty is a source of stress, even where the initial stress – the threat of getting sick – has subsided. The pandemic's long tail, we fear, could be as bad as the pandemic, albeit it will play out in another key. So, we wonder: will we ever in our lifetimes see the end of this?

No one knows. Recovery will take time. When COVID's consequences are less specifically medical (maybe a vaccine, maybe better treatments), we'll need to rebuild our economy and our social norms (have handshakes disappeared forever?). Some changes in how we work and socialize will likely be permanent, and maybe for the better (more flexibility and freedom). But it will take time to get there.

Based on the stories in *A Screen*, it's clear that we are rethinking our lives. We're contriving work-arounds – well, if I can't do This then maybe That will work. We're becoming imaginative, if only by default. We're accepting that we must rely on others; we're becoming more empathetic (how else can we justify asking others to give us a hand?). Here I'm thinking of my patient Jeremy, who comes to understand that if he approaches people, they'll cut him some slack. We're learning to subordinate our pride. It's part of a whole new protocol for interpersonal relations, starting with the elbow-bump. It's part of rebuilding community on a new, more mutually helpful basis.

In writing *A Screen*, I learned an immense amount about the importance of individual lives to our understanding of a stressed-out society. None of my patients are famous or, in themselves, could have changed much in any scalable way. Yet their lives, and their responses to personal stress provide insight into how the pandemic forced so many different people into patterns of thought and behavior that none of them ever thought they'd adopt. Collectively, their experience is instructive, therefore, if only because it demonstrates the variety of suffering that is possible during a crisis – and the variety of ways to keep going. There will never be a one-size-fits-all fix to what has happened. People will need to find a way that works for them.

Children are usually very resilient, but in this case I worry. Their educations may have been compromised, and some may be left behind. Moreover, it's not as if the kids don't know this. Some of the essays in *A Screen* deal with the issue. Thus, even where kids don't get sick, they can suffer. One of the tasks of recovery will be to monitor kids, and to ensure that the ones who do suffer receive special attention. This will be difficult as scarce public resources are allocated to the most acute problems; parents will have to follow up closely, and not leave anything to the "experts" to whom they might once have deferred.

Of course, so much will come down to money – who has it, who doesn't. As I wrote *A Screen*, I realized over and over that people with money did better in this pandemic, and will do better afterwards. Perhaps my most personal essay, in Part IV, acknowledges how I finally came to understand that my patients are atypical insofar as few are in immediate financial danger. Most are pretty comfortable, in fact. I had to look outside my frame of reference to fully grasp the magnitude of suffering of people in this country. The causes are many, not just COVID-19, but the pandemic has exacerbated the others and pushed people towards homelessness and hunger. When all of this is past (or more or less past), we'll have to rethink the fundamental structure of our society from healthcare to a living wage to some form of stakeholder capitalism. We can no longer ignore the social fissures that the pandemic exposed.

We are left with so many things to think about, and ideally to fix, in a world of scarcer resources and fewer options. It won't be easy. But I think that as individuals who've been through so much, we're in a good position to try – or we will be, once we shake off our residual exhaustion. Think about how different you are than you were, say, in February 2020 before the pandemic. You're likely more serious, more focused, more aware of the people with whom you share this planet. You know that you'll need their help. You know that the *status quo ante* is kaput, so there's really no choice but to rebuild more wisely. It's a start. *A Screen* attempts to offer some feasible, relatable models.

Now that I've come out the other side of this project, I'm grateful that I took it on. I'm grateful to my patients, who spoke to me with a directness that sometimes surprised us both, but that allowed me to be of help. Finally, I'm grateful to Sandra Sherman, whose intelligence, drive, and creativity made this project possible. As we worked together, sometimes scrapping but always finding a way forward, I realized how people can make even daunting projects actually work. In this sense, I hope that *A Screen* is itself a model for what must come next.

Of course, "next" is a loaded word. In the past couple of weeks (i.e. as fall has settled in), New York experienced a spike in cases. In some parts of the City, schools were closed after re-opening and non-essential businesses were shut down again. Religious gatherings were limited to ten people – a rule that is being challenged in court. People are getting jumpier, after having allowed themselves to relax (however provisionally). If we do have a full-blown Second Wave, as some now predict, then *Through A Screen Darkly* could become like the Bill Murray film, *Groundhog Day* (Ramis, 1993), the template for an endless loop of maladjustment and disappointment. We have to get through the winter, somehow. Maybe pull out all the clichés: Keep calm and carry on; What doesn't kill me makes me stronger; Grace under pressure; and . . . the New York State motto, "Excelsior!" Sandra edited out the clichés in this book but, in this moment – when we need reassurance – they seem spot-on clarifying.

I wrote these Reflections in late October, 2020. Now, in early February, 2021, I am returning to them amidst a Second Wave. New York was not as hard-hit as some areas, like California, but our resources are once again under pressure. People are edgy, especially as they await a coordinated vaccine roll-out. The *Times* observed that

> Getting an appointment for a Covid-19 vaccine in New York State requires persistence, luck and, arguably, above-average computer skills. There are multiple websites and often a two-step verification process. Appointments are scarce; sitting in front of a computer and hitting 'refresh' hundreds of times a day has become a new pandemic ritual.

The consolation is that now more people have access to testing and we have better treatments. But in any case, waiting seems to be the defining predicament of this period. It's an ironic contrary to our sense of continually plodding on, hoping to get past this siege to the other side. As I observed earlier in *A Screen*, the pandemic can leave us trying to balance thoughts that don't compute.

But even though vaccination seems weeks or months away for many of us (and new viral strains are emerging), we have to hope. We have to find in ourselves the energy to be our best, and to share with everyone else. The *Times* article could hardly repress its excitement that total strangers are helping their neighbors find appointments – doing all the searching, clicking, and phoning on their behalf. It's altruism, and we have to maintain this sense of community. We're all in this together, and together we will all get through it.

COMMUNITY

References

Adams, Tim. "John Cacioppo: Loneliness is Like An Iceberg – It Goes Deeper than We Can See," *The Guardian* (February 28, 2016), www.theguardian.com/science/ 2016/ feb/28/loneliness-is-like-an-iceberg-john-cacioppo-social-neuroscience-interview

Allen, Woody (dir.), *Hannah and Her Sisters* (1986; United States; A Jack Rollins and Charles H. Joffe Production, distributed by Orion Pictures).

Allen, Woody. *Wikiquote* (n.d.), http://en.wikiquote.org/wiki/Woody_Allen.

American Psychological Association. "Building Your Resilience" (2012), www.apa.org/ topics/resilience

Bee Gees, *Saturday Night Fever* (RSO, 1977).

The Bible. *Authorized King James Version*.

Bigelow, Kathryn (dir.), *Zero Dark Thirty* (2012; United States; Columbia Pictures).

Boccaccio, Giovanni. *The Decameron* (1358).

Bradley, Martha. *The British Housewife: Or, the Cook, Housekeeper's, and Gardiner's Companion* (1756).

Bui, Q. et al. "What 5 Coronavirus Models Say the Next Month will Look Like," *New York Times* (April 22, 2020), www.nytimes.com/interactive/2020/04/22/upshot/ coronavirus-models.html

Camus, Albert. *The Plague* (Éditions Gallimard, 1947) (published in English by Hamish Hamilton, 1948).

Charney, Dennis and Southwick, Steven. *Resilience: The Science of Mastering Life's Greatest Challenges* (Cambridge: Cambridge University Press, 2012).

Chiodo, C. et al. "Caution: Wit and Humor During the Covid-19 Pandemic," *Foot & Ankle International* (April 26, 2020), https://journals.sagepub.com/doi/full/10.1177/ 1071100720923651

Defoe, Daniel. *A Journal of the Plague Year* (New York: Norton, 1722) (republished 1992).

Eliot, George. *Daniel Deronda* (London: Penguin, 1876) (republished 1996).

Eliot, George. *Middlemarch* (London: Penguin, 1871–72) (republished 2003).

Fitzgerald, F. Scott. *The Crack-Up* (New York: New Directions, 1945).

Franklin, Benjamin. *Autobiography* (San Tan, AZ: Pure Snow, 1790) (republished 2020).

Friedberg, Ahron, with Sherman, Sandra. *Psychotherapy and Personal Change: Two Minds in a Mirror* (London: Routledge, 2021).

Friedman, Vanessa. "Here to Help," cited in Clé D'Or (May 13, 2020), www.cledor.nyc/ single-post/2020/05/13/How-Do-I-think-about-Shopping-Now

Gelin, Martin. "The Pandemic has Reshaped American Fatherhood. Can it Last?," *New York Times* (June 2, 2020), www.nytimes.com/2020/06/21/opinion/pandemic-fatherhood-fathers.html

Glasse, Hannah. *The Art of Cookery Made Plain and Easy* (1745), retrieved from Eighteenth Century Collections Online.

Gopnik, Adam. "The Empty Couch," *New Yorker* (May 8, 2020), www.newyorker.com/magazine/2000/05/08/the-empty-couch

Grant, Adam. *Give and Take: A Revolutionary Approach to Success* (New York: Viking, 2013).

Hamilton, Gabrielle. "My Restaurant was my life for 20 years. Does the World need it Anymore?," *New York Times Magazine* (April 23, 2020), www.nytimes.com/2020/04/23/magazine/closing-prune-restaurant-covid.html

Harvard University Health Service, *Managing Fears and Anxiety around the Coronavirus* (n.d.), www.harvard.edu/sites/default/files/content/coronavirus_HUHS_managing_fears_A2%5B5%5D.pdf

Johnson, Sarah S. *The Sirens of Mars – Searching for Life on Another World* (New York: Penguin Random House, 2020).

Keller, Helen. *The Story of My Life* (New York: Doubleday, 1903).

Keshner, Andrew. "Why Gardening During a Pandemic is so Comforting," *Market Watch* (May 2, 2020), www.marketwatch.com/story/this-earth-day-especially-remember-plants-are-non-judgmental-what-its-like-to-start-gardening-during-a-pandemic-2020-04-22

Knoll, Corina. "How New Yorkers Found Resolve After 6 Months of Pandemic Hardship," *New York Times* (September 23, 2020), www.nytimes.com/2020/09/23/nyregion/new-york-city-coronavirus-six-months.html

Kristofferson, Kris, *Help Me Make It Through the Night* (Monument, 1969).

Krueger, Alyson, "'I am Blown Away': Strangers are helping strangers get vaccinated," *New York Times* (February 4, 2021), https://www.nytimes.com/2021/02/04/nyregion/coronavirus-nyc-vaccinations.html

Kuhn, Thomas S. *The Structure of Scientific Revolutions* (Chicago: Chicago University Press, 1962).

Mack, Katie. *The End of Everything (Astrophysically Speaking)* (New York: Penguin, 2020)

Melville, Herman. *Billy Budd* (1891).

NDT Resource Center (n.d.), www.nde-ed.org/EducationResources/CommunityCollege/Materials/Structure/deformation.htm

New York Public Library, "Missing Sounds of New York: An Auditory Love Letter to New Yorkers" (n.d.), www.nypl.org/blog/2020/05/01/missing-sounds-of-new-york

Niebuhr, Reinhold. "Serenity Prayer" (1932), www.beliefnet.com/prayers/protestant/addiction/serenity-prayer.aspx

Nietzsche, Friedrich. *Twilight of the Idols* (1888).

Pfaff, Donald with Sherman, Sandra. *The Altruistic Brain: Why we are Naturally Good* (Oxford: Oxford University Press, 2015).

Pinsky, Robert. *The Handbook of Heartbreak: 101 Poems of Lost Love and Sorrow* (New York: William Morrow, 1998).

Pope, Alexander. "Eloisa to Abelard" (1717), www.poetryfoundation.org/poems/44892/eloisa-to-abelard

Postman, Neil. *Amusing Ourselves to Death: Public Discourse in the Age of Show Business* (New York: Viking Penguin, 1985).

Pressman, Daniel. "Crossing the Narrow Bridge – Rosh Hashanah" (November 9, 2009), www.beth-david.org/crossing-the-narrow-bridge-erev-rosh-hashanah-rabbi-pressman/

Quote Investigator. "I Wish I Had Said That" "You Will, Oscar, You Will" (September 5, 2013), https://quoteinvestigator.com/2013/09/05/oscar-will/

Ramis, Harold (dir.) *Groundhog Day* (1993; United States; Columbia Pictures).

Reynolds, Malvina. "God Bless the Grass" (1964), performed by Pete Seeger, *Banks of Marble and Other Songs* (Folkways, 1974).

Roethke, Theodore. "Dolor," in *Collected Poems of Theodore Roethke* (New York: Anchor/ Doubleday, 1975).

Scott Fitzgerald, F. "The Crack-Up: A desolately frank document from one for whom the salt of life has lost its savor by F. Scott Fitzgerald," *Esquire* (February, 1936). Chicago, Illinois.

Seager, Sara. *The Smallest Lights in the Universe: A Memoir* (New York: Crown, 2020).

Seinfeld, Jerry. "So You Think New York is 'Dead'?" *New York Times* (August 24, 2020), www.nytimes.com/2020/08/24/opinion/jerry-seinfeld-new-york-coronavirus. html

Sloan, *Pretty Together* (Murderecords, 2001).

Smith, Eliza. *The Compleat Housewife; or, Accomplished Gentlewoman's Companion* (1728).

Solomon, Andrew. "When the Pandemic Leaves us Alone, Anxious, and Depressed," *New York Times* (April 9, 2020), www.nytimes.com/2020/04/09/opinion/sunday/ coronavirus-depression-anxiety.html

Stein, Sadie. "'You See Your Smallness: On Giving Birth in a Pandemic," *Vogue* (May, 2020), www.vogue.com/article/giving-birth-coronavirus-pandemic-advice

Stevens, Wallace. "The Man with the Blue Guitar" in *The Man with the Blue Guitar and Other Poems* (New York: Knopf, 1937).

Stirone, S. et al. "Life on Venus? Astronomers See Signal in the Clouds," *New York Times* (September 14, 2020), www.nytimes.com/2020/09/14/science/venus-life-clouds. html

Stockton, Frank. "The Lady or the Tiger" (1882).

Swift, Jonathan. *Gulliver's Travels* (1726).

The Complete Family-Piece (1736).

Thier, Aaron. *The World is a Narrow Bridge* (London: Bloomsbury, 2018).

University of Virginia Hospital. "Having a Baby During the Coronavirus Outbreak FAQs" (n.d.), https://uvahealth.com/services/covid19/birth-coronavirus-faqs

West, Kanye. "Stronger," on *Late Registration* (Def Jam, 2005).

Williams, William Carlos. "Love Song," in *Collected Poems, Vol. I* (New York: Directions, 1938).

Willis, Bruce. *If It Don't Kill You, It Just Makes You Stronger* (Motown, 1989).

Wordsworth, William. "A Sonnet", *Longman Anthology of Poetry* (Pearson, 2006).

Wordsworth, William. "Preface" to *Lyrical Ballads* (1800), www.bartleby.com/39/ 36.html

Yeats, William Butler. "The Second Coming," *The Dial* (1920), www.poetryfoundation. org/poems/43290/the-second-coming.

Index

acceptance 5, 8, 164–7
adaptation 3–4, 8, 23–4, 49, 63, 79–80, 90, 128, 170; by children 116; creativity as 56; humor as 27–30, 34, 77, 107, 134, 151, 152; risk as element of 19
Addams, Charles 34
aging 143–6
airline industry 118
all-bets-are-off mentality 18
Allen, Woody 27, 29–30, 114
aloneness 25–7
altruism 21–2
The Altruistic Brain: Why we are Naturally Good (Pfaff) 21
American Psychological Association 6
amusement 51–2
Amusing Ourselves to Death: Public Discourse in the Age of Show Business (Postman) 52
anxiety 2–4, 10, 12–13, 22, 63–5, 72; cycle of worry 87–8; developmental milestone of separation 26–7; management of 86–9; self-fulfilling 87–8; unrelenting 57. *see also* fear
anxiety disorders 3–4
apocalypse 20, 55, 155–6
art, importance of 46–7
The Art of Cookery Made Plain and Easy (Glasse) 93
"The Art of Impermanence" (Asia Society) 72
Art Students League 137
Asia Society 72
assertiveness 43–4, 88
attachment theory 27
Attention Deficit Disorder 81, 138–9
Autobiography (Franklin) 132–3

B.C. (Before Coronavirus) and A.D. (After Discovery of vaccine) 22, 23

beauty, importance of 121, 157
belief 17, 20, 58, 150
Benei Braq, Rabbis at *151*
bewilderment 53, 96, 108–9
Billy Budd (Melville) 132–3
bin Laden, Osama 38–9
Black Lives Matter protests 95, 117
Blake, William 84
Blanchett, Cate (character, *Blue Jasmine*) 149
Boccaccio, Giovanni 56
Bosch, Hieronymus 49, 82–5, *83*
boundaries 68
Bowlby, John 27
Bradley, Martha 23, 93, 94
bridge metaphor 9, 98–100; Brooklyn Bridge 97–100, *98*; Nachman of Breslov's epigram 57–9
Britain, sensory deprivation techniques used by 39
The British Housewife: Or, the Cook, Housekeeper's, and Gardiner's Companion (Bradley) 23, 93, 94
Brooklyn Bridge 97–100, *98*
Bui, Q. 18
burnout 16, 75–6, 154, 169

Cacioppo, John 26
Cacioppo, Stephanie 26
camping metaphor 110–12
Camus, Albert 47
cancer survivors 19
capitalism 5, 154, 171
Centers for Disease Control and Prevention (CDC) 43, 155
"centre cannot hold" metaphor 154
change 2–6, 9–10, 90, 127; "elasticity" vs. "plasticity" 98–100; radical 61, 63, 97. *see also* New Normal
Charney, Dennis 22

children 67–9, 86–7; adolescent
    confirmation bias 139; birth during
    pandemic 100–3; compromised
    education, concerns about 133, 138–9,
    170–1; games and play during pandemic
    162–3; hybrid school schedules and
    138–41; learning in "pods" 131–3; talking
    to 115–17, 127
Chiodo, C. 30
choice 5; about elemental needs 110–11;
    narrowing of 127–8, 132; provisional
    90–1; tough 77–80; venturing out and
    62–5, 77–80
Churchill, Winston 156
classics, online 13
cleaning 23
clergy *151*, 151–3
climate change 117–19, 155
cloistering/confinement 40–2
Cognitive Behavioral Therapy 81
collective cognition 80
Columbia pandemic model 18
commitment 5, 9, 40
community 5, 21, 43–4, 73, 89, 172;
    adolescents and 140; intellectual 79
community standards 69
commuting 80–2
compensation 5, 14, 23, 82, 112, 128
complacency, hedges against 33–4
*The Compleat Housewife; or, Accomplished
    Gentlewoman's Companion* (Smith) 94
Complete Family-Piece 94
conspiracy theories 54
continuity 101, 103
cookbooks 92–5
coping strategies 23–4
1 Corinthians 13:12 1
corona (sonnet series) 33
coronavirus, image of *134*
courage 57–8
COVID-19 pandemic (SARS COV2):
    antibodies to 21; arc of 2; arrest
    and imprisonment metaphors 8;
    asymptomatic individuals as carriers 3;
    cancellations and closures 69–73, 117;
    as cause of GAD 3; as existential threat
    77, 79; lockdown 2, 5, 24, 41, 51, 67,
    71, 99, 129, 144, 159; long-term impact
    on health 99; loss as defining attribute
    of 4; mathematical models of 17–18;
    as occupying army 122; risk and 67–9;
    second wave 71, 75, 87, 143, 155, 161,
    167, 171–2; statistics 71, 127, 155, 168;

suddenness, effect of 71–2; super carriers
    69; vaccine 5, 18, 22, 34, 92, 93, 101, 122,
    130, 131, 154, 155, 170, 172; vectors,
    concerns about 28–9; waking up to
    10–13; Wuhan outbreak 10
coziness, logic of 37
"The Crack-Up" (Fitzgerald) 41
creativity 34–5; artists and writers
    119–24, 136–8; as coping mechanism
    56; isolation's effect on 138–9; lack of
    stimulus affects 66; venturing out and 48
cyborg 35

Dalí, Salvador 84
Daniel Deronda (Eliot) 115
dating 5, 103–5, 125
death 17–18, 30–1, 33, 37, 75, 109;
    loneliness as cause of 24; poetry as way of
    thinking about 47; statistics 127, 155, 168
Death and the Miser (Bosch) *84*
The Decameron (Boccaccio) 56
Defoe, Daniel 4, 14, 18, 47, 92
delay and postponement 136–8
denialism 43
depression: burnout and 76; children's
    reaction to pandemic 132; exacerbated
    by pandemic 15; Major Depressive
    Disorder 19; sensory deprivation
    and 37–9
deprivation, sensory 37–9, 45–6
despair 122–3, 150
diary-keeping 34–5
dignity 32, 145
disappearing, sense of 81
Dish with sailing ship *131*
Dixieland band *50*
"Dolor" (Roethke) 65–7
dressing up 30–2
drinking 124–6, 129–30
"Dum Spiro Spero" ("Where there's breath,
    there's life") 77
dystopian concerns 87, 122

economy 17, 22, 54–5, 116–17, 129, 170;
    cancellations and closures 69–73, 117
ego 156–9
either/or thinking 147
"elasticity" vs. "plasticity" 98–100
election, 2020 43
Eliot, George 94, 115
"Eloisa to Abelard" (Pope) 42
emotional detachment 16
empathy 8, 15, 43–4, 55, 123

employment: home, working from 80–2; in-person meetings 159–61; office, concept of 80; return to office 112–14; searches for 60–2; small businesses 119–21; unemployment 6, 22, 55, 71–2, 115, 168
"The Empty Couch" (Gopnik) 35–7
engineering 97–100
Enlightenment excesses 55
entertainment vs. information 52
epidemiology 3–4, 17–18, 142
essential workers 73–4, 96, 158. *see also* physicians
European Court of Human Rights 39
existential concerns 19, 77, 79, 102, 117–19
exposure therapy 136

face recognition capacities 38
fantasies 82–3, 163
fashion magazines 32
Father's Day 85
father-son relationships 106–7, 147
fear 3, 4–5, 61; legitimate 79; PTSD 63; rationality and action as antidotes to 88–9; responsibility for 57–9. *see also* anxiety
feedback, lack of 53–4
finances 91, 102
Fire-stones *117*
Fitzgerald, F. Scott 41
flu pandemic of 1918–19 155
focus, decline in ability 14
Foot & Ankle International journal 30
fragility 52
Franklin, Benjamin 132–3
Freud, Sigmund 81, 108
Friedman, Vanessa 17

gallows humor 30
games *161*, 161–4
gardening 73–5, 93
Generalized Anxiety Disorder (GAD) 3
germaphobia 133–6
gifts 33, 74
Give and Take: A Revolutionary Approach to Success (Grant) 22
glacier metaphor 62–3
Glasse, Hannah 93
globalism 74
goals, setting 40
Gonne, Maud 61
Gopnik, Adam 2, 35–7

government, silence of during pandemic 53–5
Grant, Adam 22
gratefulness 85–6, 171
Great Depression 6
Great Plague of 1665 (London) 4, 14, 18, 47, 92–4
Greenfield, Emily 22
grief/mourning 85, 108–10, 127, 149, 151–2; acceptance stage 166
Groundhog Day (film) 171
The Guardian 24
guilt 4–5, 10, 68, 86, 90, 102, 121; about protecting others 21, 29, 95, 109, 128; physicians and 77; survivors' 21
Gulliver's Travels (Swift) 55

habits of mind 55–7
Hamilton, Gabrielle 20
The Handbook of Heartbreak: 101 Poems of Lost Love and Sorrow (Pinsky) 44–5
Hanks, Tom 21
Hannah and Her Sisters (Allen) 27, 29–30
Harleth, Gwendolyn (character, *Daniel Deronda*) 115
Harvard University Health Service 86, 87–8
The Hay Wain (Bosch) 84
"Help Me Make It Through the Night" (Kristofferson) 124
herbal medicine *92*, 92–5
Hiroshige, Utagawa *57*
HIV-AIDS 44
holidays 85
home, working from 80–2
honesty 12–13, 42–4, 64
hope 9, 116, 151; self-confidence and 76–7
hortus conclusus (secluded garden) 75
Hosoda Eishi *70*
household, as defense against disease 92–5
humor 27–30, 34, 77, 107, 134, 151, 152

identity 66, 77–8, 136–7, 147; ego and 156–8
"I did not know I'd miss you as I do" (1903) *25*
"If it feels good, do it" (Sloan) 34
imagination 47, 66, 82, 104, 112, 119, 163; poetic 108
immune system, suppressed by stress 15
impermanence, as steady state 72–3
in-person meetings 159–61
insight-oriented psychotherapy 19, 81
insurance industry 115

intentions 82
isolation 5, 24–7, 41, 66; creativity, effect on 138–9; physicians and 75–6

Jewish congregations 151; humor 152
Joergensen, Esben Staerk 163
Journal of the Plague Year (Defoe) 4, 14, 18, 47, 92
judgment, consequences of 91

Keller, Helen 133
Keshner, Andrew 73
Kristofferson, Kris 124
Kuhn, Thomas 97
Kyoto Station, (Hiroshige) *57*

"The Lady or the Tiger" (Stockton) 64
Last Clear Chance doctrine 62
LEGO Education 163
Lehrer, Tom 34
lemons to lemonade metaphor *38*, 39
letting go 83–4
limits, setting and enforcing 5
local focus 117
lockdown 2, 5, 24, 41, 51, 67, 71, 99, 129, 144, 159
London, post-World War II 117
London plague (1665) 4, 14, 18, 47, 92–4
loneliness 24–7, *25*; aloneness (solitude) vs. 25–7; physical touch and 27; types of 26
loss 4, 15–16, 45, 50, 65, 109–10, 117
Louis XIV's Hall of Mirrors 53–4
love, as sustaining 117
"Love Song" (Williams) 45–7
Lydgate, Tertius (character, *Middlemarch*) 94

Madison Avenue shops 95–6
managing 5
Managing Fears and Anxiety around the Coronavirus (Harvard University Health Service) 86, 87–8
"The Man with the Blue Guitar" (Stevens) 108–10
masks 10, 30, 40, 65, 68–9, 85, 140–1; difficulties with 40, 43; N95s 16, 22, 59; politicization of 84
mastery 88–9
mathematical models of pandemic 17–18
medications 76, 81, 136
Medieval scholastics 56
meditation 39
Melville, Herman 132–3
Memorial Day weekend 58, 59

memory 42
Middlemarch (Eliot) 94
Missing Sounds of New York: An Auditory Love Letter to New Yorkers 38
moral incoherence 97
moral relativism 41
mother-daughter relationships 116
mountain image 17
Munch, Edvard 39
muse, virus as 33–5

Nachman of Breslov 57–9
nature, integration with 74
NDT Resource Center 98–9
Negative Capability 41, 42
neuroscience 38
New Normal 4–5, 44, 54, 67, 73, 90–2, 126, 166–7, 169. *see also* change
New Permanent 128
New York City: acceptance and 164–7; Brooklyn Bridge 97–100, *98*; cancellations and closures 69–73, 117; pandemic statistics 71; small businesses 119–21; subway system *165*
New Yorker 2, 35
New York Public Library 38
New York Times 51, 77; "How New Yorkers Found Resolve After 6 Months of Pandemic Hardship" 164–6; "'I am Blown Away': Strangers are helping strangers get vaccinated" 172, "The Pandemic has Reshaped American Fatherhood" 86; on risk measurement 18; "So you think New York is 'Dead'?" 166; "When the Pandemic Leaves us Alone, Anxious, and Depressed" 16
Niebuhr, Reinhold 165
Nietzsche, Friedrich 6, 136
Niwa no hanami (*Women Resting in a Park*) (Hosoda) 70
Norton Anthology of Modern Poetry 151
No-Win mentality 49
"number crunchers" 55–7
numbers, pristine beauty of 57

Obsessive Compulsive Disorder (OCD) 135–6
obsessiveness 133–6
Oedipus Complex 81, 106–7
One Percent 95–6, 102
online relationships and groups 66, 79, 89, 122–3, 125–6; YouTube classes 157. *see also* relationships

online therapy 1, 35–7, 49; intensity of remote psychiatry 1–2, 8, 10–11, 36–7, 169–70
operant conditioning 111
opportunism 148
opportunities, missed 148–50
optimism 62

pandemic. *see* COVID-19 pandemic (SARS COV2); plague
"The Pandemic has Reshaped American Fatherhood" (Gelin) 86
panic 12
panic attacks 3, 4
paradox 8
parents 67–9; elderly 105–8
parody songs 34
Partnership for New York City 119
past accomplishments, as source of strength 17
patterns 90
performance: belief as 17; honesty and 42–4
Pfaff, Donald 21
Phony War of 1939 10
physicality, psychiatry and 81–2
physical touch 27
physicians 4, 6, 58–9; COVID contracted by 82; self-confidence and 75–7; stress of 15–17. *see also* essential workers
physiological responses 15, 24
Pinsky, Robert 44–5, 46
plague: 14th century 5; 17th and 18th centuries 5; Great Plague of 1665 4, 14, 18, 47, 92–4; herbal recipe for prevention of 93–4; Marseilles, 1720s 92
Plague, 17th and 18th centuries 13–15
Plague of Frogs (Medieval Haggadah) *15*
The Plague (Camus) 47
plasma donation 21
plausibility 40
play *161*, 161–4
"*Plus ca change, plus la meme chose*" (French saying) 100–2
poetry 4, 33, 108; abstracts from experience 65; corona (sonnet series) 33; reinterpretations of 46–7; sonnets 33, 41–2; structure through 65. *see also specific poets*
politeness 42–3
Pope, Alexander 42
population studies 117–19
possibility 4, 9, 32, 124, 142
Postman, Neil 52

post-pandemic world, sharing 50–2
Post-Traumatic Stress Disorder (PTSD) 63, 64, 169
poverty 155–6
pregnancy and childbirth 100–3
prerogatives of friendship 44
Pressman, Daniel 58
pride 19, 41, 74, 115, 140, 170
priorities, re-evaluating 96
progress 4, 40, 71, 73, 76, 126, 158
protests, United States 155
psychiatric practice: curiosity, role in 122; as holistic 36; intensity of remote 1–2, 8, 10–11, 36–7, 169–70; interpersonal vs. intrapsychic experience 2, 36; physicality of 81–2, 114; process of 108–9; shared concerns 12–13. *see also* online therapy
psychiatrists: as "clergy with medical degrees" 151; emotional detachment, concern with 17; physicians, empathy with 15–16; reality, version of 1–2; role in interpreting reality 108–9; stories spun about patients 26
Psychology Today 2, 91
psychopharmacology 19
Psychotherapy and Personal Change: Two Minds in a Mirror (Friedberg) 169
Puritans 35
purpose, sense of 20, 22, 25, 73, 84, 123, 145; religious beliefs and 153

rapture of the deep 43
rational action 88–9
rational thought 51, 88
reality: manipulation of 83; psychiatrists' role in interpreting with patient 108–9; psychiatrists' version of 1–2; willed 110
rebuilding 51
re-entry 48
refugees 77–8
reinventing oneself 148–50
relationships 100; dating 103–5; games and play during pandemic 161–4; maintaining connections 6, 9, 14–15, 19, 43–4; reliance on others 72–3; remoteness of connections 54–5; strain on 43, 67, 129–31; with therapist 33. *see also* online relationships and groups
relaxation 15–16, 39–40, 50–1, 73
religious feelings 86, 151–3
remoteness 54–5
resilience 4, 46, 119, 151, 169; assigning meaning and purpose to life 22;

"elasticity" vs. "plasticity" 98–100; fantasy life and 83–4; hope and 9; practices for building 6; preparing for future 75; re-entry and 48; renewing connections 19; sharing with others 72; social thinking 22

Resilience: The Science of Mastering Life 's Greatest Challenges (Charney and Southwick) 22

resources 21, 101–2, 105; self as 9, 14, 48, 51, 56, 62, 73–5, 90, 93; strain on 171–2

Restricted Environmental Stimulation Therapy (REST) 39

retro art forms 35

rhetorical questions 76

risk 17–20, 67–9; collective assessment of 79; dating and 105

rituals 113–14

Roethke, Theodore 65–7

Romance of the Rose 103

Roosevelt, Theodore *60*

rushing, recovery and 22

sadness 23

scientists, uncertainty and 12

"The Scream" (Munch) 39

screen persona 4

"The Second Coming" (Yeats) 153–6

second wave of COVID-19 71, 75, 87, 143, 155, 161, 167, 171–2

Seeger, Pete 164

Seinfeld, Jerry 166

self, as resource 9, 14, 48, 51, 56, 62, 73–5, 90, 93

self-awareness 107

self-care 16–17, 23, 91

self-confidence 75–7

self-consciousness 36

self-control 58

self-facilitation 37

self-knowledge 22–4

self-presentation 17, 30–2

self-protection 63

sensory deprivation 37–40

September 11, 2001 10, 11

sexuality 91, 104, 145

sheltering in place 19–21, 27

Sherman, Sandra 171–2

shopping *95*, 95–7

sibling rivalry 157–8

silence 53–5, 61

simplification of life 5

Sloan (rock band) 34

smart people, dumb actions 40–2

Smith, Eliza 94

social consciousness and responsibility 141–3

Solomon, Andrew 15

somehow-factor 91

sonnets 33, 41–2

Sophocles 106–7

Southwick, Steven 22

Statue with no face *144*

"Stayin' Alive" (Bee Gees) 34

Stein, Sadie 102

Stevens, Wallace 108–10

Still Life with Lemon and Cut-Glass Wine Goblet (van Os) *38*

Stockton, Frank 84

The Story of My Life (Keller) 133

stress 4; acute and chronic 15; burnout 16, 75–6, 169; generosity lowers stress hormones 22; multiple facets of 107; religious approaches to 151–2

String Fever (marionette) *28*

structure: hybrid schooling and 138–9; through gardening 73–5; through poetry 65

The Structure of Scientific Revolutions (Kuhn) 97

suicide 77

Sullivan, Anne 133

supply chain 20

surrealism 49, 83–4

survival: all-purpose mechanisms for 57; choices and 111–12

survivalists 20

survivors 53, 62, 116

survivor's guilt 21

Swift, Jonathan 55

techno-survivalists 20

Teddy the Old Dutch Cleanser 60

television 51

tensile strength 100

Thier, Aaron 58

thinking outside the box 62

Thunberg, Greta 143

time, sense of 8–9, 13, 22–4

tort law 62

torture, sensory deprivation as 38–9

tragedies 10

Trump, Donald 43, 155

Twilight of the Idols (Nietzsche) 6

uncertainty 2–5, 9, 128, 171; COVID-19 as moving target 12; impermanence as

steady state 72–3; inability to focus 14; of risk measurement 17–20; in Victorian novels 114–15
Uncertainty Principle 12
University of Virginia Hospital 102
unkindness 84

vaccine 5, 18, 22, 34, 92, 93, 101, 122, 130, 131, 154, 155, 170, 172; access to 172
"value," economic, of human life 51
Van Os, Maria Margaretha *38*
Van Gogh, Vincent 30
vectors, concerns about 28–9
Versailles 53–4
Victorian novels 114–15
vigilantism 141–3
Vogue 102
volunteering 51
Volunteers of America 51

Warhol, Andy 137
weltanschauung 71
"We Shall Overcome" 164

"What does not kill me makes me stronger" cliché (Nietzsche) 6–7
Whistler, James McNeill 108
Wilde, Oscar 108
Williams, William Carlos 45–7
Winnicott, Donald 26–7
women, as family pharmacists 91, 92–6
Wordsworth, William 41–2, 168
The World is a Narrow Bridge (Thier) 58
World War I (Great War) 155
World War II 155
worry, cycle of 87–8
writer's block 122–4
writing the pandemic 55–7
Wuhan outbreak 10

Yeats, William Butler 61, 153–6
"'You See Your Smallness': On Giving Birth in a Pandemic" (Stein) 102

Zero Dark Thirty (movie) 38–9
Zoom meetings 21, 34, 43, 62, 105, 126, 152